the *RECONSTRUCTION DESEGREGATION* debate

Rhetoric and Public Affairs Series

Eisenhower's War of Words: Rhetoric and Leadership
Martin J. Medhurst, Editor

The Nuclear Freeze Campaign: Rhetoric and Foreign Policy in the Telepolitical Age
J. Michael Hogan

Mansfield and Vietnam: A Study in Rhetorical Adaptation
Gregory A. Olson

Truman and the Hiroshima Cult
Robert P. Newman

Post-Realism: The Rhetorical Turn in International Relations
F. A. Beer and R. Hariman, editors

Rhetoric and Political Culture in 19th-Century America
Thomas W. Benson, editor

Frederick Douglass: Freedom's Voice, 1818–1845
Gregory P. Lampe

Angelina Grimké: Rhetoric, Identity, and the Radical Imagination
Stephen Howard Browne

Strategic Deception: Rhetoric, Science, and Politics in Missile Defense Advocacy
Gordon R. Mitchell

Rostow, Kennedy, and the Rhetoric of Foreign Aid
Kimber Charles Pearce

Visions of Poverty: Welfare Policy and Political Imagination
Robert Asen

General Eisenhower: Ideology and Discourse
Ira Chernus

the *RECONSTRUCTION DESEGREGATION* debate

The Politics of Equality and the Rhetoric of Place, 1870–1875

Kirt H. Wilson

Michigan State University Press
East Lansing

∞ The paper used in this publication meets the minimum requirements of ANSI/NISO Z39.48–1992 (R 1997) (Permanence of Paper).

Michigan State University Press
East Lansing, Michigan 48823–5202

Printed and bound in the United States of America.

ISBN 978-1-61186-450-2 (paper)

LIBRARY OF CONGRESS CATALOGING-IN-PUBLICATION DATA

Wilson, Kirt H., 1967–
The reconstruction desegregation debate : the politics of equality and the rhetoric of place, 1870-1875 / by Kirt H. Wilson.
p. cm.—(Rhetoric and public affairs series)
Includes bibliographical references and index.
ISBN 0-87013-617-8 (cloth : alk. paper) — ISBN 0-87013-617-8 (cloth : alk. paper)
1. African Americans—Civil rights—History—19th century. 2. African Americans—History—1863-1877. 3. Reconstruction. 4. Segregation—Southern States—History—19th century. I. Title. II. Series.
E185.61 .W745 2002
973'.0496073—dc21

2002006969

Cover design by Heather Truelove Aiston
Book design by Sans Serif, Inc.
Cover photo is reproduced from the collection of the Library of Congress, Prints and Photographs Division, LC-USZ62-2247.

Visit Michigan State University Press on the World Wide Web at:
www.msupress.msu.edu

In Memoriam
Vidian Joseph Smith
1910–1999

Dedicated to Janice A. Wilson

Contents

Acknowledgments

During the course of writing this book, I have incurred debts that I never can repay. The first drafts were prepared for David Zarefsky, Thomas Goodnight, and my advisor, Michael Leff, at Northwestern University. Their assistance went well beyond the responsibilities of a dissertation committee. Not only did they steer me around potential problems and through difficult terrain, their faith that this study could make a contribution to our field was inspiring. I am also extremely grateful to the Speech-Communication Department at the University of Minnesota. Under the leadership of Karlyn Kohrs Campbell and Donald Browne, the department provided summer stipends in 1996 and 2000 and research assistants during the summer months of 2000 and 2001. Edward Schiappa and Robert L. Scott offered invaluable advice about the publishing process. Dean Hewes extended his friendship and moral support. One could not ask for more helpful senior faculty. Bea Dehler supplied the kind of administrative help that is essential to a major research project. I am grateful to Joan Lund whose sharp eyesight and editing skills caught many errors that I missed. Martin Medhurst has been a patient editor. I also owe a debt to the University of Minnesota for its support with the President's Faculty Multicultural Research Award, 1997–1998. This grant provided summer release time and the resources I needed to visit the Library of Congress and the Moorland-Springarn Research Center at Howard University.

Throughout the project many people have offered their criticism, advice, and friendship. Sometimes they knew that they were being helpful but just as often they did not. I want to thank Terence Morrow, an old friend and colleague who always is close to my mind and heart. The faith and interest of Angela Ray, Joshua Gunn, and Kristin Brown-Owens were deeply appreciated. It is much easier to be a scholar when your students and colleagues believe that that is what you are. Aric Putnam and Michael Kramer were exemplary research assistants. Their initiative and hard work deepened the critical and historical scope of this manuscript. Friends such as Jeff and Shelly Drake reminded me of the life that exists beyond the page.

I want to convey my deepest gratitude to Denise Bostdorff, Michael Leff, and Karlyn Kohrs Campbell. I owe my professional beginning to these incredibly talented scholars. Professor Bostdorff was a model educator who taught the value of organization, methodology, and hard work. Professor Leff demonstrated how a subtle mind can tease not only meaning but also significance from a text. Professor Campbell has been my mentor and friend during the sometimes daunting transformation from graduate student to professor. These individuals are my exemplars, and if I absorb only a portion of their skill, I will consider my professional career successful.

My family has been the most important influence during the life span of this project. Mary and Larry Humphrey, Dave and Joann Solak, and my grandparents, Vid and Isabelle Smith, never doubted my ability or the eventual publication of this work. The prayers of Jerry Elve, and, in particular, my mother Jan have made all the difference in the world. I learned the meaning of fortitude from her. Most of all, I am thankful to Janice and Cameron, my wife and our son. Rhetorical criticism is more than what I do; it is who I am. Janice understands and accepts this truth even when it makes our lives together complicated. Janice, your patience and encouragement make accomplishments possible, and your love gives meaning to success—thank you.

Preface

Few periods of United States history have received the amount of attention that has been focused on the thirteen years from 1865 to 1877. Labeled by defenders and detractors alike as the "Reconstruction," historians have studied this era from many perspectives, using a variety of methods. In the preface to his monumental work *Reconstruction: America's Unfinished Revolution*, Eric Foner summarizes the divergent interpretations of this controversial period.[1] Of particular interest is his account of the differences between the traditionalists of the early twentieth century, the revisionists of the 1950s and 1960s, and the more recent histories that date from the 1970s. The first influential histories of Reconstruction were written by William Dunning, John Burgess, and Claude Bowers.[2] Remarkable for their scope and the enduring power of their interpretations, these histories argued that the wisdom of Abraham Lincoln and Andrew Johnson was ignored by a vengeful and unscrupulous group of politicians, the radical Republicans. Using the 1867 Reconstruction Acts, the radicals wrested control from Johnson, subjected the South to military rule, disenfranchised the region's white elite, and replaced it with incompetent and corrupt governments dominated by African Americans, carpetbaggers, and scalawags. Through the valiant efforts of the Democratic Party and an organized militia that defended the homes and property of whites, the traditionalists described how the South eventually was "redeemed."

A new generation of scholars embraced the task of reinterpreting the Reconstruction, rescuing the period from the biased interpretations of the traditionalists. James McPherson, LaWanda and John H. Cox, David Donald, John Hope Franklin, and Eric McKitrick argued that the period was a time of social revolution, not unlike the modern Civil Rights Movement. The revisionists compared the 1860s with the 1960s, suggesting that the upheaval of their own moment might have been avoided if the federal government had stayed the course in the nineteenth century. According to this history, Reconstruction's idealists, confronted by a hostile Southern white populace, fought to make the Declaration of Independence a practical verity. The future for African Americans grew brighter with each constitutional amendment and civil rights law. Blacks exercised their new political and economic rights prudently, and although exceptions existed, they were not statistically significant. Most certainly, argued the revisionists, Dunning was incorrect to claim that African Americans and Republicans abused their power for personal gain or vengeance.[3] If any group was responsible for the period's upheaval, it was the Southern redeemers who resisted black equality.

A third group of historians, represented by August Meier, Harold Hyman, William Gillette, and Michael Les Benedict and followed by Eric Foner, concluded that the revisionists had been too optimistic. This postrevisionist interpretation also departed from the traditionalist view, but it argued that Reconstruction's political culture was determined by conservatism and racism. Republican idealists did exist, but their efforts to transform race relations in the United States were compromised by moderates and conservatives within the party. Furthermore, presidents Grant and Hayes failed to enforce statutes designed to protect African Americans from violence or even discrimination. With the *Slaughter-House Cases* (1873), *U.S. v. Cruikshank* (1876), and the *Civil Rights Cases* (1883), the Supreme Court played an active role in limiting the effects of the Thirteenth, Fourteenth, and Fifteenth Amendments. Finally, the political and economic elite of the prewar South, assembled under the moniker Southern conservative, reaffirmed its control through violence and intimidation. In short, the Reconstruction was a *failed* revolution; few whites, Northern or Southern, cared to interact with blacks on an equal basis, and people of color never obtained sufficient power to protect their own interests.[4]

The Politics of Equality and the Rhetoric of Place exists in-between the revisionist and postrevisionist histories described above. It is not a complete accounting of the Reconstruction era, nor is it an attempt to reconcile the tensions that exist in the period's historiography. This book is an analysis of rhetoric's power to raise the hopes and aspirations of a community while it simultaneously affects political judgments that narrow opportunity. If someone was black in America between 1863 and 1877, chances are her or his life was changing in a significant way. Whether this change was permanent or even positive depended on factors as material as a region's habits of economic production and as abstract as the Supreme Court's interpretive philosophy. Still, one of the greatest changes in that person's life was likely to be a growing belief that perhaps the "new world" of the European continent might become his or her world, too. For many freedmen and women, this dream was expressed in new behavior. Some demanded wages in exchange for their labor. Many others decided to seek political office. Still others sued railroad companies when their agents refused to seat them with the other first-class ticket holders.

Regardless of how it became manifest, the dream of equality and public respect had a tremendous impact at the local, state, and national levels. This book attempts to understand some of the national and political consequences of the Reconstruction period by analyzing the public discourse over its most radical policy, desegregation.

Introduced in 1867, passed into law in 1875, and ruled unconstitutional by the Supreme Court in 1883, the Civil Rights Act of 1875 was the first national racial desegregation law in the United States. On the one hand, this act represents the kind of egalitarian revolution that the revisionist historians both see and desire for the period. On the other hand, it represents a fatal compromise with prejudice that postrevisionists view as an exemplar of the era's hypocrisy. This book argues that both of these views are correct; the rhetoric that accompanied the bill's passage created both a radical and a conservative vision for interracial relations. As Congress debated the wisdom of desegregating public transportation facilities, restaurants, hotels, inns, cemeteries, juries, and even public schools, it reflected the incongruities in America's attitudes about race and rights. Furthermore, its debate created the political and discursive norms that would shape future judgments and race relations into the next century.

The 1870s controversy over desegregation had a significant effect on the evolution of race relations in this country. Not only did it provide an opportunity to define the scope of black civil rights in the aftermath of emancipation and Reconstruction's constitutional amendments, but it also made space for African Americans as participants in the debate. Blacks, abolitionists, and a majority of Republicans advocated a politics of equality that would have transformed the fabric of public life. Others, most especially Southern whites, viewed this "politics of equality" as a threat. To counteract the Republican's agenda, Southern conservatives resurrected an old idea, the notion of place, creating a rhetoric that maintained the appearance of reconstruction while it reaffirmed disparate power relations between African and European Americans. The desegregation controversy would lead to a new civil rights law, but in the post-Reconstruction era, the rhetoric of place was the real winner as gradually the nation's political culture accepted the norms and symbolic meanings of the moderate Democrats' rhetoric.[5]

This book pursues a mode of analysis known variously as rhetorical criticism, public address criticism, and rhetorical history. It assumes that "the study of history is an indispensable aspect of the process of rhetorical criticism," but it also maintains that though the analysis of history and rhetoric are closely intertwined, a rhetorical perspective differs from other approaches to our collective experience.[6] When critics analyze events rhetorically, they ask different questions and gain different insights than if they used a traditional, Marxist, psychoanalytic, comparative, or political economy orientation. The rhetorical critic approaches the past to interpret how discourse shaped the meanings of past events. She understands rhetoric not as a by-product of political judgments, but as a constitutive part of the same. Of course, the connections between rhetoric and policy are not always clear. Political discourse plays a role in the processes of government, but the nature and significance of that role is disputed. This book takes the position that discourse or rhetoric has considerable power. It assumes that reality has meaning only as humans associate reality with symbols and articulate them in public talk.

One consequence of this position is that the rhetorical critic sees legislation, the end result of political judgments, as a discursive creation. This is not to suggest that material resources, administrations, institutions, and political economies do not matter. Instead, the critic sees these elements as an inextricable part of a symbolic network that defines and describes a political culture. Politics is largely, but not solely, the act of connecting meanings to supposedly stable material realities. As political actors state reasons for their positions and negotiate the appropriate criteria for judgment, they construct motives for the judgments they advance. No scholar can ever be certain that the expressed motives of a politician are honest or complete, but rhetorical theory suggests that these reasons become authentic as the motives are adopted by the public. Put simply, the meaning of a political judgment resides in the rhetoric that people come to accept about that judgment.[7]

A rhetorical approach to the 1875 Civil Rights Act is appropriate, particularly because the policy involves one of the most important discursive constructs of the modern era: race. From the sixteenth century forward, western leaders have tried to categorize the phenomenon of difference that we label as race. In the mid-nineteenth century, for example, physical traits such as skin color, hair texture, and skull size were signs of racial difference. The twentieth century replaced the biological with ideas such as culture, history, and ethnicity. The idea of race changed, because each generation differed in its discursive formulation of the concept. Despite centuries of effort, a single material definition of race was impossible, because race cannot be defined empirically. As a concept and linguistic term, it is a social invention, a constructed idea that shifts with the passage of time and the changes of public rhetoric.[8]

To approach race as a discursively created idea is to understand civil rights issues in a particular way. Critical race theorists have argued that the judicial and legislative branches of the United States have failed to rid society of racial inequities, because these institutions remain tied to the belief that race and rights are objective constructs. Although politicians and jurists admit that race is a tricky concept, they continue to treat it as a matter of skin color or genetic heritage; consequently, they have failed to appreciate how racial categories are sustained in the everyday talk of society. Critical race theorists contend that racism persists because our habits of language maintain racial differences and cultural hierarchies of human worth. Haney López argues that "race must be viewed as a social construction. That is, human interaction rather than natural differentiation must be seen as the source and continued basis for racial categorization."[9] Only when politicians and the law begin to discuss race as a constructed rather than a natural phenomenon will we begin to deconstruct the differences that sustain racism. This book performs just such a deconstruction. By studying the rhetoric and political culture of the Reconstruction era, it seeks to reveal the social meanings of race and civil rights as these concepts were negotiated by the period's national politicians. Furthermore, by interpreting the rhetoric both for and against desegregation, it begins to uncover not only our civil rights history, but also our current assumptions where they pertain to equality and participation.

The United States has not resolved its tumultuous relationship with black civil rights. The modern Civil Rights Movement brought real improvements for some African Americans, but disparities grounded in race and gender differences continue. Furthermore, a number of scholars argue that the civil rights gains of the 1960s and 1970s are under attack. Well-meaning people often view the success of some blacks as proof that racism is no longer a social problem. Others, articulating old arguments about states' rights and individual responsibility, are hostile to the idea that the federal government should protect black equality.[10] David Troutt, law professor at Rutgers Law School in Newark, New Jersey, writes that the Supreme Court has engaged in a "conservative march away from the courts as the arena for determining rights, bringing them back into the political process where they are subject to the will of the majority."[11] For many advocates of social justice and students of history, this is a disturbing trend. The court's tendency, as in *Alexander v. Sandoval,* to narrow the scope of major civil rights legislation seems like the kind of retrenchment that marked the post-Reconstruction period.[12] In the absence of federal authority and without a substantial commitment to the principle of equal rights for all, African Americans were segregated, assaulted, and exploited economically. The days of Jim Crow may never return, but the discourse of that past is, at times, not so different from our own. Given this context, one can view this book as an act of intervention into our current civil rights debates. I embrace the following admonition by Cornel West: "To engage in a serious discussion of race in America, we must begin not with the problems of black people but with the flaws of American society—flaws rooted in historic inequalities and long-standing cultural stereotypes. How we set up the terms for discussing racial issues shapes our perception and response to these issues."[13] Ultimately, then, this book's purpose is to "set up the terms for discussing racial issues" by providing both a history and a critical interpretation of our civil rights past.

1

The Symbolic Meaning of Segregation

On the evening of 22 October 1883, Lincoln Hall in Washington, D.C., roared with noisy conversation. Packed closely together, some three thousand people gathered to hear two of the nineteenth-century's most celebrated orators. Those who could not find a seat were forced to stand on the edges, in the hallway, down the stairs, and outside the building. If fortunate enough to gain entry, one noticed that this was no ordinary assembly. The sheer number of people so exceeded the room's capacity that the crowd broke one or two windows. Furthermore, the audience's racial composition was diverse; European and African Americans were packed together so tightly that contact was inevitable. Before the Civil War such a large and integrated throng might have called out the district's militia. Since the conflict, these gatherings were more common; nevertheless, the assembled knew that similar audiences might become rare once again. In a way, that was the evening's topic of discussion; Frederick Douglass and Robert G. Ingersoll were scheduled to lecture about the recent Supreme Court decision, the *Civil Rights Cases*.[1]

Seven days earlier, the Supreme Court had rejected Congress's authority to desegregate the nation's restaurants, transportation facilities, hotels and inns, cemeteries, and places of public amusement.[2] Throughout the country, the decision had generated various degrees of interest. Staunch Republican papers such as the *Chicago Tribune* said that the court's decision was expected. According to the *New York Times*, it was welcome because the desegregation law actually sustained the prejudices of Southerners while doing no good for African Americans. The *Atlanta Constitution* labeled the court's decision "a triumph of law and sense," while the *New Orleans Times Picayune* called the majority opinion a "masterly and unanswerable piece of reasoning."[3]

The audience that waited anxiously in Lincoln Hall was of a decidedly different opinion. Mostly aging abolitionists, reformers, and African Americans, this audience had gained from the social changes of the last two decades. Perhaps a few had come as a curious pleasure, but most of those assembled believed that the United States Supreme Court had overturned one of the most important triumphs of the Reconstruction era. For them, the *Civil Rights* decision was not inconsequential, and it certainly was not praiseworthy; it was an error in judgment that amounted to a tragedy. Douglass was greeted with noisy applause when he rose from his chair and approached the dais. He wasted no time but quickly established his own opinion of the Supreme Court's decision: "We have been, as a class, grievously wounded, wounded in the house of our friends, and this wound is too deep and too painful for ordinary and measured speech. . . . When a deed is done for slavery, caste and oppression, and a blow is struck at human progress, whether so intended or not, the heart of humanity sickens in sorrow and writhes in pain. . . . The cause which has brought us here tonight is neither common nor trivial. Few events in our national history have surpassed it in magnitude, importance and significance. It has swept over the land like a moral cyclone, leaving moral desolation in its track."[4] Douglass's grave assessment was persuasive; he was the acknowledged leader of what might be called America's first civil rights movement.

With the Civil War and then the Emancipation Proclamation and the Thirteenth Amendment, Douglass had seen the dream of abolition fulfilled. Yet freedom for the South's black population had not transpired in the manner that he preferred. In 1869 Douglass argued that slavery had not "died an honest death," because its destruction had resulted from military advantage rather than the mortification and redemption of white Americans. He explained, "the legal relation of master and slave is abolished; but that out of which slavery sprung, that by which it was sustained, the selfishness, the arrogance of the master, still remain; the ignorance and servility of the slave still remain."[5] Because the causes of slavery were not dead,

Douglass's reform efforts continued, even as many abolitionists ceased their agitation. Desegregation was a policy that Douglass had championed during the years that separated the Thirteenth Amendment and the 1883 *Civil Rights Cases*.

Douglass's advocacy for civil rights stemmed from his personal experiences. Since the war he had attained some power in Washington, D.C. He was included, for example, in a delegation that President Grant sent to Santo Domingo. While there, Douglass was treated as an equal, and, along with the rest of the commission, the government of Santo Domingo entertained him as a diplomat. On his way home, almost within sight of Washington, D.C., circumstances changed. When the commission entered the dining hall of the U.S. mail steamer *Georgiana*, the ship's steward stepped forward and blocked Douglass's entry. The captain was summoned quickly, and he informed Douglass that this steamer maintained a segregation policy. He could not allow Douglass to enter the dining hall until all of the white guests had exited. Douglass said that if he could not eat with the rest of the Santo Domingo delegation, he would not eat at all. He returned to his cabin.[6]

A cursory investigation of this event might conclude that Douglass was excluded because of his color; however, an analysis of the rhetoric that surrounded this incident reveals a deeper motivation. According to an editorial letter that appeared in the *National Standard*, "the objection to Mr. Douglass was that he had no right to be a gentleman, or to be treated like one in the public conveyances of his own native land!"[7] The dining hall employed black waiters, after all, and they moved about the cabin with impunity. It was not Douglass's color but his status as the equal of whites to which the ship's steward and captain objected. This interpretation of the incident was not lost on the black abolitionist. In his 1883 speech condemning the *Civil Rights Cases*, Douglass declared: "When a colored man is in the same room or in the same carriage with white people, as a servant, there is no talk of social equality, but if he is there as a man and a gentleman, he is an offence. What makes the difference? It is not color, for his color is unchanged. The whole essence of the thing is a studied purpose to degrade and stamp out the liberties of a race. It is the old spirit of slavery, and nothing else."[8] On the evening of 22 October 1883, before a large and agitated crowd, Douglass offered an interpretation of segregation that few beyond Lincoln Hall cared to hear. Segregation was not a pragmatic policy to provide separate but equal facilities to the black and white races. Segregation was not a benign method for maintaining interracial harmony.

Segregation was, instead, an expression of prejudice, a symbolic affirmation of white supremacy. When publicly sanctioned and practiced, it was nothing less than the manifestation of a racially biased class system. Therefore, from Douglass's perspective, when the Supreme Court overturned the desegregation provisions of the 1875 Civil Rights Act, it breathed new life into the ideological and political foundation that had created slavery and that might now create something just as horrible and difficult to abolish.

Segregation before the Reconstruction Era

Too often accounts of nineteenth-century race relations in the United States focus solely on slavery. Slavery was the penultimate institution that regulated the interactions between blacks and whites, but it was not the only or even the most pervasive expression of racism during the century. According to the 1790 census, more than 27,000 free African Americans lived in the North while 32,000 lived in the South. By 1830 the total number had grown to 319,000, and then to 488,000 by 1860. Maryland (83,900), Virginia (58,000), and Pennsylvania (56,000) contained the largest populations. Free people of color were fortunate to live without shackles and chains, but they did not escape other forms of servitude that were onerous. Delaware (1792), Kentucky and Ohio (1799), and New Jersey (1807) withheld suffrage from free blacks. Other states that initially allowed black suffrage took back the franchise, including Maryland (1810), Connecticut (1818), Rhode Island (1822), Tennessee (1834), North Carolina (1835), and Pennsylvania (1838). The Midwestern states of Indiana, Illinois, Michigan, and Iowa never instituted black suffrage. In New York African Americans could vote if they owned property worth two hundred fifty dollars. This restriction meant that only 100 of the 11,840 African Americans in New York City could exercise the right. Only in Maine, New Hampshire, Vermont, Massachusetts, and, after 1842, Rhode Island were people of color allowed to vote.[9]

The most pervasive forms of discrimination during the antebellum involved efforts to keep blacks in carefully controlled spaces. Leon Litwack argues:

> In virtually every phase of existence, Negroes found themselves systematically separated from whites. They were either excluded from railway cars, omnibuses, stagecoaches, and steamboats or assigned to special "Jim Crow" sections; they sat, when permitted, in secluded and remote corners of theaters and lecture halls; they could not enter most hotels, restaurants, and

> resorts, except as servants; they prayed in "Negro pews" in the white churches, and if partaking of the sacrament of the Lord's Supper, they waited until the whites had been served the bread and wine. Moreover, they were often educated in segregated schools, punished in segregated prisons, nursed in segregated hospitals, and buried in segregated cemeteries.[10]

Segregation was not monolithic, but in those regions with a significant or even potential free black population, European Americans usually enforced a distance between the races.

The first tactic used by states both North and South was to restrict immigration. Virginia serves as an early example. After the Revolutionary War state legislators feared the consequences of a large, free black population, so they prohibited immigration (1793). Despite the prohibition, the black community grew, giving Virginia the second largest population of freedmen and women. In 1850 the state altered its constitution to force black emigration: any freedman or woman who remained for more than twelve months would be returned to bondage. Virginia was not atypical in its effort to control black mobility. Georgia politicians in 1829 prohibited free black sailors from communicating with anyone on shore. In the city of Augusta visiting African Americans had to register within ten days of their arrival and pay a fee of two hundred dollars. Missouri outlawed black immigration in 1847, and between 1851 and 1857 Delaware, Indiana, Illinois, Iowa, and Oregon amended their state constitutions to either prohibit or sharply control the immigration of free blacks. In Ohio, a state that was slow to enact restrictions, local citizens vowed to take up arms, lining the Ohio River with men and muskets to stop the entry of freed slaves.[11]

In those locations where a free black population already existed, whites enacted both formal and informal policies of segregation. In what is widely recognized as the most important and controversial account of segregation, C. Van Woodward notes that "hotels and restaurants were generally off limits for all Negroes, free or slave, and Negroes were usually discriminated against in public conveyances, though the races were mixed in some towns and Negroes were entirely excluded in others."[12] Although segregation existed in every state, its most rigid forms were found in the North. The first association of the words "Jim Crow" with public accommodations transpired in Massachusetts when railroad officials used the term to refer to a car reserved for black passengers. In New York people of color were excluded from the omnibuses, and a fully paid fare only allowed them to ride on the outside platform of the horse-drawn cars. Thomas Downing, one of the wealthiest African Americans in New York City, was beaten by agents of the Harlem Railroad when he tried to ride that line. Cincinnati, like some Northern cities, had no official statutes excluding blacks from museums, galleries, and places of amusement; nonetheless, local custom enforced segregation. In Cincinnati this meant complete exclusion, but in other Northern cities it meant separation to special "colored" galleries.[13]

African Americans encountered various degrees of separation when they tried to acquire an education as well. Maine admitted black students to its public schools, but Connecticut did not. In 1829 Ohio barred blacks and individuals of mixed heritage from its public schools; Indiana did likewise in 1850. Massachusetts allowed each city to determine its own policy, and for the first half of the century nearly all were segregated. Prior to 1822 black families in Pennsylvania paid taxes into a school fund, but they received no monies to attend the segregated institutions that were their only option. When the state established public schools, it gave the old and often degrading facilities to the black community. In a number of regions, whites opposed any form of black education, because they feared that even segregated institutions would bring African Americans to their town. The citizens of Canaan, New Hampshire, used almost one hundred oxen to tear a private school founded by abolitionists from its foundation. The community was unwilling to allow the building's existence, because it might encourage people of color to move to their region. These and similar instances lead Woodward to conclude that "racial discrimination in political and civil rights was the rule in the free states and any relaxation the exception."[14]

Although segregation was a widespread phenomenon, it is important that one not overgeneralize its consequences. Just as the absence of legislated segregation did not mean that blacks enjoyed equal access, the presence of segregation laws did not preclude black success. For example, virtually every Midwestern and Western state prohibited free black immigration, but these laws were enforced sporadically. Even when city and state officials enforced segregation, African Americans found ways to cheat the system. New Orleans was the South's largest city, and it had an extensive list of segregation statutes. In 1806 city officials passed a law prohibiting African Americans from presuming themselves to be "equal to whites." In 1816 New Orleans segregated theaters and public exhibitions. The Lake Pontchartrain Railroad provided transportation for free blacks and Creoles but only in separate cars, and an 1833 attempt to integrate the whites-only car resulted in a small riot, complete with gunfire. In 1835 the city segregated its cemeteries, and during the 1850s it enacted regulations to outlaw almost every conceivable form of public contact between the races. Yet despite this legislation, the city's black and biracial citizens thrived. The total number of free people of color decreased by almost one-fifth during the 1840s; nevertheless, the 1850 census revealed that 650 of them owned property averaging 3,623 dollars apiece. Prosperous by any standard, these landowners possessed real estate totaling 2,354,950 dollars in value. Anecdotal accounts of New Orleans' life complicate the issue further. Despite the official regulations, the races mixed with considerable freedom. Herbert Aptheker notes that the city's white, black, and Creole populations were determined to intermingle at masked balls, taverns, and dance halls. In fact, the city fortified its segregation laws in 1856 and 1857 precisely because neither race seemed willing to forgo contact with the other.[15]

This evidence suggests that one cannot simply equate racial animosity and segregation. Racism in the nineteenth century was not a simple or single entity. According to some historians, it was not universal. Class, region, and the personal experiences of individuals altered how and to what degree white supremacy influenced interracial relationships. New Orleans is a case in point. Segregation as legal proscription and informal custom did not keep freedmen and women from acquiring capital; nor did it prevent members of each race from having relationships. Slaveholders were quick to remind Northerners that in the South, where the black population was largest, whites and blacks enjoyed cordial friendships. Southern whites had little choice but to trust certain servants and slaves to administer plantations and farms. Relationships between white merchants and black artisans were not uncommon, and, at times, the alliances born from expediency or personal history blossomed into something greater. According to Gary Mills, the 1860 census reveals that 78 percent of Alabama's free black population was biracial. Some of these free blacks were the children of women who had been exploited by white men, but a good portion of the "mixed" population came from marital or common law relationships. Mills notes further that 51 percent of the state's interracial relationships involved white women. Aptheker concludes that European Americans, especially in the South, feared the anonymity of black mobs, but they trusted individual blacks with their lives and property.[16]

Yet despite the spectrum of interracial relationships that existed in the nineteenth century, there *is* a correlation between segregation and racism: even under the best of circumstances, segregation communicated white supremacy. Douglass understood this message only too well. Early in his abolition career, the officials of the Eastern Railroad line had thrown him from that train when he had defied its segregation policies. Reflecting on his experiences, he explained: "Yet people in general . . . will say they like colored men as well as any other, *but in their proper place.* Who is to decide what is their proper place? *They* assign us that place; they don't let us do it for ourselves, nor will they allow us a voice in the decision. . . . They treat us not as men but as dogs . . . That's the way we are liked. You degrade us, and then ask why we are degraded—you shut our mouths, and then ask why we don't speak—you close your colleges and seminaries against us, and then ask why we don't know more!"[17] Segregation, according to Douglass, was an undeserved expression of privilege that whites exercised over people of color.

Douglass was not alone in this interpretation; black and some white abolitionists of the antebellum period linked the fight against slavery in the South with the fight for civil rights in the North.[18] On 25 February 1842, for example, Charles Lenox Remond addressed a Massachusetts legislative committee to discuss the issue of segregated conveyances. He provided several personal illustrations, arguing that when he traveled in Great Britain he was treated with respect. When he traveled in America, he received inferior accommodations because of his race. He explained, "The grievances of which we complain, be assured, sir, are not imaginary, but real—not local, but universal; not occasional, but continual, everyday matter-of-fact things—and have become, to the disgrace of our common country, matter [*sic*] of history."[19] The amazing efforts of black abolitionists and radicals such as William Lloyd Garrison and Wendell Phillips were rewarded on occasion. In the first quarter of the century, Massachusetts was a segregated state, but starting in the late 1830s, white and black abolitionists began a campaign to eradicate even "separate but equal" institutions. In 1842 the state's antimiscegenation law was repealed. By 1844 abolitionists had pressured the state's railroads to get rid of the Jim Crow cars. In 1855 the state legislature desegregated Boston's public schools after an extensive campaign by the abolitionists.[20] These victories were extremely important to the free blacks of Massachusetts, and they illustrate that the abolitionists of the state viewed segregation as an important part of their movement. For these reformers, especially the black abolitionists, slavery and civil rights were equated; they were both expressions of the same attitude. The black activist Theodore Wright was critical of some of his white colleagues, because, despite their efforts to abolish slavery, they shared the prejudices that sustained the "peculiar institution." Wright expressed the sentiments of free blacks when he declared that the goals of abolitionism would be accomplished only when every individual "annihilate[d] in their own bosoms the cord of caste. . . . Let every man take his stand, burn out this prejudice, live it down, talk it down, everywhere consider the colored man as a man, in the church, the stage, the steamboat, the public house, in all places, and the death blow to slavery will be struck."[21]

The speeches of Remond, Wright, and especially Douglass are significant, because they illustrate that segregation evoked a *symbolic* meaning that went well beyond its practical effect. In locations such as New Orleans, some freedmen and women enjoyed good economic and social relationships with whites. Furthermore, the practice of segregation cannot be dismissed as prima facie evidence of racial animosity. But despite the good will of particular whites, and regardless of the variances created by class and region, white Americans preferred to have blacks and whites separated in public spaces, and this system of differentiation, whether enacted through legislation or local custom, declared that African Americans were distinct and inferior. To be sure, not every person of color interpreted segregation in this way. Blacks, especially in the postwar South, sometimes preferred separation from the white community. Still, for a sufficient number, the segregation of public accommodations was interpreted as an act to keep free blacks in their proper, that is, unequal place.

As race relations evolved from 1800 to 1900, African Americans became increasingly defined as not only different but also as a social problem that impinged upon the fabric of society and the rights of European Americans. W. E. B. Du Bois explained the consequence of differentiation in his eloquent book *The Souls of Black Folk.* Writing in 1903, he argued: "Between me and the other world there is ever an unasked question: unasked by some through feelings of delicacy; by others through the difficulty of rightly framing it. All, nevertheless, flutter round it. They approach me in a half-hesitant sort of way, eye me curiously or compassionately, and then, instead of saying directly, How does it feel to be a problem? They say, I know an excellent colored man in my town; or, I fought at Mechanicsville; or, Do not these Southern outrages make your blood boil? At these I smile, or am interested, or reduce the boiling to a simmer, as the occasion may require. To the real question, How does it feel to be a problem? I answer seldom a word."[22] By the end of the nineteenth century, to be a black American was to be defined as a "problem," a kind of political and social illness that necessitated treatment.[23] How did race relations in the United States devolve to the point where the very presence of blackness was a public dilemma? The march toward this status was not linear. In fact, the rhetoric of the post-Civil War years articulated a very different vision of U.S. race relations. Between the feudal arrangements of the Southern antebellum era and the violent racism of the early twentieth century was a interval of transition when race relations were more fluid and governmental policy seemed to be constrained by the ideal of equality.

Reconstruction: The Politics of Equality and the Rhetoric of Place

From 1863 to 1877 various political factions clashed as they rebuilt a nation that had collapsed almost completely. After the Civil War sections of the South lay in ruin, increasing class conflict. Death and injury had devastated families and communities. An expanded federal government threatened the system of American federalism, and the status of the seceding states remained uncertain, as did the future of Southern representation in Congress.[24] Among these problems two questions were always at the edge and often at the center of debate: to what extent are African Americans now "equal" with European Americans, and how shall that notion of equality be implemented? The statesmen and activists that framed these questions came to various answers. Abolitionists and radical Republicans, sometimes referred to as Reconstruction's "equalitarians," argued that the black and white races now stood as equals. Differences might persist at the individual level, but these differences resulted from the oppressive slavery system and the limited opportunities apportioned to freedmen and women. In principle, the two races were the same, and, according to the equalitarians, government was the proper vehicle for creating a public sphere where even individual variances could disappear. Moderate and conservative Republicans, as well as the majority of America's white citizens, did not adopt such an extreme position. Broad differences of opinion existed, but the general consensus was that African Americans remained, as a race, inferior. Nevertheless, the most remarkable thing about the Reconstruction era is that the nineteenth century's racial attitudes did not lead to the conclusion that blacks deserved no rights. The Emancipation Proclamation and the military service of black soldiers had shifted Northern attitudes. A solid majority in Congress and beyond the Southern states believed that blacks deserved at least "limited absolute equality." Material equality might be impossible; the two races might always exist at unequal levels of civilization, yet those who wielded power at the close of the Civil War argued that freedmen and women deserved the rights inscribed within the Declaration of Independence.[25] The process of transforming the Declaration's principles into public policy and legal statute constitutes what I have termed the politics of equality.

The politics of equality began even before the Civil War had ended. On 31 January 1865 Congress passed the Thirteenth Amendment, which stated: "Neither slavery nor involuntary servitude, save as a punishment for crime whereof the party shall have been duly convicted, shall exist within the United States, or any place subject to their jurisdiction." This language was unambiguous; it guaranteed freedom to the slaves. The amendment's second section, however, was slightly more controversial: "Congress shall have power to enforce this article by appropriate legislation."[26] The Republicans who controlled Congress at the end of the Civil War viewed this language as a positive affirmation of their duty to guarantee freedom.[27] The party was divided over what legislation actually was necessary, but as the years from 1865 to 1877 unfolded, Republicans enacted stronger and stronger laws in the name of black liberty. The 1866 Civil Rights Act and the Fourteenth Amendment (1868) established that people of color were national citizens with constitutional rights. The first Reconstruction Act (1867) called for new Southern governments that included African Americans. The Fifteenth Amendment (1870) gave black citizens the right to vote. Enforcement Acts in 1870 and 1871 signaled the federal government's willingness to protect freedmen and women from violence. These acts and amendments had a profound effect on the political culture of that era. To justify each successive bill, Republicans voiced a rhetoric that placed African and European Americans on greater and greater terms of equality. One historian concludes that during the Reconstruction era, "racial equality, equal rights, and the use of national authority to secure both were living ideas," much as they are today.[28]

For African Americans, the Civil War and the years immediately thereafter were like the dawn of a new age. W. E. B. Du Bois writes that "when the Northern armies entered the South they became armies of emancipation. It was the last thing they planned to be"; still, African Americans viewed their coming as a salvation, and they began to exercise their newfound liberty immediately.[29] Many celebrated the day of Jubilee by simply leaving the plantations that had kept them hostage. The act of walking from county to county, following the Union Army or in search of one's family, became a physical expression of freedom. After 1865 the former slaves returned to the regions that they knew best, and many aspired to recreating in their own homes the lives that they witnessed among white people. Black families sent their children to the new Freedom Schools, taught by Northern schoolteachers who, with missionary fervor, tried to correct the intellectual devastation of slavery. Many freedwomen stayed at home, enjoying a domestic life that slavery had denied them. Black men went looking for work and wages, assuming that the races would now cooperate to create a new economic system. After the 1867 Reconstruction Act, black men became involved in politics. They debated the important issues of the day in political clubs such as the Union League. A good number sought public office, from the county tax assessor to the state senator and governor.[30]

Of course these events, the results of what I term the politics of equality, did not exist within a vacuum. As the Republicans in Congress and people of color throughout the states aspired to create a new vision of "We the People," the plantation leadership or "conservatives" who had lost the Civil War fought to regain their way of life. Joel Williamson writes that the South's culture, prior to the Civil War, had as much in common with the feudal systems of medieval Europe as with the industrial society of the North. The Deep South, reacting to the threat of slave insurrections, had created a strict caste system in which every member of society occupied a very specific position, socially and geographically. Plantation owner, local merchant, free black artisan, and field slave were constrained by norms that determined exactly how they lived their lives and interacted with one another. At the center of this culture was the concept of "place." Place existed as a kind of condensation symbol; it signified a person's identity and location within the organic communities of the South. Individual and communal, place determined the spaces that a person could occupy and how one could interact, privately or publicly, with others. It even determined a person's civil rights. As the South's white elite worked to rebuild a society that war had devastated, they returned to the notion of "place," using it as the centerpiece of their political rhetoric. Williamson writes that "'place' was the key word in the vocabulary of Conservatism, and place applied not only to blacks, but all people and all things. One Southern white perception of Radical Reconstruction was that it seemed to be precisely a concerted attempt to put things out of place. It was a horrendous effort, not simply to destroy the Conservative world but to make of the social order in the South a monstrosity."[31] The rhetoric of place articulated by the Democrats of the South had important consequences for public policy.

After the war the Southern governments established by Presidents Lincoln and Johnson legislated the economic and social relationships that would exist between the races. The "black codes," as they were known, acknowledged that people of color were no longer slaves, but the codes continued to reinforce the places that had existed in the antebellum era. For example, South Carolina's black codes stipulated what kind of language should appear on all labor contracts between blacks and whites: "All persons of color who make contracts for service or labor, shall be known as servants, and those with whom they contract, shall be known as masters."[32] The terms "master" and "servant" were crucial, because they reinforced the places that each race had occupied before the war. The North might call the former slaves "freedmen," but South Carolina law would maintain the caste system that defined "servants" in very different terms than their "masters."

One common dimension of the black codes was their effort to regulate the mobility of African Americans. Several Southern states passed or revised their vagrancy laws in the wake of the Thirteenth Amendment. Mississippi, for example, permitted civil officers to arrest any black "servant" who quit his position or walked away from the place where he was working. Fines were apportioned based on the distance between one's point of arrest and the property line of one's master. Individuals who failed to obtain a labor contract were deemed vagrants and could be arrested, fined, and forced to work for the very person who had owned him or her before the war. Finally, the black codes gave enormous discretion to local officials to determine the "place" that individual blacks would occupy within the community. If a district judge in Mississippi determined that a parent was "of notoriously bad character" or if that parent was not teaching his or her children good habits of industry, then the judge had the authority to "apprentice" the children to a local landowner.[33]

The black codes were onerous, but they were not the only vehicle used to keep blacks in their proper place. Violence and terror were also effective. The historian Stetson Kennedy argues that the Civil War did not end at Appomattox. In the name of white purity, justice, and self-defense, Confederate soldiers traded their uniforms for the masks of night riders and engaged in guerrilla actions that proved more successful than the war's open hostilities.[34] Whites injured or killed African Americans for seemingly slight offenses, especially when the perceived affront reinforced black autonomy. In one case, a black man was beaten for "claiming the right of whipping his own child" rather than recognizing the right of his former master to do the same.[35] Such informal cases of violence were horrible, but they paled in comparison to the organized violence fomented by groups such as the Ku

FIGURE 1.

Klux Klan, the Knights of Camelia, the White Brotherhood, and the '76 Association.[36] In robes and hoods, these groups "broke up Republican meetings, threatened radical leaders, whipped Negro militiamen, and drove Negroes away from the polls. They were guilty of shootings, murders, and plundering," and they vowed to use whatever force was necessary to regain control of local and state governments.[37] Congress documented the violence against African Americans in hearings during the summer and fall of 1871, and the nation's black community was informed of these problems by newspapers such as Frederick Douglass's *New National Era*.[38] White Republican newspapers and magazines also ran stories on Southern violence. On 12 January 1867 *Harper's Weekly* published a lithograph that juxtaposed the violence against blacks before slavery and after the Emancipation Proclamation. It ran with the caption, "Slavery Dead?" (See figure 1.)[39]

The notion of place confronted the politics of equality with an intense challenge; nevertheless, for the "equalitarian" politicians who viewed the Reconstruction era as an opportunity to reformulate the nation's laws and racial attitudes, the period held enormous promise. Advocates for black equality knew that removing two centuries of inequity would take time; the key was to begin well. It was in this grand spirit that Massachusetts senator Charles Sumner proposed the first national desegregation measure in United States history. Sumner's bill was the zenith of Reconstruction's equality politics: it called for federal authority to eliminate racial segregation in hotels, trains, restaurants, churches, transportation facilities, cemeteries, and public schools. At first the measure encountered little success, but then in December of 1873 several factors revitalized Congress's interest. Sumner's ill health and eventual death in 1874 garnered support as a memorial to his political service. Mississippi, Louisiana, Arkansas, Florida, Alabama, New York, and Kansas either passed or proposed similar bills.[40] Seven African Americans obtained seats in Congress, and they became vocal advocates for desegregation.[41] Finally, as the Democrats "redeemed" the South, endangering Republican control, Republicans wondered whether desegregation was necessary to protect the hard-won liberties of America's newest citizens.

The congressional debate that surrounded the 1875 Civil Rights Act is one of the most remarkable discussions of civil rights principle and policy in any era. When the Republicans came together to support the measure, they gave some of the most egalitarian political speeches of the nineteenth century. Proponents argued that African Americans deserved more than limited forms of equality. Desegregation was the penultimate expression of the Declaration of Independence. The policy would allow the freedmen and women to achieve the intellectual and cultural heights of European Americans, and, according to the Republicans, the rights of the black minority had to be protected from the prejudices of the white majority. In response to and in conjunction with their improved position, the Democrats opposed desegregation with a fervor that had marked their antebellum defense of slavery.

The 1875 act was a milestone in the evolution of America's civil rights history, and the debate over its passage was nothing less than a crucible in which the thoughts and judgments that would determine the future of race relations were formed. By analyzing the rhetoric of this debate, we come to a deeper understanding of the period's political culture and the trajectory of racial policy into the twentieth century. Perhaps, finally, we also get a glimpse into the failures of Reconstruction and why race remains such a difficult issue.

Conclusion

In 1883 Frederick Douglass mourned the Supreme Court's decision to nullify the Civil Rights Act of 1875, because he understood that the bill was unique in United States history. The act's significance was not tied to its effectiveness, nor was its importance limited by compromises that, as we shall see, undermined its scope. Douglass argued:

> It is said that this decision will make no difference in the treatment of colored people; that the Civil Rights Bill was a dead letter, and could not be enforced. There is some truth in all this, but it is not the whole truth. That bill, like all advance legislation, was a banner on the outer wall of American liberty, a noble moral standard, uplifted for the education of the American people. . . . It expressed the sentiment of justice and fair play, common to every honest heart. Its voice was against popular prejudice and meanness. It appealed to all the noble and patriotic instincts of the American people. It told the American people that they were all equal before the law; that they belonged to a common country and were equal citizens. The Supreme Court has hauled down this flag of liberty in open day, and before all the people, and has thereby given joy to the heart of every man in the land who wishes to deny to others what he claims for himself.[42]

The 1875 Civil Rights Act represented the culmination of Douglass's work. More "honest" than the Emancipation Proclamation, it articulated the principle of equality with words meant to teach and inspire. Perhaps the bill had been largely symbolic, but it was also the nation's final chance to learn how to transform the Declaration of Independence into the "practice of everyday living."

2

The Legislative History of the 1875 Civil Rights Act

The history of the 1875 Civil Rights Act is complex, so before an analysis of its congressional debate can ensue, one must first untangle the legislative process that led to its passage. Extremely unpopular in the South and even throughout much of the North, it is remarkable that the desegregation measure survived at all. Much of the credit for its success can be attributed to a vocal minority who kept the measure alive despite considerable opposition. Among the Democrats there was unanimity; they denounced the bill in every particular. Faced with strong opposition, desegregation's advocates justified their proposal with strongly egalitarian claims that were heightened by the voice of several black congressmen. Yet in spite of this rhetoric, at several moments in the bill's evolution, moderate and conservative Republicans demanded compromises that undermined its effectiveness. In short, the legislative history of the 1875 Civil Rights Act is an exemplar of the period's political culture—it illustrates how the era's legislation became trapped between principle and the expedient demands of racial politics.[1]

The Origins of National Desegregation

The Civil War, the Emancipation Proclamation, and the Thirteenth Amendment put enormous pressure on racial segregation. The bravery and sacrifice of African Americans during the war had altered, ever so slightly, the prejudices of some Northern whites. This feeling led to the dismantling of Jim Crow in the North during the 1860s and 1870s. In the South segregation had been a cultural norm rather than a legislative system. With the abolition of slavery, Texas, Mississippi, and Florida moved quickly to pass laws that bolstered segregation. Most of the Southern states were more cautious, however. Howard Rabinowitz and C. Vann Woodward disagree about some of the particulars, but both historians contend that Jim Crow began first in the newer urban centers, spread slowly to the South's older cities, and eventually reached a fevered pitch in the last decade of the nineteenth century. Of particular interest is that segregation, whether through law or custom, actually *improved* the daily lives of some urban blacks during the Reconstruction period. Before the Civil War, public services such as education, welfare, and health care had excluded people of color; slavery had made these services either irrelevant or dangerous to the region's systems. As segregation moved from a cultural practice to legal proscription, it created new opportunities. Faced with either exclusion or segregation, African Americans accepted the latter. Blacks desired the full range of their constitutional rights, but they also understood the difficulty of exercising liberty in a hostile environment.[2]

People of color were less willing to accept the segregation of trains, stagecoaches, steamboats, restaurants, and theaters. When the 1867 Reconstruction Act allowed blacks to participate in the new state governments, the freedmen demanded complete access to most public accommodations. Louisiana's 1868 constitution, drafted with the help of African Americans, desegregated conveyances and other institutions licensed by the state. In 1868 Arkansas's General Assembly passed a law that forbade the discrimination of first-class accommodations because of race. In the next three years, similar provisions were introduced in the state legislatures of Florida and Mississippi. Arkansas passed a second, more sweeping act in 1873.[3] The black community sent Congress thousands of letters and petitions calling for a national civil rights law. Black newspapers such as the *New National Era* and the *Elevator* insisted that the Republicans finish the purpose of the Fourteenth Amendment by making desegregation a national policy. Frederick Douglass and other abolitionists used their influence to persuade the country that new laws were necessary.[4]

A second group, the radical Republicans, also pushed for new civil rights legislation after 1870. Exactly who comprised this political minority is a matter of debate among historians. According to David Donald, there is little definitive evidence to suggest exactly who and what constituted a radical Republican. Examining the voting records of Congress from 1863 to 1867, he concludes that radicalism was a function of one's constituency. Politicians who consistently voted for radical proposals tended to come from strong Republican districts, whereas moderates came from mixed districts where they were forced to solicit votes from a broader spectrum of voters. Given these findings, some scholars have argued that radicalism represented the core beliefs of the Republican Party during and immediately after the war. David Montgomery focuses on the ideology of Reconstruction's politicians to identify the radical Republican. Radicals, he argued, blended the Whig notion of an activist state, the Jeffersonian principles of majority rule, and the economic ideal of free labor. Michael Benedict distinguishes between legislative and political radicals. Legislative radicals used the principles identified by Montgomery to make judgments; political radicals wanted the power that accompanied radicalism, but they did not always vote for equalitarian policies if it seemed as though a bill might undermine their authority in Congress or at home.[5]

Regardless of who or what constituted the congressional radicals, several senators of the Forty-first Congress acted on their principled idealism, introducing four civil rights bills in the second session. One of the bills, S. No. 916, was introduced by Senator Charles Sumner of Massachusetts. Sumner was known as a champion of black civil rights, and he had a lengthy history with desegregation. In 1849 he had argued a school desegregation case before the Massachusetts Supreme Court (*Roberts v. City of Boston*). In his brief, he stated that the "fundamental right of all citizens" was "Equality before the Law." Sumner maintained that segregated institutions created harmful psychological and sociological effects on the children of both races, who were separated for no reason other than the color of their skin. The doctrine of "separate but equal" was not only false, he had explained, it was also harmful to the community and the principles of democracy.[6] On 13 May 1870 the Massachusetts senator proposed a bill that applied this argument to hotels, trains, steamboats, stagecoaches, restaurants, churches, cemeteries, houses of public amusement, and public schools. The measure also empowered the federal government to levy jail terms and monetary fines against offenders.[7]

Sumner's bill faced powerful opposition within his own party. Senator Lyman Trumbull (Illinois) was the chairman of the Senate Judiciary Committee, and he made no pretense about his dislike for the measure. In 1866 he had been a driving force behind the first Civil Rights Act and the Fourteenth Amendment, but since then his politics had become more conservative. On 7 July 1870 Trumbull reported the bill adversely from his committee and recommended its "indefinite postponement." Several historians argue that Trumbull was not alone in his distaste; moderate and conservative Republicans believed that desegregation was a political liability, and they wished to table it without discussion.[8] Sumner, however, was not easily dissuaded, and he reintroduced the bill during the next session, 20 January 1871. The bill was again referred to the Judiciary Committee, again Trumbull reported the measure adversely, and again the session ended before the bill reached the floor for discussion. When Sumner tried a third time, during the first session of the Forty-second Congress, 9 March 1871, he tried to maneuver the bill around Trumbull: "This bill has already been twice reported adversely upon by the Committee on the Judiciary. I think, therefore, it will not be advisable to refer it again to that committee. It is a very important bill; nothing more important could be submitted to the Senate; and I submit that Congress ought to act upon it before we go home."[9] Sumner's desire that Congress at least discuss the merits of desegregation went unfulfilled, and when the Senate again referred it to the Judiciary Committee, most everyone assumed that it would meet its past fate.

When the Senate returned in December for the second session, it was greeted by a House bill that granted universal amnesty to all of the Confederate leaders who remained under congressional disabilities.[10] Sumner, writes Jager, "seized upon this as an opportunity to bring his Civil Rights Bill to a vote by introducing it as an amendment to the amnesty measure."[11] Encouraged by scores of letters and petitions, sent primarily from African Americans, Sumner argued that charity for the South must be linked with justice for people of color. His proposal met with immediate opposition. Senator Joshua Hill, a Republican from Georgia, objected to the association of "irrelevant amendments" to the amnesty measure.[12] Furthermore, he argued: "If there be a hotel for the entertainment of travelers, and two classes stop at it, and there is one dining-room for one class and one for another, severed alike in all respects, with the same accommodations, the same attention to the guests, is there anything offensive or anything that denies the civil rights of one more than the other?" Sumner responded: "The Senator mistakes substitutes for equality. Equality is where all are alike. A substitute can never take the place of equality."[13] Hill was not the only Republican senator to object to Sumner's amendment. Orris Ferry, a Republican from Connecticut, was also an outspoken champion of separate but equal institutions. Trumbull interrupted the exchange between Sumner and Hill to argue that desegregation was not the appropriate topic for discussion. The House had sent the Senate an amnesty bill, and Trumbull fumed that Sumner should not be allowed to derail amnesty's consideration and passage.

The amendment to combine Sumner's Civil Rights Bill and the amnesty provision quickly became embroiled in a political contest that pitted one Republican against another. After 1870 the Republicans had divided into several factions. A group known as the liberal Republicans argued that it was time to move away from the inflammatory policies of 1867 and 1868. They wanted less intrusion into Southern politics and more economic reform. The amnesty provision was an important step in their bid for power, because it would solidify a coalition with the Democratic Party. A second group, the regular or "Grant" Republicans, maintained the party's antipathy toward the Democrats. They distrusted the liberals, and although they had mixed feelings about the future of Reconstruction, they were not yet ready to see it end. Eric Foner writes that divisions had existed from the beginning of congressional Reconstruction: "For Radicals, [congressional Reconstruction] represented the culmination of a lifetime of reform. For others, it seemed less the fulfillment of an idealistic creed than an alternative to prolonged federal intervention in the South, a means of enabling blacks to defend themselves against abuse, while relieving the nation of that responsibility."[14] After the Fifteenth Amendment had passed, party discipline had weakened, and without clear opponents against which to unite, Republicans fought amongst themselves. In 1872 those Republicans who opposed the liberals or simply disapproved of amnesty for the Confederates saw Sumner's amendment as an opportunity. Grant Republicans voted to unite amnesty and the Civil Rights Bill, knowing that the Democrats could never vote for a measure that would mandate desegregation.[15]

On 9 February 1872, the Senate was deadlocked, twenty-eight to twenty-eight, over Sumner's amendment. Casting the tie-breaking vote, Vice President Schuyler Colfax supported the amendment and the two bills became one. Sumner's victory was short lived, because the Democrats and liberal Republicans withdrew their support from the revised bill, and the combined measure failed to gain the two-thirds majority that it required. In May a second amnesty provision came to the Senate, and again it was amended with Sumner's Civil Rights Bill. Trumbull was incensed, and he tried to disallow the amendment, arguing that the civil rights measure required only a majority to pass whereas the amnesty provision required two-thirds. Since the votes necessary for passage of the bills differed, they could not be combined. Trumbull's effort failed, and, on 9 May Colfax broke another twenty-eight to twenty-eight tie; nevertheless, the combined measure was defeated a second time.[16]

A week later a dubious political maneuver killed Sumner's bill for the rest of the session. On 21 May 1872 a Republican senator who had opposed Sumner's bill introduced his own measure to "declare and enforce the civil rights of citizens of the United States." The language of Matthew Carpenter's (Wisconsin) measure was less forceful than Sumner's, and it excluded the original's provisions regarding public schools and juries.[17] As the day's session moved into the evening and then into the morning of the next day, Carpenter and several colleagues prevented the Senate from adjourning. Around five o'clock in the morning, with few senators in attendance, Carpenter made a motion to take up Sumner's desegregation measure. When asked his intention, he replied that he wished to replace the majority of Sumner's bill with the language of his own measure. Democrats on the floor were wary, but Carpenter assured them that their cooperation would lead to an immediate consideration of yet another amnesty provision. Supported by George Edmunds of Vermont, Carpenter argued that if the Senate passed the altered Civil Rights Bill *and* the amnesty provision separately, amnesty would most certainly become law. The Senate voted to take up Sumner's measure.

With Sumner not in attendance, the Southern Republican George E. Spencer (Alabama) condemned Carpenter's tactics: "I am very much afraid that the civil rights bill is going to be this morning in this thin Senate entirely emasculated and rendered practically useless. It is unfair and unjust to take a vote upon this bill during the absence of the Senator from Massachusetts." Carpenter was unsympathetic: "The Senator from Massachusetts has been sent for and requested to attend. He has had fair notice. This matter has been discussed for several days. Now do let us settle it." When the question was called, Carpenter's bill was substituted for Sumner's language, twenty-two to twenty. Thirty-two members of the Senate, including Sumner and Trumbull, were absent. Several vocal opponents of desegregation, including Thomas Norwood (Democrat from Georgia) and Allen

Thurman (Democrat from Ohio), supported Carpenter's amendment, while the radical Republicans Henry Wilson (Massachusetts), James Nye (Nevada), and Frederick Frelinghuysen (New Jersey) opposed it. The revised measure passed before eight o'clock in the morning. The Senate immediately proceeded to consider the latest amnesty provision, but within moments Sumner arrived on the floor. Informed of the situation, he offered his original Civil Rights Bill as a rider to the amnesty provision. His proposal was defeated thirteen to twenty-nine. When amnesty came to a final vote moments later, only Sumner and Nye voted against it. Afterward Sumner addressed the floor: "All this winter I have stood guard here making an ineffectual effort to secure those rights, insisting always that they should be recognized side by side with those of former rebels. Many Senators agreed with me, as I understood, but now at the last moment comes the sacrifice. . . . Sir, I sound the cry. The rights of the colored race have been sacrificed in the Chamber where the republican party has a large majority—that party by its history, it traditions, and all its professions bound to their vindication. Sir, I sound the cry. Let it go forth that the sacrifice has been perpetrated. Amnesty has been adopted, but where are the equal rights of the colored race?"[18] When the amnesty bill became a law, it did so without the civil rights amendment. In the House Representative William Frye (Maine) had introduced his own version of Sumner's bill, but its opponents had blocked its consideration.[19] The Republicans were unable to muster the two-thirds majority they needed to suspend the rules and vote on Carpenter's version of the desegregation measure. Despite attempts in May and June, Carpenter's bill, though it lacked provisions desegregating schools and juries, died.

The Congressional Debates of 1874

On the first day of the Forty-third Congress, Sumner, whose health had slipped dangerously, proposed two measures: his national Civil Rights Bill (S. No. 1) and a bill to desegregate Washington, D.C., schools.[20] The previous year had given him some hope. Mississippi, Arkansas, Florida, New York, and Alabama had passed legislation that desegregated public accommodations and transportation facilities, and Kansas was on the verge of doing likewise.[21] Desegregation had several new proponents, as well. President Grant voiced his support, and several congressmen such as Benjamin Butler of Massachusetts and the more moderate House Speaker, James A. Blaine, agreed that suffrage was insufficient. Perhaps only a civil rights act

FIGURE 2.[23]

---

could secure Reconstruction's gains, they reasoned. Summarizing the attitudes of Republicans, William Gillette writes that "despite the measure's continuing unpopularity and perennial failure, there was a new feeling on the Republican side of the aisle during spring, 1874, that a supplementary bill mandating civil rights ought to be passed."[22]

One symbol of this new outlook was manifest in the composition of the House itself. Looking down from the galleries in December of 1873 one could not help but notice the seven African Americans who stood proudly before the speaker. Joseph Rainey (South Carolina), John R. Lynch (Mississippi), Richard H. Cain (South Carolina), Robert B. Elliott (South Carolina), James Rapier (Alabama), Alonzo J. Ransier (South Carolina), and Josiah Walls (Florida) brought a new urgency to the issue.[24] Sumner's voice may have faded, but these men were outspoken advocates for desegregation. Their own experiences seemed to justify the bill's need; several had been forced to ride in second- or third-class coaches as they traveled to Washington, D.C. As one of these representatives explained, "Here a foreigner can learn what he cannot learn in any other country, that it is possible for a man to be half free and half slave, or, in other words, he will see that it is possible for a man to enjoy political rights while he is denied civil ones; here he will see a man legislating for a free people, while his own chains of civil slavery hang about him."[25]

The African American representatives of the Forty-third Congress altered the congressional debate in subtle yet important ways. First, for the Republicans in Congress, their presence demonstrated that equality politics could work. Lynch, Rainey, and Walls had been slaves.[26] That fact more than anything else signaled the drastic change that had overtaken the country's political order. Throughout the 1874 debate, supporters of civil rights pointed to their black counterparts and asked why these men could be seated as equals in the House but not in a restaurant or stagecoach. Second, for the opponents of desegregation, the presence of the black members illustrated the folly of ignoring one's proper place. Forced to interact with African Americans on equal terms, several Democrats became irate. According to a 5 February 1875 article in the *New York Times,* their presence infuriated the Kentucky Democrat John Brown; he refused to address any black member. He preferred to remain silent rather than ask a representative of color to yield the floor.[27] The *New National Era* reported the sullen comments of a New York representative, Samuel Cox, when Joseph Rainey defended the Republican government of South Carolina. After the black representative's speech, he received applause to which Cox replied: "This applause proceeds on the principle, I presume, on which the artist received credit for making a wonderful painting. The painter, although his work was a wretched daub, was applauded because he painted it with his toes."[28] How one judged Reconstruction after Congress gained control in 1867 determined how one viewed the presence of these black men. They were small in number and lacked the experience and power of their colleagues, but Rapier, Elliott, and the others forced Congress to confront the implications of the Fourteenth and Fifteenth Amendments. They were catalysts, encouraging Republicans to extend the politics of equality and causing the Democrats to unite against the same.

The House Debate, 1874

Sumner's measure was not the only desegregation bill that session; Benjamin Butler reported a version from the House Judiciary Committee on 18

December 1873.[29] While the Senate referred Sumner's proposal to its Judiciary Committee, yet again, the House took up Butler's bill. Formal consideration of the measure (H.R. 796) transpired on 19 December 1873 and 5–7 January 1874; however, individual representatives addressed the issue throughout the first session.

Prior to a discussion over the bill's substance, opponents and proponents contested the debate's structure, and that discussion reveals the partisanship that marked the ensuing conflict. Butler wanted the House to move quickly. He proposed a single day of debate with a vote before eight o'clock P.M. on 19 December, but as he announced this schedule Democrats objected, arguing that the bill's complexity necessitated an extended discussion. In a terse exchange, Butler declared that the House was familiar with the issue; therefore, a debate was superfluous. Democrats, represented by James Beck (Kentucky) and the newly seated Alexander Stephens (Georgia), countered that the matter was too grave to rush. They proposed an open-ended debate with sufficient time for both parties. Eventually Butler and the Democrats reached a compromise: the debate would continue until the second day after the holiday recess, provided that each speech not exceed twenty minutes. With the format determined, each side established its position.[30]

Butler began by providing a brief summary in favor of the bill. According to him, the measure was meant to enforce the rights that black citizens already possessed under the new constitutional amendments. Moreover, he argued that the bill reflected the mission and purpose of the United States:

> Whether it is wise or not to have given these equal rights is a question which no man can answer to-day, because we are trying an entirely new experiment in government. . . . We take in nations or parts of nations; we take in peoples or parts of peoples wholly diverse from us; and instead of throwing our laws over them and holding them by force, we have always given them equal rights of citizenship with us and rights of self-government; and not only the right of governing themselves but of assisting in governing us. This great experiment, for the first time tried in the history of the world, has not yet been concluded so that any man can say with certainty that it is the very summit of human wisdom. Certain it is, however, that it is the best emanation of human wisdom yet shown in government.[31]

James B. Beck, a Democrat born in Scotland, countered Butler's ideas with the primary arguments of bill opponents. Quoting the 1873 *Slaughter-House Cases* decision and the Bill of Rights, he argued that his state had the right to establish separate but equal facilities if it wished. The South would educate the former slaves, but it would do so on its own terms and in its own way. He concluded:

> I will say, however, that I see one evil purpose in all this legislation. Many of the gentlemen on this floor perhaps do not see it; but the purpose is, I fear, by this Federal legislation, to impose laws so obnoxious on the States in which there are large numbers of colored persons that they will, whenever the proper occasion arises, be goaded on to demand their rights in the most offensive form. It will happen, for course, that in some localities these offensive demands will be resisted or grudgingly given. Arrests will be made; imprisonments will follow; fines will be inflicted; the cry will be raised that these men are disloyal and not in obedience to the Constitution of the United States. . . . While, perhaps, no gentleman on this floor intends that, my word for it, that is the meaning, the intent, the purpose, and the object of driving this legislation through now, and under these circumstances time will prove the truth of what I say. Of course, it will be denied now.[32]

One final speaker addressed Congress on this first day, and it is appropriate that it was the voice of a former slave. Joseph H. Rainey, a representative from South Carolina, declared that the Civil Rights Bill was more than just a question of law. Congress had to approach the issue in the "light of humanity" and the progress of civilization. The bill was designed to protect his race from prejudice, especially in states such as Mr. Beck's Kentucky. He declared:

> We, sirs, would not ask of this Congress as a people that they should legislate for us specifically as a class if we could only have those rights which this bill is designed to give us accorded us without this enactment. I can very well understand the opposition to this measure by gentlemen on the other side of the House, and especially of those who come from the South. They have a feeling against the negro in this country that I suppose will never die out. . . . They, sir, would not give to the colored man the right to vote or the right to enjoy any of those immunities which are enjoyed by other citizens, if it had a tendency to make him feel his manhood and elevate him above the ordinary way of life. So long as he makes himself content with ordinary gifts, why it is all well; but when he aspires to be a man, when he seeks to have the rights accorded him that other citizens of the country enjoy, then he is asking too much, and such gentlemen as the gentleman from Kentucky [Beck] are not willing to grant it.[33]

With this speech, the debate was held over until after the Christmas recess. Three distinct personas had articulated three distinct positions. A white radical, a white Democrat, and a freedman had given their opinions. The debate that followed extended from these points.

On the first day of debate after the holiday recess, there were two moments of considerable drama. John T. Harris began the day's discussion, and he argued, in rational, controlled tones, that desegregation was inexpedient and unconstitutional. As the Virginia Democrat continued the style of his oratory changed, and his arguments became more extreme. At one point, he declared that desegregation was wrong because it was based on an incorrect and immoral principle. He said, "It is based upon the purpose, the theory, of the absolute equality of the races. It seeks to enforce by law a doctrine which is not accepted by the minds nor received in the hearts of the people of the United States—that the Negro in all things is the equal of the white man. And I say there is not one gentleman upon this floor who can honestly say he really believes that the colored man is created his equal." At this moment Alonzo Ransier, a black representative from South Carolina, interrupted Harris to state: "I can." Harris immediately replied, "Of course you can; but I am speaking to the white men of the House; and, Mr. Speaker, I do not wish to be interrupted again by him."[34] Later Harris affirmed that racial prejudice was natural and that white children were born with the knowledge of their superiority. Ransier again interjected, saying "I deny that," to which Harris replied, "I do not allow you to interrupt me. Sit down; I am talking to white men; I am talking to gentlemen."[35]

This exchange was both dramatic and revealing. It illustrated with sharp relief that the contest over desegregation was a fundamental conflict between the politics of equality and the ideology of place. The Republicans of the Forty-third Congress entertained various opinions as to the "perfect equality" of blacks and whites, but they had reached a widespread consensus that Harris's action was indecorous. The *Chicago Times* ran editorials against the Civil Rights Bill, but it also felt compelled to editorialize that "Mr. Harris unfortunately spoiled the effect of a good argument by an ill-timed and ill-tempered display of plantation manner."[36] The discursive norms that were a part of the master-slave relationship were no longer viable in the halls of Congress. The politics of equality had altered the political culture, and no white representative had the right to silence a black representative in the manner that Harris attempted. As we shall see, there were other members of Congress whose style and substance matched Harris's vitriolic statements, but they were in the minority. Moderate Democrats quickly realized that they would need to modify their rhetoric if they were going to sustain the definitions of place that made whites superior to blacks. Perhaps Alonzo Ransier was also thinking about the idea of place when he addressed the House later that day. He said that he was glad that things had changed in Congress, but he declared that slavery remained alive and well in the South. Those politicians who opposed desegregation proved that slavery existed by their actions in Congress. If African Americans had been equal enough to fight America's wars, nurse Southern children, and warm their masters' beds, why should Southern whites be concerned about "social interactions" now, he asked?[37]

A second dramatic moment transpired later in day when the former vice president of the Confederacy, Alexander Stephens, addressed the House. When the 1872 amnesty provision became law, Stephens became eligible to fill the vacancy caused by the death of Ambrose R. Wright. He arrived in Washington, D.C., on 1 December 1873. Never considered by the Republicans to have been a radical Confederate, the Georgia representative was praised for his attempt to keep the South from seceding.[38] At the same time, Stephens clearly represented the elite planter class of the antebellum era and its notions about place. During the war he had said that slavery was the Confederacy's cornerstone, and although he had opposed the black codes and had argued for reconciliation, he also had reaffirmed the South's right to secession.[39] In an edition of his book, *A Constitutional View of the Late War between the States,* given to Great Britain's earl of Rosebery, Stephens inscribed: "The Earl of Rosebery will find in this work a very thorough exposition of the causes, character, conduct and results, so far, of the late war between the States of the North American Union. . . . [The writer] also trusts that in it His Lordship will see a complete vindication of the *Rightfulness* [emphasis his] of the Southern Cause."[40] In 1874 Stephens was an icon of the old South: "Like a ghost of some earlier time, Confederate Vice President Alexander H. Stephens, now representing Georgia in the House, delivered the major speech in opposition," writes Foner.[41]

The House's leadership granted Stephens an hour to speak, provided that Robert Elliott, a black member of Congress, receive equal time for rebuttal.[42] According to the *Chicago Tribune,* "Stephens took a position near the final row of seats on the Democratic side, and spoke with his smoking cap on, as before, leaning on a pile of Congressional Globes, so arranged as to bring his manuscript near the level of his face." He was elderly and feeble; yet he possessed a shrill voice that could fill the entire chamber, and when he rose to speak, the Democrats' side overflowed and the galleries were packed. In a telling decision of either indifference or insult, hardly twenty Republicans remained seated to listen.[43] Those that remained heard a speech devoted to three primary arguments: 1) the Civil Rights Bill was unconstitutional, 2) the policy of desegregation was inexpedient, and 3) if left alone, African and European Americans in the South would prosper.

The reaction to Stephens's speech was mixed. His papers contain many letters expressing gratitude and requesting copies of his address. A Mrs. H. Whitsill wrote, "the Southern people have at length found a person who represents them in Congress with beaming dignity and ability."[44] Most of the Democratic press heralded his constitutional arguments as an example of reasoned statesmanship and learning.[45] The Republican papers, however, called the address a magnificent failure,[46] and at least one Northern Democratic press admitted that the speech did not meet expectations, because Stephens's voice was weak and strained.[47] Still, he had offered the strongest attack on desegregation to date, and his claims were effective. In the ensuing speeches, Democrats would state repeatedly that Stephens had expressed their own position completely, and most of the speakers modeled their own arguments after his. At the day's end Robert Elliott secured the floor to offer the Republicans' response.[48] Rather than begin his speech, he heightened the dramatic tension by allowing the House to adjourn until the following day.[49]

Whereas Stephens had represented the conservative opposition to the Civil Rights Bill, Elliott represented Republican idealism and, fairly or not, the entire black race. The principal representative among four blacks from South Carolina, Elliott had made a profound impression on his white colleagues as a freshmen member of the Forty-second Congress. His skin was dark and his facial features were so distinctively African that he had shocked his colleagues. Despite his British education, his blackness brought home the uncomfortable truth that a member of the "inferior race" occupied a position equal to their own.[50] Now, almost three years after he had entered Congress, Elliott rose to address the chamber and an overflowing gallery. Reportedly, the capacity crowd was 95 percent black, as many of the city's people of color had come to see one of their own refute the former vice president of the Confederacy.[51] The physical contrast between the young black representative and the aged statesman was extreme. Not more than thirty-two years of age, when Elliott addressed the crowd on 6 January he must have noticed Stephens, who had entered that morning in a wheelchair.

Opponents of desegregation, at both the national and state levels, often argued that African Americans did not have the intelligence or refined sensibilities to enter the public sphere as the equals of whites. In a sense one can view Elliott's address as a kind of test. Could an African American politician rise to the occasion and refute one of the country's most noted statesmen? Elliott began by expressing two regrets: that he should have to rise to advocate equal rights for American citizens, and "that the dark hue of my skin may lend a color to the imputation that I am controlled by motives personal to myself."[52] He then proceeded to deal with each of the controversy's most important issues—the constitutional question, the expediency theme, and black equality. In a comment aimed directly at Stephens, Elliot declared that the nation needed no instruction about human rights from one who had been so recently a traitor, and while Stephens had learned much since 1861, he was a laggard still. In response to Harris's speech of the day before, he said, "Let him feel that a Negro was not only too magnanimous to smite him in his weakness, but was even charitable enough to grant him the mercy of his silence."[53]

According to most accounts, Elliott passed his exam with flying colors. Peggy Lamson writes that when Elliott concluded, "the roar of applause was prolonged and deafening; so many Republicans (and even a few of the liberal Democrats) swarmed forward to shake Elliott's hand that they actually 'formed in line in the aisle and moved up to his seat in a column.' Everyone was talking about the nobility of his appeal to reason, the eloquence of his style, the dignity of his bearing, and the brilliance of his grasp of the constitutional issues."[54] Newspapers across the nation praised the speech. The *Chicago Tribune* stated that Elliott "commanded the attention of the House to an extent seldom achieved by any man. . . . The speech undoubtedly had great influence, and was worthy of it. The remark was common everywhere that there were probably not more than 20 of the 300 men in the House who could pretend to equal it."[55] The more conservative *New York Times* noted that the text was "well written" and "delivered with the earnestness and eloquence of a natural orator." Furthermore, the *Times* wrote that Elliott had given the Republicans several innovative arguments in support of the bill's constitutionality.[56] Thomas Nast memorialized the event with a stunning lithograph. In the center panel, Elliott is seen addressing the House, while on flanking panels full-length statues of Abraham Lincoln and Charles Sumner appear.[57] Even the Democratic *Chicago Times* admitted that Elliott had performed well, and in an editorial the following day, the paper felt it necessary to defend a prior article that had argued that no "full-blooded negro" had ever attained a high state of intellectual development.[58] Perhaps the greatest distinction Elliott received was that the white Republicans who spoke after him used his speech as definitive proof that African Americans were the equal of European Americans.

Elliott was not the only person of color to speak on behalf of the Civil Rights Bill. On 10 and 24 January a former minister of the African Methodist Episcopal Church, Richard Cain, added his voice to the debate.[59] Josiah T. Walls of Florida spoke on 6 January, and although his speech lacked Elliott's studied eloquence, it was remarkable for its passion and vision.[60] Ransier addressed the House several times. Not only did he speak on 5 January, but he also offered additional comments on 7 February and 9 June. A 9 June speech by James Rapier rivaled Elliott's text in its forcefulness and persuasive power.[61] Born in Florence, Alabama, in 1837, Rapier, like most of the black representatives in the House, was biracial. A "Free Negro" before the war, he was educated by private tutors supplied by his father. Sent North in 1857, he studied at Montreal College and later at the University of Glasgow in Scotland. He had been a teacher, a newspaper correspondent, and a farmer, and this last occupation became his primary job when he returned to Alabama to take over the family farm. He was popular among people of both races, and his neighbors asked him to serve as their representative to Alabama's Constitutional Convention.[62] Elected to the Forty-third Congress, he reduced the entire desegregation controversy to one concise statement: "Either I am a man or I am not a man."[63]

Compared to the exchange between Stephens and Elliott, the remaining debate was anticlimactic. In the end, Butler returned the measure and twelve amendments to the House Judiciary Committee. According to some accounts, moderate and conservative Republicans were pressuring Butler to "bury the bill." White Republicans from the South warned that it would destroy the party's chances in the fall elections. Privately, Northern Republicans worried that the Democrats might be right about the measure's effect on public education. If Congress desegregated public schools, perhaps public education would die as parents removed their children from the classroom.[64] Butler withdrew the bill, but before he did he offered a scathing critique of his opponents and a heartfelt defense of the bill. In the final moments of the debate, he declared: "Now, Mr. Speaker, these men have fought for their country; one of their representatives [Robert Elliott] has spoken, as few can speak on this floor, for his race; they have shown themselves our equals in battle; as citizens they are kind, quiet, temperate, laborious. . . . They have industry, they have temperance, they have all the good qualities of citizens, they have bravery, they have culture, they have power, they have eloquence. And who shall say that they shall not have what the Constitution gives them—equal rights?"[65] With these comments the formal debate ended. What began with promise concluded with enough frustration that Democrat and former New York city mayor Fernando Wood complained that the debate had been "fruitless." Despite Butler's best efforts to salvage the situation, the bill's supporters shared Wood's opinion. Several of the black members of Congress would offer speeches throughout the session, but most of the equalitarians, both within Congress and without, turned to the Senate. Perhaps, they hoped, the upper chamber could succeed where the lower had failed.

The Senate Debate, 1874

Sumner's Civil Rights Bill, minus its church desegregation clause, remained with the Senate Judiciary Committee through the winter months. Then, on 11 March 1874, Charles Sumner died. Just before his death, he had entrusted the bill to Senator Frederick Frelinghuysen of New Jersey, and reportedly his final words were, "You must take care of my civil rights bill—my bill, the civil rights bill, don't let it fail."[66] Whether it was in respect to Sumner's memory or because Lyman Trumbull no longer controlled the Judiciary Committee, the committee reported the bill favorably on 14 April 1874. *Harper's Weekly* demanded that the Republicans finish what Sumner had started, and it seemed that Senator Frelinghuysen was prepared to follow that advice.[67] A member of the Senate Judiciary Committee, Frelinghuysen expanded the bill by altering its enforcement mechanism to provide federal courts with exclusive jurisdiction over all civil rights cases.[68] Other moderate Republicans, perhaps to revive their moral authority or as a testament to Sumner's memory, backed the measure. The historian Bertram Wyatt-Brown suggests that "there is good reason to believe that the Senate momentarily succumbed to a contrite sentimentalism," as members of Congress who had remained silent previously became champions of desegregation and Sumner's memory. A legal historian, Michael McConnell, counters that the Senate's support for desegregation was genuine. His study of congressional voting records shows that a majority of the Republicans had voted for desegregation since 1872. Regardless of the motive, the bill was now popular, and Democrats were forced to use various tactics to weaken its provisions.[69]

The Senate debate was a halting affair. Most of the discussion transpired on 19 April and 20–22 May, although one can locate speeches on 30 April and 4 May. On the first day Frelinghuysen declared:

> We were told that to give the colored people freedom was to subject the whites of the South to murder, rapine, and violence. But instead of this—while not forgetting those from whom they had received the boon of freedom—they as a general rule had a tender regard for the comfort and well-being of those to whom they were formerly enslaved . . .
>
> We were told that if you placed them in the Army they would not fight; but in the front ranks they gave proof of their claims to high manhood.
>
> We were told that they would abuse the elective franchise; but unless a large majority of the Senate are in error, they have most wisely employed their privilege.
>
> So now, invest them by this bill with full and unqualified privileges, and they will so enjoy them as not to provoke, but so as to remove prejudice.[70]

Not surprisingly, the Democrats disputed Frelinghuysen's claims. For example, Senator Thomas Norwood of Georgia responded: "Nine years ago four million slaves were set free; the next year, clothed with civil rights; the third, armed with the ballot, like blind Polyphemus with his club; the fourth, makers of laws, of governments, and rulers of men, their former masters. Within this brief time they were graduated in the school of republican statesmanship, passing at a bound to the degree of doctor of their learned laws; and in ten States the whites were dismissed from office, and these learned republican doctors were set up on end like ten-pins, and put in charge. History furnishes no parallel to this triumph in the plastic art since God made man of clay."[71] Norwood's speech would be the last for several weeks. On 8 May 1874 the Republican caucus decided to postpone discussion and address other measures. According to the *Chicago Times*, the decision was made to give party stalwarts time to deal with internal dissension.[72] The Republican leadership was determined that the measure would pass, and they were willing to postpone the decision so that reluctant Republicans could be persuaded. The debate opened again on 20 May, and it continued for three days.

As the debate extended into the afternoon of 22 May, Democrats continued to vilify the measure and those who supported it. Lewis Bogy (Missouri), Henry Cooper (Tennessee), and Eli Saulsbury (Delaware), for example, punctuated their repetitious arguments with angry outbursts. Among these speakers the threat of miscegenation became an increasingly prominent theme.[73] At 9:30 P.M. Timothy Howe of Wisconsin offered the last speech in favor of desegregation. The Democrats, unwilling to concede defeat, sent a series of senators to the floor in an effort to exhaust their opponents.[74] This strategy continued until 3:00 A.M.[75] Despite these efforts, the opposition had little hope of wearing down the Republicans, who lounged in the cloakrooms or on couches in the back of the chamber. A bare quorum remained on the floor, and during this period, no more than twenty members—at times only three Republicans—were present. Those who remained wrote letters, read the newspaper, or, like the colorful Texan James W. Flanagan, fell asleep.[76]

When it was clear that the Republicans would not allow the Senate to adjourn, opponents tried to weaken the measure through amendments. A Republican senator from California offered the most popular of these amendments. Senator Aaron Sargent argued that states and school districts should have the right to maintain separate but equal schools. The amendment appealed to several Republicans who, like their House counterparts and Sargent himself, worried about the political consequences of school desegregation. A brief verbal battle ensued, but a sufficient number of Republicans followed the party's leaders, and the amendment was defeated by a five-vote margin, twenty-one to twenty-six.[77] Senator John Gordon's (Georgia) proposal to remove the school desegregation clause altogether was defeated as well, fourteen to thirty. Sargent then proposed to replace the word "schools" with "school systems," but Republicans quickly recognized that the motion would make it difficult to desegregate specific institutions, so after another lively exchange, the Senate rejected this amendment, sixteen to twenty-eight.[78] Without another motion on the table, Republicans called for a final vote, and almost twenty hours after the day's debate began, the bill passed with twenty-nine yeas and sixteen nays. Matthew Carpenter, the senator who had destroyed Sumner's efforts in 1872, Arthur Boreman (West Virginia), and John Lewis (Virginia) were the only Republicans to vote against the measure.[79] Adjourning after seven o'clock that morning, the Senate sent Sumner's modified Civil Rights Bill to the House.

To make the bill a law two actions were now necessary: The House had to alter its legislative rules to place the measure on the calendar, and it had to pass the bill. Since Sumner's death, the bill had sustained a regular majority, but when Butler tried to place it on the calendar, he fell short of the two-thirds he needed for the rule change.[80] Among Southern Republicans there was a general concern that passing the bill would doom the party's chances in the fall election. On 16 June 1874 Chester B. Darrall (Louisiana) chided his Southern colleagues: "I was not prepared to see gentlemen on this floor, members of the republican party, who come here representing southern constituencies . . . have any doubt as to the wisdom of passing this bill—indeed have so much doubt that they have even gone so far as to vote against the reference of it to the proper committee."[81] The bill returned to the House Judiciary Committee where it languished. According to McPherson, "Adoption of the law [in the Senate] was probably intended as a memorial to the dead senator, but the House, perhaps less affected by Sumner's passing, refused to concur in the Senate's action before adjournment."[82] Many Republicans remained interested in desegregation, but, at least according to *Harper's Weekly,* the public school clause remained a major stumbling block. Meanwhile, the white public had ceased to care. The *Chicago Tribune* reported, "there is very little enthusiasm for the bill in any quarter except among the colored people themselves." If Southern newspapers are an accurate indication of Southern feeling, white Southerners were outraged that the bill had achieved even this limited success. The Louisville *Courier-Journal* predicted a "war of the races." The *Atlanta Constitution* declared that every good white and black citizen deplored the Senate's action.[83]

The Fall Election of 1874

Perhaps the *Tribune* was correct; in the elections of that fall, the Democrats won a landslide victory. Every state but Iowa, Kansas, Maine, Vermont, and South Carolina rejected the Republicans. Corruption allegations and an economic downturn contributed to the Republicans' loss, but civil rights and especially desegregation were major issues in the campaign. The sponsor of desegregation in the House, Benjamin Butler, and several prominent party members lost their seats. Most distressing for the Republican idealists was that the election turned the Republican's two-thirds majority in the House into a seventy-four vote deficit. In 1874 the House contained eighty-eight Democrats and two hundred three Republicans (two seats were vacant). When the Forty-fourth Congress was scheduled to convene on 6 December 1875 there would be one hundred eighty-one Democrats and one hundred seven Republicans. Senate Republicans maintained their majority, but they lost eight seats, dropping from fifty-four to forty-six.[84]

One can interpret the 1874 election as the beginning of the end for Reconstruction's politics of equality. Not only did the Democrats take control of the House, but they also solidified their position throughout the South. Southern "redemption" had begun almost with the Reconstruction Acts of 1867, and the election of 1874 secured some important gains. Arkansas's and Florida's legislature were redeemed, and Alabama became the second "black belt" state—Georgia was the first—to return to Democratic rule. Southern conservatives won over two-thirds of the region's House seats, and even in states that remained Republican, the pending Civil Rights Bill had dampened the support of whites. The years of Republican control were coming to an end quickly. As the Forty-third Congress returned to start its second session, many of the men who had taken control of Reconstruction from President Johnson knew that their own tenure was short; consequently, two realities were painfully obvious when they arrived on 7 December 1874. Support for desegregation had hurt the party, and the problems of discrimination, racial prejudice, and violence remained, especially in the South. What the Forty-third Congress would choose to do with this information was unclear.[85]

The Congressional Debates of 1875

The House Debate, 1875

When the House Republicans began the second session, Benjamin Butler and other "stalwarts" in the party decided to use their final months in Congress to shore up Reconstruction's flagging policies. Their agenda included the Civil Rights Bill, a new enforcement act that expanded the president's power to suppress election violence and conspiracies, legislation to expand the jurisdiction of federal courts, and various appropriation measures to enhance the stature of departing Republicans.[86] This ambitious agenda faced a united Democratic front that interpreted the 1874 election as a mandate. When the gavel dropped and the session began, a Democratic filibuster seemed inevitable.

The Republican idealists had only one chance to pass new reconstruction legislation. They had to amend the rules of parliamentary discussion so that the House Democrats could not use procedural motions and open-ended debates to block the Republican agenda. In a fascinating synthesis of principle and politics, Butler decided to make desegregation the key. He would use a weakened Civil Rights Bill as a justification for the rules change, galvanizing Republican support behind the principle of equal rights. After its passage, Butler intended to move on the rest of his legislative agenda. On 16 December 1874 he reported a version of the Civil Right Bill that permitted "separate schools and institutions giving equal educational advantages in all respects for different classes of persons entitled to attend such schools."[87] The separate but equal language was a compromise to gain the support of Republicans who, in the broad daylight of the fall election, expressed reservations about the bill. Democrats immediately paralyzed the House through numerous motions to adjourn. Butler demanded that the House suspend the use of dilatory motions for the rest of the session. He then became irate when fifteen Republicans voted with the Democrats, and the motion failed to achieve the necessary two-thirds for a rules change. The situation moved from bad to worse when the Democrats began a full-scale filibuster on 27 January. With the roll called seventy-five times on procedural motions, "the Democrats stalled, deadlocking proceedings by repeating the same monotonous routines over and over. Since the House chamber had become the temporary home of the representatives, it soon began to resemble a disheveled campground."[88] The House stayed in continuous session for three days. In the middle of the morning on 29 January, the Republicans conceded defeat and allowed the House to adjourn. At that moment, it seemed as though desegregation was doomed.

The situation remained bleak until James Blaine (Maine), Speaker of the House and chairman of the Committee on Rules, suggested a compromise. The House would alter the rules to restrict dilatory motions to one day, but the motion would apply exclusively to nonfinancial legislation. The compromise would allow Republicans to get business to the floor with only a simple majority. It was backed by the influential Ohio representative and future president, James Garfield.[89] The proposal did not please Butler, however. It prohibited an appropriation measure that would have sweetened his departure.[90] But despite his negative vote, the compromise achieved a two-thirds majority, and the road was cleared for another debate over desegregation. The House discussion began on 3 February, and it involved two days of harsh language and extremely personal attacks.[91]

Butler began the debate by re-explaining the bill's goals and ideals. In the process, he exchanged remarks with William Niblack, a Democrat from Indiana, who questioned the wisdom of using federal rather than state courts to adjudicate civil rights cases. Butler responded that federal intervention was necessary so that the "banditti," "horse-thieves," and night-riding murderers of the South could not pervert justice. These comments incensed Texas congressman William McLean, who, according to one partisan newspaper, had been drinking.[92] McLean had entered the Confederate Army as a private, had been promoted to captain, and then eventually major. Believing that Butler had called a majority of Southerners horse thieves, bandits, and murderers, McLean, in reference to Butler's military career, muttered that the former Union general was the only murderer on the floor. Pandemonium ensued when Butler heard McLean's comment and brought it to the attention of the House.[93] After considerable effort, the speaker reestablished order, and in a final statement of defiance Butler declared, "if the gentleman said I was a murderer because I hanged a man at New Orleans, that so far from taking offense I glory in it, and the trouble has been that I did not hang more then than I did."[94] With this statement an acrimonious tone was set that would dominate the debate.

As before, black representatives played a crucial role. John R. Lynch of Mississippi argued that school desegregation was "harmless," and that the opposition's claims that it would destroy the South's educational system were absurd.[95] As the evening session wore on, a crowd remained in the galleries but few representatives stayed on the floor.[96] Among those who did were Richard Cain and Joseph Rainey. Both men challenged the claims of their white colleague, Representative Thomas Whitehead (Virginia), who argued that his state did not practice discrimination. The discussion that passed between the black representatives and Whitehead is interesting, because it reveals the degree to which both sides talked past one another. When asked whether Richmond streetcars excluded blacks, Whitehead responded that they did not. Rainey then detailed a recent instance when he had been ejected personally from a Richmond streetcar within the city limits. Unmoved by Rainey's personal testimony, the Virginia representative continued to insist that racially based segregation did not exist in Richmond.[97]

National newspapers characterized the previous day's debate as disgraceful, and the *Chicago Tribune* stated that Butler had set a horrible precedent with his "guerrilla and bush-whacking style." The *New York Times* compared the rancor between Butler and McLean to the conflict of the Civil War.[98] The confrontations of 3 February would prove to be minor compared to the uproar that transpired on the fourth. Charles Eldredge, a Democrat from Wisconsin, argued that African Americans were an inferior race and that Reconstruction had ruined the South's majesty and pride. In South Carolina, he said, educated and refined men and women were dominated by an "uneducated, semi-barbarous African race" whom Republicans had forced into power.[99] John Brown of Kentucky extended the arguments of his Northern colleague by accusing the Republicans of conspiring to overthrow the constitution. Brown declared that Benjamin Butler was full of falsehood, fraud, and meanness. In a personal attack of his motives, Brown compared Butler to an 1829 Scottish criminal that had smothered his victims and sold their bodies for medical dissection.[100] Brown's analogy "brought the members to their feet with as much suddenness as if a bomb had exploded over their heads."[101] The *Chicago Tribune* reported, "There has never been a time since the hot war when there was such a fever-passion that the very air seemed nervous. . . . there was a flush upon the face of every man."[102] Representative Hale, although he would vote against the measure, immediately proposed to censure Brown. Eldredge, James Beck, and Samuel Cox defended Brown, stating that Brown's comments were similar to Butler's. Republicans countered that Brown had "forgotten his decorum as a member," because his statements were premeditated. Accordingly, they argued that a strong penalty was necessary.[103] Hale's proposition passed and the speaker publicly censured the Kentucky congressman.[104] Fernando Wood, who had been serving as a Democrat since 1841, reflected: "When I first had the honor to be a member of Congress we had order, we had quiet, we had deliberation, we had discussion; but now we have none at all. It is continual excitement, continual disorder, and continual disturbance; that is God's truth."[105] The commotion actually seemed to work to the Republicans' advantage; the extreme rhetoric of Democrats such as Brown, Beck, Eldredge, and Cox united the party in a way that policy could not. A few conservatives, such as Simeon B. Chittenden of New York and James Sener and J. Ambler Smith of Virginia, vocally opposed the measure, but a majority agreed to vote in its favor, provided a compromise could be reached over its school clause.[106]

Three different approaches to the school proposition existed by 4 February. The first proposal, offered by Butler and the House Judiciary Committee, retained the school clause in a weakened state that reflected a separate but equal philosophy.[107] A second proposal—to substitute the Senate bill for the House bill—would have reinstated the original clause to desegregate public schools. A third suggestion by the Republican Stephen Kellogg (Connecticut) eliminated the common school language completely. Kellogg argued that if the clause remained in any form, Southerners could use it as a pretext for racism. Several Republicans agreed. Barbour Lewis, a Republican from Tennessee, explained that "while it is right that the colored man should have the same privileges in schools as the white; while nothing can be said against it on principle, still you must remember that legislation cannot always control public sentiment and at once mold and fashion and recreate great communities in their ideas, their thoughts, their habits, customs, and modes of life."[108] Even one of the black representatives testified that "[African Americans were] willing to accept anything which is deemed necessary to the welfare of the country. Spare us our liberties; give us peace; give us a chance to live; give us an honest chance in the race of life; place no obstruction in our way; oppress us not; give us an equal chance, and we ask no more of the American people."[109]

When the speaker called for a vote on Kellogg's amendment, one hundred twenty-eight yeas and forty-eight nays (many abstaining) were heard; the House removed the bill's clause to desegregate public schools. An amendment to allow separate but equal facilities for all of the institutions covered by the bill also was rejected, ninety-one to one hundred fourteen. In a final effort to reestablish school desegregation, the Pennsylvania radical John Cessna moved to substitute the Senate's 1874 bill for the House version. The house rejected the amendment that would have returned the bill to its original standing, one hundred fourteen to one hundred forty-eight. Finally, the speaker called the question on the bill itself, and one hundred sixty-two to ninety-nine, with twenty-eight representatives abstaining, H.R. 796 was sent to the Senate.

The Senate Debate, 1875

The Civil Rights Bill came before the Senate on 6 February 1875, and the upper chamber sent it to the Judiciary Committee, where it remained until the end of the month. Although desegregation's advocates had a majority, its passage was not guaranteed. Some expected the Senate, which had passed a more radical version in 1874, to reject the House measure which did not contain the school provision.[110] These fears were unfounded, and although the Republicans postponed the vote until 27 February, they stood solidly behind the bill. Without the school clause, desegregation's opponents attacked the bill less vigorously. Southern conservatives continued to oppose the measure, but they used the debate as an opportunity to discuss their positions on constitutional interpretation, states' rights, and the policies of Reconstruction. Indeed, for Senate Democrats, desegregation represented all of the political folly that they had endured over the past nine years.

Eventually, the Republicans moved to conclude the debate. Allen Thurman (Ohio) presented an amendment to remove the jury clause, but it was defeated after a lively exchange between Thurman and George Edmunds of Vermont.[111] Other amendments were introduced, but each failed in turn.[112] To conclude the discussion, and, one might add, the legislative prospects for civil rights during the Reconstruction era, Senator Edmunds offered a final speech. A skilled constitutional lawyer, he argued that the Democrats had demonstrated their true feelings not only in this debate but also since Reconstruction had begun. He said, "[the Democrats] have stood, therefore, with a persistence that would be worthy of a good cause, that slavery should not be abolished. They have said that citizens of the United States should not have the equal protection of the laws. They have said that race and color should still stand in this Republic and be made tests for the exercise of the rights of citizenship"; they are, he concluded, completely unrepentant.[113] With a vote of thirty-eight yeas to twenty-six nays, the Senate then passed the bill. Seven of the negative votes came from Republicans, and an additional nine senators abstained. On 1 March President Grant signed the measure, and it became the Civil Rights Act of 1875.[114]

The Civil Rights Act in the Post-Reconstruction Era

When he closed the debate, Edmunds expressed the hope that the Civil Rights Act would remove the inequities of slavery that had continued despite the institution's demise. The act did not have the effect Edmunds desired. Just before its passage the *New York Times* declared, "there is nothing left in the bill passed which is of very great consequence to the Negro or the white race."[115] A majority of historians and legal scholars seem to agree. James McPherson argues that the act had very little influence on Southern racial practices and that segregation continued as the norm.[116] A good portion of the bill's failure resulted from its enforcement mechanism. Although it gave broad power to federal courts, the bill required that the offended party first file a lawsuit. With little political power, scarce economic resources, and scant authority in their communities, most blacks could not seek redress. Moreover, federal attorneys encouraged them to take civil action rather than pursue the matter in federal court. With the uncertainty of a positive verdict, the number of cases dropped sharply after an initial flurry; subsequently, the South ignored the law with impunity.[117]

In 1883 the Supreme Court ruled in the *Civil Rights Cases* that the 1875 act was unconstitutional.[118] Writing for the majority, Justice Bradley affirmed that the Fourteenth Amendment did not empower Congress to regulate individual action; it only prohibited state action. Bradley did, however, spare the statute's jury section, and it alone survived until the next civil rights act in 1957. Justice John Harlan dissented, arguing that his colleagues had sacrificed the substance and spirit of the Fourteenth and Fifteenth Amendments.[119] Reaction to the decision was mixed. Southern politicians and the majority of European Americans seemed to agree with Bradley. According to Weaver, the Southern politicians of both parities praised the decision, because the act had only "hindered Negro progress and Negro-white relations."[120] The *New York Times* reported that the decision was greeted with cheers in Atlanta, while in the North it was met with little regard, since, according to the *Times*, it would not alter the condition of African Americans.[121] Republicans in Congress condemned the decision. Senator John Sherman said the justices had undermined the "cornerstone of Republican principles." The former secretary of the interior, Samuel J. Kirkwood, called the decision a terrible mistake. Louis T. Michener of Indiana called on President Arthur to support a constitutional amendment that contained the language of the 1875 act. Senator Benjamin Harrison, soon to be president himself, promised blacks that something would be done. Five bills, including a constitutional amendment, were introduced to replace the Civil Rights Act. It is difficult to determine the depth of this feeling, however, because President Arthur made only a tepid statement in favor of new legislation, and Congress never debated or voted on any of the measures.[122]

The primary repercussion of the court's decision was on Jim Crow. Ironically, the decision caused Republicans beyond the South to seek relief in state legislation. Eighteen states passed or amended their civil rights laws, and many of these were modeled after the 1875 act. Connecticut, Iowa, New Jersey, and Ohio passed statutes in 1884. Colorado, Illinois, Indiana, Massachusetts, Michigan, Minnesota, Nebraska, and Rhode Island did likewise in 1885. In these and other states, equal rights leagues were formed, and some African Americans in the North enjoyed a new sense of freedom. Nevertheless, despite the flurry of new laws, important differences remained between law and social practice. People of color sometimes won antidiscrimination suits, but the penalties were usually slight. Enforcement was haphazard, and it was not uncommon for African Americans to experience abuse from proprietors or patrons who were willing to flaunt the law. For the most part, "local traditions prevailed, and these accorded Negroes a place of inferiority."[123]

It is difficult to discern with certainty what motivated the civil rights initiatives of the Reconstruction and post-Reconstruction periods. Legal historians such as Robert Kaczorowski, J. Morgan Kousser, and Michael W. McConnell argue that the Republicans truly wanted African Americans to have every right and privilege of citizenship. They contend that Reconstruction's civil rights initiatives, including desegregation, resulted from the party's moral and ideological commitments to the Declaration of Independence.[124] When the Republicans found their agenda blocked at the national level, they acted pragmatically, turning their attention to state and local relief. While these claims have merit, most scholars contend that the support for radical legislation such as desegregation, even in the North, was mixed.[125] Stephen Riegel's study of lower federal court rulings between 1865 and 1896 found little difference between decisions in the North and in the South. The judges of both regions interpreted segregation as an adequate implementation of the Fourteenth Amendment. The lower courts took seriously the notion of equal, separate institutions; nonetheless, even Republican judges saw no contradiction between the "equal protection" of citizenship rights and the act of segregation.[126] Ward McAfee argues that the educational reforms in the Northeast, including Republican efforts to desegregate public schools, were motivated by religious and ethnic prejudices. In urban centers such as New York, whites did not want their children educated with blacks, but they feared a Catholic cultural takeover even more. The Republicans took advantage of these attitudes by instituting school reforms that forced Catholic children, especially those of Irish descent, to attend institutions controlled by state and federal governments. The party's leaders argued that school reform would protect Protestantism.[127] The sometimes contradictory evidence suggests that there was no consensus in the North about whether and to what degree racial desegregation should be enforced. In the South, the vast majority of whites and even some blacks believed that segregation was either a necessary evil or a positive good.

The demise of the 1875 Civil Rights Act was a portent of Jim Crow's triumph in the South. Tennessee took the lead in 1881 by segregating its railroad cars. In 1883 Arkansas segregated the hospital wards of its mental institutions, Florida segregated its railway system in 1887, and, in 1888 Savannah, Georgia, resegregated its cemeteries. This small trickle of legislation was followed by a second Supreme Court decision, *Louisville, New Orleans, and Texas Railroad vs. Mississippi* (1890). According to the court, states had the right to segregate transportation facilities, and that same year Louisiana moved to protect its Jim Crow cars. Georgia segregated its prisons in 1891. Then, in 1896 the Supreme Court gave official sanction to the "separate but equal" doctrine in *Plessy vs. Fergusson.* Arkansas, Alabama, Virginia, North Carolina, and Florida all adopted more stringent Jim Crow laws over the following seven years.[128]

Conclusion

For a number of historians, the omission of the school provision, the absence of a strong enforcement mechanism, and the Supreme Court decision of 1883 make the 1875 Civil Rights Act little more than an anomaly in the history of race relations during the nineteenth century. Gillette cynically writes that neither party was "taken in" by the radical orators who used the Declaration and spoke about liberty, equality, and first principles.[129] Wyatt-Brown comments that "Northerners and Southerners had come to agree, as they had in the 1830s, that basically the Negroes were undeserving of first class citizenship." He concludes, "if the bill could claim any significance, it lay in its demonstration of the bankruptcy of Republican Reconstruction principles. Rather than being a true memorial to Charles Sumner and his cause, it was a travesty of racial justice, because neither the white public nor its representatives expected or wanted the Act's enforcement."[130] Foner is less critical about the Republicans' motives, but he too concludes that the measure was a "dead letter" prior to the 1883 *Civil Rights* decision. Howard Rabinowitz has repeated this position in a review of segregation history and the work of C. Vann Woodward.[131]

In the chapters that follow, I acknowledge that the compromises in 1875 weakened the bill, but I also argue that this measure is extremely important. As C. Vann Woodward notes, its immediate effects were minimal, but it had a powerful symbolic presence within the African American community. In addition, the rhetoric that surrounded the bill's passage reveals a great deal about how the politics of equality had altered Reconstruction's political culture and about the innovative skills of moderate Democrats who modified the notion of place into a new rhetoric that co-opted much of the Republicans' position. The next chapter explores the egalitarian dimension of the act's symbolism by examining the advocacy of Charles Sumner. More than any other member of Reconstruction's Congress, Sumner influenced the politics of equality. His colleagues rarely embraced his radical proposals, at least in the forms that he introduced; nevertheless, his advocacy helped shape the political culture of the nineteenth century. By appreciating how this bill was initially the expression of an amazing career and rhetorical persona, one can begin to understand the complexities of this important moment in American history.

Conclusion

3

The Politics of Equality in Charles Sumner's Prophetic Vision

On 15 January 1872 Senator Charles Sumner explained Reconstruction's effect on African Americans and public policy: "Ceasing to be a slave, the former victim has become not only a man, but a citizen, admitted alike within the pale of humanity and within the pale of citizenship. As a man he is entitled to all the rights of man, and as citizen he becomes a member of our common household with equality as the prevailing law."[1] These words describe how Sumner viewed the changes of Reconstruction and the politics of equality. Compared to the norms of the antebellum, the nation had undergone a revolution. Property had become human and those who were once slaves were now citizens. For Sumner, these changes were a sign that equality was now a fundamental criterion for political judgment. Prudent policy and, by extension, wise deliberation required that equality be used as "the prevailing law," a law designed to make other laws.

This chapter focuses on the discursive origins of the 1875 Civil Rights Act. To appreciate Reconstruction's desegregation controversy, it is important to understand that Sumner's career and the norms of his political judgments were constituted by a discursive practice that challenged the nineteenth-century's political culture. I interpret Sumner's tumultuous career as the enactment of interpretive prophecy, and I use that lens to view his desegregation measure as the culmination of a prophetic agenda. Although the politics of equality had several proponents in Congress, Charles Sumner was its prophet and champion. He sought to return America to its revolutionary origins of participatory democracy.

The Tumultuous Career of Charles Sumner

According to Ronald Jager, Sumner's character was so complex and his personality such a paradox that he was an enigma even to his contemporaries.[2] His early life provides little evidence for the type of social and political agitator he became. Born in 1811 to a family of modest means, he approached his education with a seriousness that secured a place at Harvard University. There he earned the reputation of a studious pupil, though not an intellectual giant, graduating in 1830 and entering Harvard Law School soon thereafter. Although he graduated near the top of his class, he was never a successful lawyer. Easily distracted, he often lapsed into broad abstract speeches before the bench that had little to do with the case. Sumner was a talented legal scholar, and his law school mentor, Judge Joseph Story, hoped that he would return to Harvard as a professor, but in 1837 Sumner traveled to Europe where he acquired other goals.[3] Exposed to Britain's system of governmental administration and its social scene, he came to realize that he too could blend public service with social refinement.

In 1840 Sumner returned to America, and his life quickly turned toward politics. He found abolitionism to be the perfect outlet for his studious and philosophical character; reportedly his first newspaper subscription was to William Lloyd Garrison's *Liberator*.[4] By 1842 he had published several antislavery essays, including one that disagreed with the popular Daniel Webster.[5] His popularity grew as a consequence of his antislavery writing and his relationships with Boston's leaders. In 1845 city officials asked him to deliver the Fourth of July oration. He chose as his thesis the principle that "in our age, there can be no peace that is not honorable; there can be no war that is not dishonorable."[6] This was an odd theme given the rhetorical situation; his audience expected an epideictic address that celebrated the Revolution. Those expectations did not coincide with Sumner's sense of propriety, however. He stated, "The subject may be novel, on an occasion like the present; but it is comprehensive, and of transcendent importance.

It raises us to the contemplation of things not temporary or local, but belonging to all ages and countries—things lofty as Truth, universal as Humanity."[7]

With a transcendent truth as his object, Sumner stood before a large group of military personnel and "thundered at them on the wicked barbarism of their profession." He called war a degradation of human nature, and he affirmed that the standard for society's conduct always must be justice and benevolence. Not content with this verbal thrashing, he even included "contemptuous flings at the gay trappings of which the militia soldier is so proud."[8] His speech was so extreme that it both fascinated and distressed his friends, who were transfixed by his devotion to pacifism and his methodical oration that went well beyond the occasion's proprieties and existing opinion. After the speech, when Sumner, city officials, and invited guests retired for a Fourth of July dinner, "thirteen toasts were given, and nearly all the responses showed hostility toward Sumner and his ideas."[9] According to the *Daily Evening Transcript*, a Captain Park proclaimed that Boston was known for its odd notions, yet Sumner's ideas were the strangest he had ever heard.[10]

The address itself had several consequences. Politically, it established Sumner beyond the moderate perspectives of mainstream Whigs or Democrats, but it also brought many new speaking invitations. He soon became popular among a growing group of social activists. The allegiance of Sumner's new friends stemmed not from some uncommon depth that he possessed, but rather from his moral certainty and the honesty he displayed while speaking.[11] Philosophically, Sumner conflated personal and social propriety. Because the true standards of conduct were transcendent, they applied to individuals and societies equally. He stated, "The True Greatness of nations is in those qualities which constitute the true greatness of the individual."[12] Rhetorically, Sumner believed that no argument or mode of expression was indecorous if it spoke the truth and brought others into compliance. Reacting to the criticism his oration prompted, he wrote Robert Winthrop: "The customary tone of reference to the war of the Revolution is in a spirit which would be considered indelicate with regard to any private or personal experience; &, it seems to me, well worthy of consideration, whether the time has not come for nations to put aside their habits of boasting, as indecorous, if not unchristian. It seems to me that the propriety of this course must commend itself, not only for those, who may regard the conduct of the Fathers of the Revolution as questionable, but even to those who think it entirely justifiable."[13] Sumner did not perceive decorum as an extension of social practice or audience expectation. Propriety resulted from a correct perspective. This idea was reflected in his speech when he described his purpose: "I wish to expose an irrational, cruel, and impious custom, sanctioned by the law of nations." Regardless of international law, regardless of social custom, war was an evil that must be overthrown.[14] This stand brought Sumner to the attention of Theodore Parker, a radical transcendentalist. Parker thanked him for the speech, saying that it was a great service to humankind. Parker was not the only member of that New England social movement to notice Sumner. He became acquainted with over thirty-five transcendentalist thinkers, maintaining friendships with Parker, William Ellery Channing, William H. Furness, Margaret Fuller, and Ralph Waldo Emerson. These individuals were willing to overlook Sumner's affectations, which were many, because of his obvious sincerity and dedication to ideals.[15]

Owing to his moral philosophy, Sumner was a "Conscience Whig," although his oratory and political position labeled him as an outright abolitionist.[16] Along with others of similar mind, he tried to transform the Whig Party into an antislavery vehicle for change, against the objections of a second faction known as the "Cotton Whigs." After a rather public dispute with Robert Winthrop over the war with Mexico, Sumner refused to support Winthrop's re-election. Subsequently, Boston's elite completely excluded him from the social gatherings that he had enjoyed hitherto, and the Whig leadership turned on him as a renegade. The historian Anna Dawes writes, "especially sensitive to slights and social neglect, he suffered keenly. To the end of his life he remembered the sting and suffering of this time."[17]

By 1847 Sumner faced a difficult decision. He could alter his position, obtain absolution, and return to New England's circles of power, or he could maintain his principles and be forced to society's margins among the abolitionists. To solve this dilemma, Sumner found a third alternative. He became a member of the Free Soil Party. While his older Whig friends, such as John G. Palfrey, Charles F. Adams, and Attorney General Caleb Cushing, attributed his defection to ambition, his move toward the Free Soilers also coincided with his own vision of the truth. He was troubled by slavery's growth, especially through the harsh fugitive slave bill proposed in Clay's 1850 compromise. When, in April of 1851, he received his Senate seat from a loose coalition of Free Soilers and Northern Democrats, Massachusetts's citizens perceived him to be stubborn, uncompromising, and openly critical of politics.

Sumner's Senate record was mixed. He produced little legislation himself, and his critics complained that despite his considerable education, his constitutional arguments were less than precise.[18] But as his oratory grew more elaborate and his arguments more radical, his symbolic importance, especially for the cause of black rights, grew ever brighter. One of his earliest biographers, Moorfield Storey, proclaims, "Sumner brought into the Senate a new force. . . . He was no politician in the ordinary sense. He saw clearly what was right, and he devoted his life with absolute singleness of purpose and unwavering courage to the pursuit of the ends which his conscience approved. . . . His gaze was fixed on a distant goal, and he did not stoop to look at what lay in the path."[19] Two incidents, one prior to the war and one after the conflict, illustrate Sumner's rhetorical power and his almost cavalier inclination to exceed social and rhetorical conventions.

"The Crime against Kansas"

The Compromise of 1850 had forced an unstable peace concerning slavery. A few politicians hoped that the issue was settled; however, circumstances in 1854 quickly proved that slavery remained a volatile problem. Seeking to facilitate western expansion and a northern railroad line through Chicago, Stephen Douglas introduced the Kansas-Nebraska bill to organize Nebraska into two territories. To avoid the thorny issue of slavery, Douglas proposed that the territories should decide whether to permit the institution, and he described this policy with a term coined by Lewis Cass—"popular sovereignty."[20] Sumner believed, as did his colleague Salmon P. Chase, that popular sovereignty would spread slavery throughout the country; subsequently, during the spring of 1856, he purposed to give a "great philippic" on how congressional policy had ruined Kansas. For months armed proslavery Missouri raiders had disrupted Kansas elections and intimidated antislavery residents. That May, eastern papers reported that the raiders had increased in number, were actively disarming free-state men, and had taken prisoners.[21] Sumner used these reports as an opportunity to deliver his address: "The Crime against Kansas."[22]

Sympathetic biographers describe the speech as "a terrible indictment of a policy which should have been impossible in a free country" and as "an unanswerable presentation of eternal truths against the falsehoods of the hour."[23] Glen Stocker counters that Sumner's performance was a strange mixture of moral condemnation and insult. Sumner attacked Douglas unmercifully, at one point calling him a "noisome, squat, and nameless animal" who allowed a "perpetual stench of offensive personality" to proceed from his mouth.[24] His insults were so extreme that several members of Congress accused him of violating congressional decorum; even those who agreed with him felt that the address was indecent. Still, the entire incident might have been forgotten if it were not for the events that transpired two days later. On 22 May Sumner sat at his desk on the Senate floor, franking copies of his "Crime against Kansas" speech. He was approached by Preston Brooks, a South Carolina representative and relation to one of Sumner's foes. Brooks declared that the speech had been "a libel on South Carolina and on Mr. [Andrew P.] Butler, who is a relative of mine."[25] Brooks then attacked Sumner, repeatedly striking his head with a walking cane. Sumner, "eyes blinded with blood . . . then made a mighty effort to rise, and, with the pressure of his thighs, ripped the desk from the floor."[26] According to Storey, "Sumner's head was bruised and gashed, and the flow of blood was so copious as to drench his clothes and those of the men who helped him, but the thickness of his hair apparently prevented a fracture of the skull and saved his life."[27] Melodrama aside, the extent of Sumner's injuries remains unclear, but he did not return to the Senate for three years.

Scholars often reference this incident, but they confine its meaning within a narrow critical context. For example, Stocker's analysis is constrained by a specific and detailed history of the event and the events prior to the speech. Less explicit but also evident is a context of congressional norms about what constituted decorous debate. Based on that emphasis, he concludes that Sumner's attacks negated the logic and reason in his speech. Put simply, the speech was a failure.[28] Historians have taken a similarly narrow look at this event. Pierson argues that historians treat this incident as a clash of personalities; accordingly, they fail to consider its social significance.[29] I want to emphasize two aspects of this conflict that are largely unexplored.

First, this incident allowed Sumner to construct his persona as a prophet. Rhetorical critics have explored the role and function of prophecy as a type of speech. Critic Margaret Zulick writes, "prophecy, both as stylized speech and as dramatized public character, is an enduring deep source of American rhetorical consciousness that taps into the wellsprings of our religious and social imagination."[30] Sumner was able to tap into this prophetic voice. Not only did he use condemnation to reveal the sins of individuals and the nation, but he also had withstood evil and received the pains of his righteousness. Prophets are, of course, extraordinary "suffering servants" who possess special knowledge: "The prophet's burden is to make the extraordinary, invisible, and personal understandable, visible, and public."[31] Suffering becomes one means to accomplish and legitimate that knowledge, and Sumner's caning negated the eccentricities of his personality. Indeed, both Sumner and Brooks became mythic champions that had fought for the legitimacy of their respective camps. Public response to this incident reinforces this interpretation. Southerners sent Brooks ornate canes to replace the one he broke over Sumner's head, and although the House removed him from office, South Carolina immediately re-elected him. Northerners saw Sumner as a martyr, as "virtually every Northern city held a public meeting to protest the assault."[32] Among his friends, the transcendentalists, Sumner's speech was greeted enthusiastically. Parker praised it, declaring his hope that Sumner would keep his integrity always. Emerson called Sumner's condemnation of the Kansas-Nebraska bill "brave, temperate & sound," and he urged the senator to stand fast.[33]

Second, this conflict represents a growing tension in the antebellum political culture that led to the Civil War and continued during the Reconstruction era. Sumner's speech and the subsequent conflict were repudiations of the dominant political sensibility of that century. The rhetorical critic James Jasinski writes that Henry Clay helped to define a pattern of political judgment that dominated the antebellum era.[34] This form made compromise a virtue; consequently, political judgments were constrained by the need to balance regional and economic interests. Any idealism, other than the primacy of union, became dangerous because it threatened to upset this careful balance. In the antebellum era's political culture, Sumner was a dangerous person. More abolitionist than senator, his speech inverted prudence, making accommodation not only imprudent but also evil. Accommodation sustained slavery. No amount of compromise would make slavery right, and according to Sumner nothing could be settled which was not right.

The discursive sensibilities of Sumner's "Crime against Kansas" speech foreshadowed the Civil War and Reconstruction. When accommodation became imprudent, division was inevitable. Paradoxically, the South reached this position before the North did. Regardless, once the war began both sides eschewed the prudential accommodation of the past in favor of various principles—states' rights, union, slavery, emancipation, and, eventually, redemption. Once the war was over, a number of politicians refused to return to the standards of the past. These individuals were uninterested in compromise; after all, compromise had only postponed what they saw as an inevitable conflict. Not surprisingly, Sumner was at the forefront of this struggle, as his opposition to the Fourteenth Amendment demonstrates.

Sumner's Opposition to the Fourteenth Amendment

Throughout the Reconstruction era, Sumner worked for the civil and political rights of African Americans. After Johnson reestablished the Southern state governments without black representation or suffrage, Sumner quickly joined the chorus of radical voices against the president. Despite his prominence, Republican leaders thought Sumner too unpredictable to join the Joint Committee on Reconstruction.[35] His colleagues knew him well. In February of 1866 Sumner spoke repeatedly against one of the early versions of the Fourteenth Amendment. As he did before the war, he declared that the proposal was yet another example of accommodation. A revealing portion of the text reads: "I am at a loss to understand the origin of a proposition which seems to me nothing else than another Compromise of Human Rights, as if the country had not already paid enough in costly treasure and more costly blood for such compromises in the past. I had hoped that the day of compromise with wrong had passed forever. Ample experience shows that it is the least practical mode of settling questions involving moral principles. A moral principle cannot be compromised."[36] To Gerrit Smith he wrote, "To my mind it is the meanest & wickedest proposition every brought into Congress. Its baseness is colossal."[37]

Along with this criticism, Sumner extolled the amendment's egalitarian ideal, but his praise did not save him from censure. According to Donald, "the oration was a grand discourse on principles," but the Republican leadership viewed the speech as indecent:

> Among Republican leaders, Trumbull considered Sumner devious and unscrupulous; Grimes called him "a cold-blooded, selfish, dangerous man"; and Fessenden regarded him as a "malignant fool." Fellow Radicals, too, sharply disagreed with him. Even the genial Wilson was unwilling to follow him in opposing the Fourteenth Amendment. Wade, after listening to one of Sumner's hyper-classic speeches which, he said, only proved the obvious, remarked despairingly: "It's all very well, Sumner, but it has no bones in it." The equally Radical Zachariah Chandler could not endure Sumner's lecturing and when he began piling precedent upon precedent, quotation upon quotation, would leave the Senate chamber, growling: "Sumner is one of them literary fellows."[38]

In a sense, Trumbull was correct. Sumner was unscrupulous according to the political standards of the pre-Civil War era. He resisted the antebellum patterns of judgment. Using the Declaration of Independence as a sacred text, he declared on 6 February 1866: "Our fathers solemnly announced the Equal Rights of all men . . . and now the moment has come when these vows must be fulfilled to the letter. . . . A failure to perform these promises is moral and political bankruptcy. It is a repudiation of moral and political duties."[39] In Sumner's view, Congress faced a propitious moment in the nation's history. Now was the time to implement a radical understanding of the Declaration into the country's structure and culture. Anyone who disagreed with his position was compromising with slavery.[40]

Lessons for Desegregation

This brief sketch of Sumner's political career has relevance for the Civil Rights Bill he introduced in 1870. Sumner became, at least in his own mind, a moral prophet and the embodiment of principle.[41] This characterization is both descriptive and critical. The Fourth of July incident reveals Sumner's sense of decorum, which was inextricably linked to moral righteousness. His "Crime against Kansas" speech and the subsequent clash with Brooks illustrates his embodiment of antislavery ideals and suffering service. His attack on the Fourteenth Amendment demonstrates his tendency to ignore the requirements of politics when they conflicted with his beliefs. If analyzed individually or with reference only to the historical facts, these events constitute Sumner as an ideologue who failed to comprehend the norms of political office. But when Sumner is approached as the constituted subject of certain social forces, he becomes a moral prophet with an agenda to reformulate the nation's political culture.

Sumner's career should be approached critically, from the perspective of interpretive prophecy. According to Michael Walzer, prophecy involves a form of critique that combines inspiration with a "poetic version of what must have been at least sometimes, among some significant part of the prophet's audience, ordinary discourse." The prophet's goal is "to arouse remembrance, recognition, indignation, repentance." [42] In Sumner's case, he combined an inspired vision of black equality and rights with a dramatic interpretation of the United States' purpose and principles. He made the egalitarian dimensions of the Declaration of Independence the foundation of society, and he called Americans back to that moral code. Although his political agenda was revolutionary, he shaped his message by the retelling of past values from which society had departed. That he had reinterpreted the tradition to suit his goals and new circumstances did not lessen their power as historical proof.

Walzer notes that the interpretive prophet gains authority from his or her situated stance. That is, the prophet exists within particular social boundaries, and while she may play at detachment, her discourse is grounded in the moral codes of the society to which she belongs.[43] Jeremiah, not Jonah, is the archetype here. According to Zulick, Jeremiah's prophetic voice was dialogic—constituted by his own multiple consciousnesses as a member and critic of Jewish society. As a result, "the prophetic ethos in Jeremiah is multivocal and socially constituted" at its core.[44] Likewise, Sumner derived his authority from his status as a senator—a representative of the people. His voice was also multivocal, representing the ideals of abolitionism, the classical values of a Harvard scholar, and the philosophy of the transcendentalists. He was both a reflection of and a reaction against the political culture of the antebellum era, but, more than that, Sumner's prophetic voice was a catalyst for the political changes that began in 1865.[45] A lithograph of Sumner published by Henry Schile summarizes the moral significance of the senator's political career. A youthful looking Sumner stand with one hand in his vest and the other pointing to a document that reads: "Equal rights to all." Published the year of his death (1874), the image portrays Sumner as the champion of equality. (See Figure 3) In the early years of the Reconstruction era, Sumner, along with a few other radicals, insisted that African Americans receive every conceivable right—political, legal, and public—that was granted to European Americans. From 1865 to 1875 Congress moved slowly in that direction, and although many members of Congress never embraced the principle of equality as fully as he, Sumner was instrumental in goading his colleagues further, in leading his people to repentance.

Sumner's Politics of Equality

Sumner's defense of desegregation was more than an expression of his radicalism; it was also the penultimate declaration of his persona and career. In arguing for the Civil Rights Bill, Sumner extended the politics of equality, which, thanks to his discursive agitation, was a legitimate dimension of the political landscape. First, he established the notion that segregation, regardless of its intent or motive, could never be truly "equal." Second, he combined a new national policy for race relations with the traditional values of human equality and rights. Finally, he advocated a system of jurisprudence grounded not only in precedents and original intent, but also in the social realities of the present. Sumner's 15 January 1872 speech not only defended his decision to amend the Amnesty Bill with the Civil Rights Bill, it also foreshadowed the vision of civil rights that we maintain today.

FIGURE 3.

Equality versus Inequality

The opening moments of Sumner's address are important, because they invoke a distinction between material appearances and a metaphysical reality. He declared: "Mr. President, slavery, in its original pretension, reappears in the present debate. Again the barbarous tyranny stalks into this Chamber, denying to a whole race the equal rights promised by a just citizenship. Some here thought slavery dead. This is a mistake. If not in body, at least in spirit or as a ghost making our country hideous, the ancient criminal yet lingers among us, insisting upon the continued degradations of a race."[46] With these words, Sumner established a proposition that characterized the logic of his judgment to support desegregation—put simply, "slavery" persists. From that assumption Sumner argued the following: slavery must be abolished; equality must become manifest in daily life; and only desegregation can achieve these goals.

Sumner's comments reveal how the speaker's assumptions differed from the larger public. In the aftermath of the Civil War it seemed reasonable to assume that slavery was dead. Indeed, even before the war's end, newspapers and magazines described the institution's demise. An illustration by Thomas Nast, which appeared in *Harper's Weekly* only weeks after the Emancipation Proclamation, is instructive. Across the top of two pages, the word "E M A N C I P A T I O N" appears. The left page, which comprises a distinct panel, portrays the slavery system with all of its iconic horrors—slave auctions, whipping, hot irons, chains, and so forth. The right page features a panel with black men and women receiving wages, young children hurrying off to school, and a cordial greeting between black workers and a white foreman. In the center, between the slavery past and freedom's future, Nast draws a happy black family, relaxing by a warm stove.[47] This illustration was not accurate, of course. As many historians note, the Emancipation Proclamation was narrow in its scope.[48] More to the point, the title of the lithograph, "The Past and Future," communicates the symbolic nature of the picture's images. The illustration that appears in *Harper's Weekly* and a second version that Nast published in 1965 are ideal representations of the "emancipation moment." They announce the triumph of freedom gained by the sacrifices of civil war and the brave pronouncement of President Abraham Lincoln. (See Figure 4)

Republicans took great pride in the fact that slavery was dead. The North's victory was, in part, a victory of ideology. Central to the Republicans' belief system was the idea that slavery was the explicit denial of economic self-determination.[49] Most Americans understood slavery only in

FIGURE 4.

connection to the chains and whips that Nast depicted in his illustration. Because these icons were absent, the labor system was dead; slavery was abolished. Sumner's text, however, implied that chains and whips were only symbols. Through metaphor, he suggested that slavery's spirit, its essence, existed even though its corporal body had decayed. He declared that the "slave is free" but only in part, "No longer a chattel, he is a man justly entitled to all that is accorded by law to any other man." Furthermore, Sumner acknowledged that "the *slave* testifies; the *slave* votes." "But," he declared, "this is not enough." Blacks remained slaves despite their access to certain legal and political rights. Despite this limited freedom the African American was a slave, because "the denial of any right is a wrong that darkens the enjoyment of all the rest."[50]

Central to Sumner's rhetoric was a basic dissociation between the idea of slavery and the traditional manifestations of slavery. Slavery's chains were rusted through, yet "little children are turned away and forbidden at the door of the common school, because of the skin. . . . the indignity offered to the colored child is worse than any compulsory exposure, and here not only the child suffers, but the race to which he belongs is blasted and the whole community is hardened in wrong."[51] Sumner asked his colleagues to comprehend segregation as yet another of slavery's manifestations. This was a departure for many of his colleagues, since they had adopted an antislavery stance not from any particular appreciation for African Americans, but because of slavery's economic repercussions. In contrast, Sumner argued that slavery was an evil that transcended its symbols. It was a particular ideal that allowed European Americans to cry out, "I am better than thou, because I am white. Get away!'"[52] The doctrine of white superiority was the essence of slavery, and any legislation that sustained that was another incarnation of the same.

In his own words, Sumner wanted to rid the nation of its racial caste that had its basis in slavery's broad philosophy; thus he expanded, or one might say reduced, slavery to inequality's presence and sanction within the public sphere. To provide evidence for slavery's continued presence, Sumner identified examples of discrimination involving Frederick Douglass and Louisiana's lieutenant governor, Oscar Dunn.[53] Furthermore, Sumner read aloud from the numerous letters and petitions he had received from African Americans. Quoting from a letter of a black man from Georgia, Sumner said, "In whatever direction we [African Americans] go, whether it be in public places of amusement, in the street cars, upon the railroad, in the hotel, or in the way-side inn, we encounter the invidious distinction of caste and oligarchy. . . . we would be less than men if we did not everywhere, and under all circumstances, utter our earnest and solemn protest against this inhuman outrage upon our manhood."[54] Citing similar evidence from the North and the South, from Virginia to Pennsylvania, Sumner concluded that people of color were still slaves.

Sumner's redefinition of slavery allowed him to benefit from the term's persuasive history. Slavery had been a condensation symbol or ideograph since the American Revolution.[55] Although most rhetorical scholars have focused on terms such as liberty and property, slavery played a crucial role in revolutionary rhetoric. Celeste M. Condit and John L. Lucaites declare that an abhorrence of personal enslavement was the single most prevalent position shared by all of the colonists.[56] Sumner recognized slavery's rhetorical force. Before their estrangement, he had written Winthrop that the colonies' "grievance, their slavery, was the necessity of paying a few pence more or less on certain things, under the direction of a Parliament in which they were not represented. No just or humane person can fail to perceive that all this was as a feather compared with the rod of oppression, now held by our country over *more than three millions of fellow-men.*"[57]

Sumner, like Frederick Douglass, understood that "there is not a man beneath the canopy of heaven that does not know that slavery is wrong *for him*."[58]

The genius of Sumner's text was that he contrasted slavery with equality. During the American Revolution, liberty was slavery's antonym. Although equality increased in prominence with the conflict, the terms liberty and property constrained the egalitarian dimension of equality along the lines of race, gender, class, and citizenship. Most mid-nineteenth-century Americans valued the idea of equality, but they defined it narrowly. Even the Great Emancipator had adhered to narrow assumptions, maintaining various and seemingly contradictory positions.[59] Most of those who had opposed slavery saw liberty as slavery's opposite. In contrast, Sumner's text made equality slavery's antithesis. In the ideal world of his political and moral reality, slavery and equality were agonistic, and each defined the other. In a revised version of this speech that Sumner edited for a collection of his speaches, he explained, "the denial or abridgement of Equality on account of color is also part of Slavery. So long as it exists, Slavery is still present among us."[60]

Grounded in Enlightenment philosophy, Sumner utilized the notion of human equality to form the transcendental basis of desegregation. He argued, "The various colors of the human family belong to the same mystery. There are white, yellow, red, and black, with intermediate shades, but no matter what their hue, they are always MEN, gifted with a common manhood and entitled to common rights."[61] One can locate similar comments in John Locke, David Hume, Jean-Jacques Rousseau, and Charles Buffon, because, at an abstract level, Enlightenment thinkers argued that certain qualities of human nature cut across racial distinctions. Sumner took this abstract idea and transformed it into a complex pattern to guide public action. He had argued before the Massachusetts Supreme Court, in 1849, that the "fundamental right of all citizens" was "Equality before the Law."[62] Now, in 1872, Sumner reformulated this legal principle into a political philosophy. "Equality in rights" was the first right of all citizens: "Equality in rights is not only the first of rights; it is an axiom of political truth. But an axiom, whether of science or philosophy, is universal and without exception or limitation; and this is according to the very law of its nature."[63] Equating the political and moral arenas to the truth of empirical studies, Sumner established a universal law that encompassed not only the judicial but also the personal, political, and moral dimensions of society.

Sumner's emphasis on the equality of rights influenced his memory of the Civil War. According to him, the Civil War was caused by an ideological conflict between the divergent principles of slavery and equality. Both sides in this conflict recognized that the "self evident" truth of equality was the real issue: "The Nation insisted that all men are created equal; the Rebellion insisted that all men are created unequal."[64] Quoting Jefferson Davis and Alexander Stephens, Sumner argued that the Confederacy used white supremacy as the foundation of its governmental system. Aligning himself with Lincoln and redefining the president and the Union's war goals in the process, he affirmed that Lincoln had taken up the gauntlet that Davis had thrown down. According to Sumner, Lincoln, en route to the Capital on 22 February 1861, suggested that death was preferable to relinquishing the egalitarian principle within the Declaration of Independence.[65] In reference to the "Gettysburg Address," Sumner declared that "in precise conformity with the Declaration, was it announced that our Republic is dedicated to the Equal Rights of All; and then the prophet-President, soon to be martyr, asked his countrymen to dedicate themselves to the great task remaining."[66] With inequality established as the war's cause and perfect equality described as its goal, Sumner concluded, "the victory of the war is vain without the grander victory through which the Republic is dedicated to the axiomatic, self-evident truth declared by our fathers, and asserted by Abraham Lincoln."[67]

Sumner's war narrative served several purposes. First, it added historical weight to his polar principles—equality and slavery (that is, white supremacy). When he retold the story of the Civil War, he provided flesh to the abstract bones of his principles. Equality became the Union's motive. The association with Lincoln also strengthened Sumner's argument. It did not matter that Lincoln never articulated an equality as radical as Sumner's. The late president's prestige was growing by the year; even the Democrats and former Confederates dared not assail his image. In death, Lincoln's persona became the common property, and the president's exact feelings and attitudes became obscured by the need to make sense of the war and his tragic end. Furthermore, as scores of politicians aligned themselves with the mythic figure, Lincoln's actual policies blended with the assumptions and purposes of these politicians. This process was aided by the latent paradoxes in Lincoln's own discourse. When Sumner aligned his equality with Lincoln and slavery with the Confederates, he no doubt hoped that Lincoln's symbolic power would make him seem less extreme.

Another aspect of his Civil War memory was that his account strategically aligned the North's war aims, which every Republican embraced, with desegregation as a policy. Sumner's narrative reformulated the late conflict to make room for the Civil Rights Bill. Every Republican believed in the justness of the war, and its glory was a powerful rhetorical resource. Because Sumner argued that equality in rights was the war's ultimate goal, he was able to claim that his bill was necessary to conclude the conflict. Recall his words that "the victory of the war is vain" without a victory that secures the rights inscribed by Jefferson. He declared that justice, the promise of happiness, and indeed the war's very meaning would be lost if Congress did not pass his legislation.[68] Desegregation was the final act to ensure the freedom that Union soldiers had purchased with blood.

The thesis of Sumner's 15 January 1872 text resides in its slavery-equality agon; however, his discourse does not end there. Based upon this dichotomy, Sumner defended desegregation through three distinct sets of arguments. First, he applied the equality ideal to the racial subjectivity of people of color; second, he argued that the current practices of inequity necessitated the bill; and finally, Sumner used his egalitarian philosophy to reinterpret the Constitution.

From Slave to Citizen

The words that began this chapter articulate the dramatic change that Sumner attributed to the Reconstruction era. He said, "ceasing to be a slave, the former victim has become not only a man, but a Citizen, admitted alike within the pale of humanity and within the pale of citizenship. Dishonor to him is dishonor to the Republic itself."[69] This passage argues that the politics of equality which characterized Sumner's present had altered the very being of freedmen and women. In a version of this speech edited for his public papers, Sumner expanded on this shift, claiming that Aristotle had distinguished between Greeks and barbarians by calling non-Greeks little more than plants and brutes. "This," he suggested, "is the very distinction between Citizenship and Slavery. The Citizen is of the national household; the Slave is no better than brute or plant. But our brutes and plants are all changed into men; our Barbarians are transformed into Greeks."[70]

At one level these passages engaged the primary issue of Reconstruction politics. Are African Americans equally human, and, if so, are they a part of the American community? Clearly Sumner's position coincides with that of blacks both before and after the war. But for a few noteworthy exceptions, the declaration of the National Negro Convention of 1853 is representative: "Notwithstanding the impositions and deprivations which have fettered us—notwithstanding the disabilities and liabilities, pending and impending—notwithstanding the cunning, cruel and scandalous efforts to blot out that right, we declare that we are, and of right we ought to be *American citizens.* We claim this right, and we claim all the rights and privileges, and duties which, properly, attach to it."[71] Sumner brought these arguments into the halls of Congress, and in the process he added something important to this discussion.

Social norms excluded reformers such as Frederick Douglass, Wendell Phillips, and Elizabeth Cady Stanton from mainstream politics. Because their position was marginal compared to those who controlled the public sphere, "they could not avoid forms of address that worked powerfully against them, and their ethos inevitably was both radical and compromised, black and white, female and male."[72] The texts of most nineteenth-century radicals pursued multiple purposes (for example, persuasion, identity [re]construction, and legitimization). Audience expectations were important for these speakers, because their violation might lead to further silencing. In contrast, Sumner existed *within* the United States' inner circle of political power, and this position gave him a discursive advantage. First, he could express extreme ideas, yet his colleagues could not exclude him from political debate. As a member of Congress, his right to speak was guaranteed, provided he did not violate parliamentary rules. Second, Sumner's discourse was influenced by the demands of the political process; consequently, although his agitation resembled the discourse of other reformers, he was forced to connect the rights of African Americans with the rights of other citizens. His rhetoric was more encompassing than some reformers, because he had to address the common good. With these two ideas in mind, consider the following section, which illustrates Sumner's thought as well as his prophetic voice: "Whatever he may have been, he is now the same as ourselves. Our rights are his rights; our equality is his equality; our privileges and immunities are his great possession. To enjoy this citizenship, people from afar, various in race and complexion, seek our shores, losing here all distinctions of birth, as, into the ocean all rivers flow, losing all trace of origin or color, and there is but one uniform expanse of water where each particle is like every other particle and all are subject to the same law. In this citizenship the African is now absorbed."[73] Through descriptive imagery, Sumner proposed that the varied racial backgrounds of America's inhabitants ran together into the vast ocean that was the nation. In this ocean, each stream became indistinguishable from every other. One might infer that each person's natural origins no longer mattered. In the United States, citizenship eclipsed racial difference; thus African Americans were consubstantial with European Americans. But why are they the same? In the analogy, the streams become alike, not because they undergo a material transformation, but because they exist within a new *context.* They were separate, but as they come together, they become alike in a vast ocean. The transformation that Sumner's text attributed to people of color resulted from a change *in place.* African Americans were the same as European Americans because they now occupied the same space as whites. They were Greeks not because they had transmuted into something physically different, but because they were now citizens; they were within the national sea.

By building his association between blacks and equality on the Fourteenth Amendment, Sumner separated himself once again from the moderate Republican position. Maltz contends that the philosophy of natural rights dictated the Republicans' approach to African Americans during this era. According to him, Republicans believed that nature's laws required that blacks possessed certain basic rights.[74] While this philosophy had facilitated their free labor ideology and antislavery stand, it did not move much beyond a basic support for black economic self-determination. Moreover, one might note that its focus on "nature" worked against a sense of sameness because it allowed critics to emphasize those physical—that is, natural—differences that distinguished white from black. In contrast, Sumner defended desegregation because it enacted the ideal of a human equality, but then he extended this position to argue that African Americans now enjoyed more than the equality of natural rights. Their citizenship entailed a sameness that was not determined by nature's law. For him, the Fourteenth Amendment extended the basic ideals of nature and turned them into a type of social and political contract that had no connection with the physical characteristics that kept the races apart.[75]

According to Sumner, the opponents of desegregation failed to recognize that physical "realities" did not determine a person's equality. Among his critics, the "prejudice of color" persists, he said. This prejudice "pursues its victim in the long pilgrimage from the cradle to the grave, closing the school, barring the hotel, excluding from the public conveyance, insulting at the theater, shutting the gates of science, and playing its fantastic tricks even in the church where he kneels and the grave where his dust mingles with the surrounding earth."[76] To Sumner, those who relied on physical differences to determine a person's worth misunderstood the new context that citizenship entailed. Because of citizenship, material or individual differences no longer mattered. Inclusion within the social contract guaranteed equality, regardless of a person's intellect or education. As explained through his metaphor, Sumner argued that the opponents of civil rights denied the reality of the national "ocean." They assumed incorrectly that the physical characteristics that made each race unique kept the "rivers" of America's populace ever separate.

Few arguments could have been a sharper condemnation of the cultural beliefs held by Southern conservatives. Sumner's text took the notion of place and transformed it into a vehicle for the politics of equality. Through a metaphor that established a common place, a single public space, Sumner inverted a concept that conservatives used to define and defend Southern culture. He refused to recognize the conservatives' thesis that each person and race was designed, by God, to pursue distinct public duties. Instead, Sumner posited a common purpose for every citizen. Someone's family heritage, regional location, and class affiliation no longer mattered in his broad metaphor. Furthermore, his discourse shifted attention from the freedman's person to his status as citizen; he associated equality with African Americans by avoiding completely the empirical differences that Southern conservatives used to justify segregation.

It is hard to imagine a rhetoric that conflicts more directly with the Southern ideal of one's proper place. Perhaps another metaphor, enunciated by Booker T. Washington on 18 September 1895, will illustrate the power and implications of Sumner's discourse.[77] Washington argued that in all that is "social" the races could remain as separate as fingers, but they could work together toward common goals and progress as one hand. In this metaphor, Washington described American race relations in terms of separate and static identities. Although citizens may have a common goal, they only achieve that goal by maintaining their distinctiveness as separate fingers. Sumner's common purpose was fundamentally different. His water metaphor entailed a dynamic, progressive connotation that was missing from Washington's hand metaphor. Citizenship and political liberty were not static concepts but notions that evolved as the streams of time and history brought them into convergence. In Sumner's text, the separate races moved and blended together, and, most important, they did not maintain separate identities as fingers or as any other body part. The Massachusetts senator created a vision of the public sphere in which each person was indistinguishable within a collective ocean of American identity.

It may be impossible to underestimate the ramifications of Sumner's association between African Americans and equality. His prophetic assertions called for a radical shift in America's institutional, social, political, and cultural systems. It forced into the public sphere a whole class of people that the nation, both North and South, had either excluded or segregated into distinct places. Moreover, his transformation provided the former slaves with a status that extended the legal and political ramifications of the Fourteenth and Fifteenth Amendments. One could not construe citizenship narrowly, at least not as he defined it. Citizenship granted an equality of being that physical characteristics could neither deny nor affirm. It would seem that to Sumner, intelligence, wealth, and most certainly race had no bearing on the principle of equality.

Sumner's arguments closely paralleled the claims of certain abolitionists and the black community. Well before 1863 these two groups had sought to remove slavery and guarantee equality to America's black populace. The abolitionists of New England had worked hard to eliminate various forms of segregation.[78] Within the black community, equality almost always had had a broad scope. In 1792 the freedman Benjamin Banneker wrote Thomas Jefferson to enlist his help in combating the "train of absurd and false ideas and opinions, which so generally prevails with respect to us." Banneker reminded Jefferson of the principles declared in the Declaration of Independence, and he insisted that the founder of America's original document live up to the ideals of the American Revolution. Banneker's brash letter is only one example among many. People of color throughout the early nineteenth century defended their equality, and their agitation provided an important discursive ground that Sumner adopted and utilized.[79] Recall that Sumner used the letters of African Americans, verbatim, to demonstrate the relationship between segregation and discrimination. One might note further that Sumner's arguments mirrored those of the black abolitionists. In 1869 Frederick Douglass also had argued that slavery was not dead. In a speech at the Thirty-sixth Anniversary of the American Anti-slavery Society, Douglass had used this claim to encourage the abolitionists to continue their agitation.[80] Whether Sumner was intentionally adopting the definition of slavery offered by Douglass is immaterial. The point is simply that Sumner's position and authority allowed him to articulate radical thoughts within the halls of Congress.

The Bill's Necessity

As Sumner applied his equality ideal to African Americans, he also argued that the bill was a practical necessity to safeguard the freedoms of these new citizens. His discourse established that the measure was an expedient and necessary policy. Only complete desegregation could solve discrimination. Furthermore, the bill was expedient because it would provide Americans with a new moral awareness.

Sumner had drafted the Civil Rights Bill to resolve what he saw as problems of discrimination, but Sumner's solution was not the only option. Moderate Democrats who opposed desegregation argued that a state-sponsored system of "separate but equal" facilities would address the concern expressed by some Republicans without alienating the Southern populace. When Sumner introduced his bill in 1872, Senator Joshua Hill argued that "if there be a hotel for the entertainment of travelers, and two classes stop at it, and there is one dining-room for one class and one for another, served alike in all respects, with the same accommodations, the same attention to the guests," then no civil rights were denied. Separate but equal institutions were neither offensive nor unconstitutional.[81] Sumner responded to these arguments directly. Separate but equal institutions would never meet the former slaves' needs because such a scheme was an "artificial" equality. He said: "Then comes the other excuse, which finds Equality in separation. Separate hotels, separate conveyances, separate theatres, separate schools and institutions of learning and science, separate churches, and separate cemeteries,—these are the artificial substitutes. And this is the contrivance by which a transcendent right, involving a transcendent duty, is evaded: For Equality is not only a right, but a duty."[82] Separate but equal facilities could not solve the problem of discrimination for two reasons. First, separate institutions were never truly equal. Sumner contended that black schools almost always were inferior to white schools, and that black railroad cars were less comfortable than cars enjoyed by white passengers. In his words, the "substitute is invariably an inferior article."[83] Second, separate institutions denied the very essence of equality. He explained: "How vain to argue that there is no denial of Equal Rights when this separation is enforced. . . . Separation implies one thing for a white person and another thing for a colored person; but Equality is where all have the same alike. There can be no substitute for Equality,—nothing but itself. Even if accommodations are the same, as notoriously they are not, there is no Equality. In the process of substitution the vital elixir exhales and escapes. It is lost, and cannot be recovered; for Equality is found only in Equality."[84] To deny anyone full equality was to deny the term's nature, and, he implied, the guaranties of citizenship.

These passages were remarkable for several reasons. First, they reveal another dimension of Sumner's prophetic persona; his comments foreshadowed the claims of civil rights activists in the twentieth century. The fact that Sumner had used the notion of psychological harm to oppose segregated education policies in his 1849 *Roberts* brief is even more remarkable.[85] Second, these comments reveal the very essence of Sumner's political philosophy. Equality, at least the equality that Sumner articulated, entailed an association, a sameness, a recognition of those aspects that brought Americans together. Segregation reflected a dissociation, a difference that divided individuals and communities. Sumner recognized that fact and came to a conclusion that was almost one century ahead of its time: a truly equal citizenship could not be built on segregation, no matter how "equal" the separated institutions. For Sumner, the separate but equal solution was mere form rather than a real answer. It promised equality but lacked the power to realize its own goals. His equality made different demands. As a standard of evaluation, it prohibited any legislation that might lead to hierarchical difference. As a motive for action, it invested Congress with a positive responsibility. Political leaders were responsible to discover and rectify inequality wherever it existed in the public sphere. Inaction in the face of discrimination was an abrogation of congressional duty and the denial of transcendent law.

Sumner was well aware that many whites, Northern and Southern, did not share his belief in equality, and he used this fact as a second reason for the bill's necessity. Not only did he argue that desegregation was beneficial for African Americans, but he also confirmed that those who disagreed with the transcendent truth of human equality needed a civil rights bill to transform their beliefs and opinion: "An enlightened public opinion must be invoked. . . . the law is needed now as a help to public opinion. It is needed by the very people whose present conduct makes it necessary. Prompted by the law, leaning on the law, they will recognize the equal rights of all. . . . In the absence of the law people please too often by inhumanity, but with the law teaching the lesson of duty they will please by opposite conduct. Thus will the law be an instrument of improvement, necessary in precise proportion to existing prejudice. Because people still please by inhumanity, therefore must there be a counteracting force."[86] Sumner's notion of "public opinion" differs from the view of today's political consultants who gauge public opinion through phone surveys. Sumner was not interested in the polls but in the deeper issue of social belief and sentiment. He was concerned about the nation's public morality, as dictated by communal memory and meaning. It was his purpose to alter that morality and, through desegregation, to elevate the public mind to a new level of understanding and moral consciousness. He did not believe that the measure would bring about an instant conversion among its opponents, but he did argue that public opinion, if properly constrained by law, could evolve toward a greater appreciation of equality's truth.

This argument involves two implications that are critical to the politics of equality as this mode of action was used by Republican idealists. First, it assigned a strong moral function to legislation; it was designed to sway the public toward virtue. Justice for past and current wrongs was an important aspect of the bill, but its author insisted that redemption for past wrongs was only one aspect of the measure. Desegregation was meant to transform society's beliefs about race, creating a better future for everyone. This liberal notion—law and government as catalysts to moral and social change—leads to a second implication. Sumner's perspective required an active government that used intrusive legislation to achieve moral ends. Remember that when it came to civil rights, the political culture of the antebellum era had valued limited government. Antebellum Whigs had used governmental authority to advance specific economic polices, but they had not extended this principle into the realm of personal liberty. Laws were intended to prohibit government's intrusion, not protect individual freedom. When Sumner granted to the federal government the right to "guide" social belief, he also infused it with an active moral responsibility. From our contemporary stance, after the 1950s and 1960s, a governmental mandate to alter society's assumptions about race seems unremarkable. Yet when one considers that the very first public accommodations bill also entailed a moral duty for government, one begins to appreciate a recurring dimension of civil rights legislation. That is, civil rights law is often, if not always, accompanied by increased government involvement in the everyday lives *and* moral decisions of the public.

Reinterpreting the Constitution

In 1872 it was not clear whether the Civil Rights Bill was constitutional. Lyman Trumbull, Rockwood Hoar, and Lot Morrill, all influential members of the Republican Party, expressed doubts as to whether the recently altered Constitution authorized a bill of its scope.[87] Morrill argued that the Fourteenth Amendment was only a prohibition against certain types of state action and that it did not grant additional powers to Congress. Senator Matthew Carpenter felt that the bill's jury clause was unconstitutional, and Frederick Frelinghuysen, who eventually managed the bill after Sumner's death, suggested that its church provision might violate the First Amendment's religion clause. Conservative Republicans such as Orris Ferry, John A. Logan, and Thomas Weston Tipton of Nebraska claimed that its enforcement mechanism extended the federal government's power well beyond constitutional limits.[88] Sumner tried to mollify these concerns and to place his measure within the Constitution's bounds.

To justify the bill's constitutionality was not easy. When Congress debated the Fourteenth Amendment, Republicans had said little about its impact on segregation. It is instructive, then, that instead of examining the policy, Sumner turned his attention toward the Constitution and offered an alternative interpretation of America's founding document. He began with the idea that the country originated with the Declaration of Independence. He said: "Why is the Declaration of Independence our Magna Carta? Not because it declares separation from a distant kingly power; but because it announces the lofty truth that all are equal in rights, and as a natural consequence, that all just government stands only on the consent of the governed, and these are held to be self evident. Here is the soul of republican institutions, without which a Republic is a failure, a mere name and nothing more. Call it a Republic if you will, but it is in reality a soulless mockery."[89] By calling the Declaration the nation's Magna Carta, Sumner elevated it to a status equal to if not greater than the Constitution. He reinforced this relationship by referring to the Declaration and the Constitution as our "two title-deeds of Constitutional Liberty, each interpreting the other, and being the fountain out of which are derived the rights and duties of the American citizen."[90] Indeed, Sumner associated the two so closely that they became practically indistinguishable. As a result, he broadened the term "Constitution" to include the second document. In Sumner's text, the Constitution no longer stood alone. It also entailed the Declaration. Consequently, the meaning of the Constitution was infused with the Declaration's egalitarian principle. By conflating these two very different texts, Sumner sought to justify his prophetic stand and policy.

Zarefsky and Gallagher provide some insight into why and how Sumner accomplished this hermeneutic turn. They argue that the Constitution is a condensation symbol or ideograph that Americans revere. As our sacred legal and political text, it maintains the country's social structure and identity; consequently, political leaders must justify legislation constitutionally.

Without some constitutional basis, legislation cannot fit into America's legal framework. Fortunately for politicians, constitutional arguments are relatively easy to generate because the document is ambiguous. It allows for more than one interpretation at a time. However, this same flexibility makes the Constitution incapable of resolving certain issues completely. Its flexibility as a text works against any single interpretation.[91] In this controversy, the nature of the Constitution worked both for and against the Civil Rights Bill. For instance, the Constitution's natural ambiguity allowed Sumner's opponents to offer interpretations that justified segregation. On the other hand, Sumner also exploited this flexibility; it allowed him to link the original document with the Declaration. In fact, one might conclude that Sumner subsumed the Constitution within the Declaration to direct the Constitution's ambiguity toward his perspective. Although Jefferson's creed is not precise, it does seem to express an egalitarianism that is absent from the text of the Constitution. By stressing that proper interpretation required both documents, Sumner created a meaning that favored his position.

To grasp more firmly Sumner's association between the Declaration and the Constitution, it is helpful to understand how Lincoln's "Gettysburg Address" exhibits a similar tactic. According to Wills, before the war the nation had used the Constitution as its fundamental working law. Wills argues that in the "Gettysburg Address," "Lincoln distinguished between the Declaration as the statement of a permanent ideal and the Constitution as an early and provisional embodiment of that ideal, to be tested against it, kept in motion toward it."[92] Lincoln seemed to argue, then, that the Founding Fathers created the union with the Declaration and founded the country upon its principles. Wills states, "[Lincoln] not only put the *Declaration* in a new light as a matter of founding law, but put its central proposition, equality, in a newly favored position as a principle of the Constitution."[93] Critic Martha Solomon Watson ably demonstrates that Lincoln did not originate this discursive strategy, nor was he solely responsible for the Declaration's elevation.[94] The members of the American Antislavery Society and the women of Seneca Falls used Jefferson's text as a model for their own declarations. Sumner also was an important part of the Declaration's transformation. He combined the Constitution and the earlier Declaration until the idea of America's founding document involved both texts.[95]

Once Sumner established a reflexive relationship between the Declaration and the Constitution, he used these documents to argue against inequality. He said: "And shall those equal rights, promised by the great Declaration, be sacrificed to a prejudice? Shall that equality before the Law, which is the best part of citizenship, be denied to those who do not happen to be white? Is this a white man's government or is it a government of 'all men,' as declared by our fathers? Is it a Republic of equal Laws, or an Oligarchy of the Skin? This is the question now presented."[96] The Founding Fathers did not support inequality, he argued, and as evidence he pointed to the now equally fundamental texts of the Declaration of Independence and the Constitution. He demanded that his colleagues look at its words: "the Declaration speaks of 'all men,' and not of 'all white men;' and the Constitution says, 'We the people,' and not 'We the white people.'"[97] The absence of the term white, according to our speaker, demonstrated the founders' belief in equality, and it proved that equality—as Sumner defined it—played a central part in the country's origin.[98] Again playing with the ideas of appearance and reality, he declared that skin color was a minor matter of appearance; equality was the true, transcendent, ideal.

Rhetorical critics acknowledge that it is dangerous to attribute intent to a speaker, especially one situated in a previous century; however, evidence exists that Sumner recognized and intended to reinterpret the Constitution. When he rewrote this speech for his anthology, he added the following paragraph: "Once Slavery was the animating principle in determining the meaning of the National Constitution: happily, it is so no longer. Another principle is now supreme; breathing into the whole the breath of a new life, and filling it in every part with one pervading, controlling sentiment,—being that great principle of Equality which triumphed at last on the battle-field, and, bearing the watchword of the Republic, now supplies the rule by which every word of the Constitution and all its parts must be interpreted, as much as if written in its text."[99] Sumner knew that his constitutional arguments departed from the norm, but that was his purpose. Moreover, he argued that with equality as the nation's supreme principle, interpreting the Constitution through the lens of equality was not one option among several, it was the only correct perspective. This constitutional approach, concludes Jager, was the most striking feature of Sumner's constitutional thought; it was powerful precisely because it "transcended the narrow view of an unbending rule of law" and replaced it with an interpretive practice able to "meet new considerations in a changing society."[100]

Conclusion

James Jasinski notes that nineteenth-century Whigs and Democrats were ambivalent about the American Revolution. Although Fourth of July celebrations were highly patriotic, they had "evolved into rigid, formulaic rituals, that despite a certain degree of tension, reified the nation's memory of the revolution."[101] In the antebellum era's political culture, the Revolution was less important than the historical process of which it was a part. Leaders portrayed it as a natural process in the growth of republican government. Sumner's political career and rhetorical practice upset this settled vision. For Sumner, the Declaration of Independence was a trumpet blast, an announcement of separation and a statement of political truth. It is no wonder that among the Whigs and Democrats, and then later among the regular Republicans, Sumner was unpopular. His norms of political judgment violated the antebellum era's political culture, *and,* even after the Civil War, he remained on the extreme, prodding his colleagues toward an ever-more-radical implementation of equality politics.

Sumner's sense of what constituted prudent policy was dictated by his moral belief. That is, he pursued a subversive form of prudence described by his friend and confidant, Ralph Waldo Emerson. In his 1841 essay titled "Prudence," Emerson differentiated between base prudence and true prudence. Base prudence was the prudence of outward well-being, expediency. True prudence was the natural extension of the individual who understood that circumstances were only the symbolic representations of transcendental truths.[102] According to Emerson, most of society approached poetry and politics as separate endeavors. Expediency and prudence were the domain of statesmanship while truth and beauty were in the realm of artistic expression. This dissociation was false because truth, beauty, and prudence were different dimensions of the same transcendent reality. Emerson explains, "poetry and prudence should be coincident. Poets should be lawgivers; that is, the boldest lyric inspiration should not chide and insult, but should announce and lead the civil codes, and the day's work."[103]

Sumner put Emerson's transcendental philosophy to work. Both prophet and statesman, he combined politics with a twentieth-century vision of equality. Treating the Declaration and the Constitution as sacred texts, he declared that the nation remained in sin. Despite the Civil War, slavery continued. Further judgment would surely follow unless and until his colleagues saw the Declaration's egalitarian principle as the foundation of law and society. Sumner revised America's past moral system, reformulating it to meet the needs of his political judgment, and, in the process, he called the nation to repentance. The fact that Sumner's ideas and political philosophy foreshadowed the modern era of civil rights is remarkable but not surprising, because his rhetoric made equality the supreme norm of political judgment. Repudiating states' rights, his support for desegregation required a federal authority with sufficient power to alter the beliefs and attitudes of the populace. This liberalism did not enter U.S. politics until the twentieth century, and it is impossible to know how our history might have differed if Sumner's perspective had been adopted in the 1870s. Certainly, the lives of African Americans would have been different.

Finally, it is important to note that Sumner's text reflects the argumentative themes that would mark the rest of the debate. First, Constitutional arguments became a major line of inference making for the congressional civil rights debates of 1874 and 1875. As one of the strongest themes for bill opponents, those who opposed Sumner's measure attacked its constitutionality at every turn. Once the Supreme Court decided the *Slaughter-House Cases* in 1873, critics received additional ammunition. Concerned with this potent criticism, bill advocates rallied with a variety of original explanations to locate the bill within the horizon of proper constitutional law. As a result, congressional leaders debated various approaches to constitutional authority, interpretation, and American federalism. Second, whether the bill was expedient also became an important theme in the civil rights controversy. Those Republicans who supported the bill argued that only complete desegregation would mitigate the problems encountered by African Americans. Those who fought against it characterized it as harmful because it would increase racial tension; moreover, Democrats and a small number of Republicans refuted the claim that African Americans really wanted desegregation. Third, the term *equality* and its application to the former slaves became a major point of discussion. As equality was perhaps the most important issue for the champions of civil rights, bill proponents extended Sumner's claims and argued that African Americans were the basic human equivalent and potential equal of every white man and woman. Black equality proved to be a thorny issue for bill opponents. In an altered environment where the antebellum era's racial epithets were inappropriate, moderate Democrats contrived a rhetorical middle ground where they could sustain basic racial differences without seeming overtly racist. Ironically, as we shall see, the space that these Democrats occupied was the very space that Lincoln had created in 1858.

4

Black Equality and the Civil Rights Act of 1875

"Whatever he may have been, he is now the same as ourselves. Our rights are his rights; our equality his equality."[1] When Charles Sumner spoke these words, he was giving voice to a radical dream that would have altered the very fabric of American society. The term "equal" had been a part of the Reconstruction's political culture since Lyman Trumbull introduced the 1866 Civil Rights Act, but the exact meaning of that term was still in dispute.[2] Republican idealists such as Sumner applied the term broadly to include African Americans. In his 15 January 1872 speech Sumner had stated that blacks were the same as whites on the basis of their humanity and because of their new location within the context of American citizenship. Sumner's language implied further that this state was incompatible with a caste system grounded in physical differences. It was founded, instead, in an ideal consubstantiality between the races that transcended the mundane and the material.

This chapter explores the differing interpretations of "equality" as they were expressed in the congressional debates of 1874 and 1875. Indeed, equality became a central issue as desegregation's proponents and opponents grappled with whether and to what degree the former slaves were equal citizens. In the process, three distinct discourses emerged. The first, articulated by Democrats who employed pre-Civil War arguments grounded in the old ideology of place, contended that African Americans were destined to be the white man's inferior in all respects. The second voice, represented by Republican proponents of desegregation, argued that blacks were essentially equal to whites; consequently, the law should reflect that equality in the form of a national desegregation policy. The third voice, that of moderate Democrats, claimed that although blacks were equal in some senses, they were still different. Moderate Democrats dissociated the notion of equality into three distinct parts—political equality, legal equality, and social equality. This division became the center of a broad discursive innovation that modified the notion of place into a rhetorical form that sustained racial inequities at the regional level, while it accommodated some of the egalitarian dreams of national Reconstruction politics.

The First Voice: White Supremacy and Black Inferiority

To state that racial prejudice was a factor in Reconstruction's desegregation debate is to state the obvious. The legislative history that appears in chapter 2 provides several illustrations of the racist arguments of Representatives John T. Harris, Charles Eldredge, and John Brown. Moreover, although exceptions existed and the variables of class and region altered race relations in profound ways, the ideas of black inferiority and white superiority were accepted generally. LaWanda and John Cox explain that "the roots of this prejudice ran deep in the history of the country and of the Western world, and in the 1860s prejudice was dignified by the scientific authorities of the day. When the freedman was made equal citizen, the concept of racial inequality, unlike the institution of slavery which had become an anachronism, was still growing in vigor and malignancy."[3] Yet the 1870s civil rights debate demonstrates that overt and explicit claims about black inferiority were expressed by only a few extreme Democrats. The Republicans and moderate Democrats avoided racist language. To appreciate how the extreme Democrats, or fire-eaters, approached the notion of equality, one must first investigate the economic and cultural layers of racism in that existed in the deep South.

Today social scientists concur that racism in the United States is not reducible to personal feelings or private prejudice.[4] Racism is, and was during the nineteenth century, multidimensional, with cultural, institutional, and linguistic components.[5] Pierre Van den Berghe suggests that at America's inception the nature of capitalism and its need for cheap labor produced an economic environment where racism could flourish in the form of slavery.[6] After the Civil War the system of white supremacy as well as its economic conditions were in jeopardy. William J. Wilson writes that "the ruling economic elite was frightened because the southern economy was on the verge of total collapse without slave labor." The black codes of 1865 and 1866 were intended to protect the economic interests of the wealthy planter class. Even after their demise, the planter elite maintained their control over African Americans and poor European Americans through the system of sharecropping and credit.[7]

On its face, sharecropping was equitable to both the landowner and the laborer. Immediately following the war, landowners wanted to hire wage labor to work as gangs, but black farmers refused. They wished nothing to do with the old antebellum methods, so they used the new lien laws of 1866 and 1867 to establish some measure of autonomy. The black farmer agreed to work a small plot of land either by himself or with his family in return for a share of the crop. He would receive the necessary tools and seed from the local merchant, who, in turn, would put a lien on a portion of the crop. As a consequence of this arrangement, three different parties had a claim to the fall harvest: the landowner, the merchant, and the laborer. In a good year, each of these parties would take their allotted share. That, at least, was how it was supposed to work. Before long, with almost complete autonomy over contracts and the credit system, landowners and merchants manipulated the system to their benefit. When Southern Democrats reestablished control of local and state politics, they quickly enacted laws that favored the economic interests of landowners and merchants, and as the production of cotton and other crops fell in the 1870s and 1880s, the laborer rarely received his or her share. Poor production, climate irregularities, pests, fraud, and coercion eventually transformed the crop-lien system into an exploitive means of production that kept both people of color and white farmers in debt. As industrialization spread across the South, the old planter elite and the new merchant-bankers benefited from racial tensions between lower-class whites and African Americans.[8]

The economic substructure of racism in the black belt was reinforced by the work of prominent naturalists, anthropologists, biologists, and social scientists who sought to catalog racial difference. By the mid-nineteenth century large segments of the scientific community had a clear and concise objective: to develop a theory of racial difference that explained an individual's value as well as social and cultural disparities.[9] The science of ethnology legitimized racial hierarchies, and its discourse slowly became a part of the South's cultural beliefs. The work of Samuel Morton provides one influential example. In his *Crania Americana* (1839) and *Catalogue of Skulls of Man and the Inferior Animals* (1849), Morton used craniometry, the study of facial angles and skull capacities, to argue for the inferiority of Africans and the "Negro Group."[10] When Morton died the *Charleston Medical Journal* declared: "For the present, we can only say that we of the South should consider him [Morton] as our benefactor, for aiding most materially in giving to the negro his true position as an inferior race. We believe the time is not far distant, when it will be universally admitted that neither can 'the leopard change his spots, nor the Ethiopian his skin.'"[11] Morton was not the only scientist whose work influenced the last half of the nineteenth century. Articles by Louis Agassiz and Nathaniel Shaler, prominent scholars who argued for black inferiority, appeared in popular magazines. By the end of the century racial science helped to define the ideology of a new Southern politician, the Southern radical.[12] Radicals had not achieved their ascendancy when Congress debated the Civil Rights Bill, but a minority of congressmen were eager to express the kind of vicious racism that would become typical during the 1890s.

In the civil right debate of 1874 and 1875, several Democrats argued that African Americans were uncivilized and that they existed only slightly above the level of animals. Lewis Bogy (Missouri) stated that centuries of interaction between the races had seen no improvement among those of color. In Africa the race remained practically barbaric, and its members did little more than eat, drink, sleep, and die, he said.[13] According to Representative Charles Eldredge of Wisconsin, blacks were an "uneducated, semi-barbarous," "stupid," and "ignorant" race. He implied further that while whites possessed refinement and intellect, individuals of color exhibited little more than physical strength and brute force.[14] Milton Durham (Kentucky) revealed a similar disdain for African Americans when he characterized the "true" relationship between the races. He said, "the poorest and humblest white person in my district feels and knows that he or she belongs to a superior race morally and intellectually, and nothing is so revolting to them as social equality with this inferior race."[15] Durham argued further that no one could deny black inferiority because the truth was ingrained into the hearts and minds of Americans.

When these Democrats used the term equality at all, they applied it intraracially rather than interracially. They argued that whites were equal to one another and that blacks were equal to one another. Eldredge, for instance, declared that the Fourteenth Amendment had made the former slaves absolutely equal with no one but themselves.[16] The Democrats who voiced this position actively denied any implication that either race shared something of value. This discourse was not just an explicit statement of racial animosity; it also maintained the notion of place as it was articulated at the beginning of the Civil War. For the fire-eaters, nothing of substance had changed since the antebellum period. Inequality, not equality, existed as the universal law of humanity. Representative William Robbins of North Carolina explained: "We have heard much in this debate about equality—the equality of men and of races of men. That kind of rhetoric has been fashionable in America for a century past. The illustrious Jefferson appears to have inaugurated it when he penned the celebrated sentence, 'All men are born equal.' That sentence was analyzed twenty-five years ago by another famous statesman of our country, and shown to be not only not true, but to contain more error and untruth than has ever been embodied, perhaps, in the same number of English words." Robbins continued, "not equality, but infinite inequality and variety, is the law of this universe." Jefferson's Declaration "is a sentiment which may serve very well, and often has served well, as the war-cry of revolutionists, but calm philosophy, aye, plain common sense, smiles at its absurdity."[17] Based on this foundation, the fire-eaters argued that the equality politics of Charles Sumner and the Republican idealists had corrupted the natural order.

According to several members of Congress, the Republicans had made a terrible mistake when they took control of Reconstruction from President Johnson and the state governments. As the result of either ignorance or maliciousness, Republicans gave legal and political rights to a race that was incapable of governing itself, let alone others. Barely more than savages, African Americans could not fulfill the responsibilities of leadership; consequently, the "once proud and majestic commonwealths, are in ruins, lying prostrate before us, in the very struggle and article of death—the work of your legislation."[18] According to Eldredge, Republicans had turned national reconciliation into a "war of the races."

The phrase "war of the races" is revealing; it signals a perception of Reconstruction politics that connects the political judgments of that period with the Civil War conflict. Furthermore, it illustrates that for at least some members of Congress, the Civil War was not yet over. Consider the comments of Kentucky representative John Young Brown who characterized Reconstruction policy as follows: "Onward and onward you go in defiance of the sentiment of the country, without pity and without justice, remorselessly determined, it seems, to devote these distressed southern people to complete destruction, to give their 'roofs to the flames, their flesh to the eagles.'"[19] These words reflect the horrible devastation of the Union Army's final campaigns. Much of the discourse employed by Brown, Eldredge, and Robbins used militaristic imagery and terms to reinforce the notion that the Republican agenda amounted to continued warfare against the South. Such comments are engaging, in part, because they ignored the fact that the North's influence on the South had declined significantly by 1874.

After the election of 1868, Southern conservatives had initiated a campaign to regain political power by restoring "home rule." Part of the strategy involved organized acts of violence to intimidate Republicans and African Americans, especially during elections. A second strategy was to attack the Republican state governments for corruption and abuse. The Democratic press in the South ridiculed black state legislatures, calling them "menageries" and "monkey houses." Due to these efforts, Reconstruction effectively ended in Tennessee in 1870; in Georgia in 1871; in Texas and Virginia in 1873; in Alabama and Arkansas in 1874; and in Mississippi in 1875. Because these dates reflect the point at which the governor *and* both houses of the state legislature were returned to Democratic control, one must recognize that the conservatives' influence was felt in these states well before the years they were "redeemed."[20] On 5 September 1868, *Harper's Weekly* ran a caricature of Southern Redemption and the Democratic opposition to Reconstruction. "This is a White Man's Government" portrays an unrepentant member of the Confederacy, an Irishman, and a New York businessman united to put down black rights. In the background, an African American orphanage and public school are ablaze. (See Figure 5)[21]

As the redemption rolled through the South, Democrats in Congress did not complain less about the domination of Republican interest. If anything, the congressional debates in 1875 contained even stronger denunciations of Republican intrusion into Southern life and culture. Why characterize the Republican agenda with such disdain just as the Southern Democrats were regaining their position? One answer is that this discourse was useful to Southern politicians. The Republicans had waved the bloody shirt for a decade; indeed, the memory of the war seemed to be the only means by which its leaders could maintain party unity. Similarly, cries of Northern aggression galvanized the South against policies that Democrats disliked. A second interpretation of these condemnations suggests that this discourse

"THIS IS A WHITE MAN'S GOVERNMENT."

FIGURE 5.

was an important part of the New South rhetoric. Waldo Braden argues that the postwar South witnessed a resurgence of epideictic rhetoric that valorized the Civil War and the Southern cause.[22] Southern interests assailed by Northern capital and greed was an important theme in this discourse. Still, there is a third explanation.

The Democrats generally and the extreme Democrats in particular viewed Reconstruction's equality politics as a threat to Southern culture. To use a contemporary metaphor, the opponents of desegregation believed themselves to be engaged in a "culture war." According to the history described by these politicians, African Americans were the agents of Northern aggression. After the Civil War, the Republican idealists had deceived the former slaves with the dream of perfect equality. Equality was a carrot, they argued, and because of its promise a largely ignorant population had waged a campaign against the standards of Southern culture. Representative Aylett Buckner (Missouri) explained:

> For nearly a decade [the Republicans] have been legislating for the negro by amendments to the constitution and by acts of Congress; the judicial power of the Government has been placed at his service; the Army and Navy have done police duty for him; Senate and House have been wrangling over him for years. He sits as a legislator in both ends of the Capital. His pathway to wealth, position, and place have been cleared of all obstructions. He is king of South Carolina, Florida, Louisiana, Mississippi, and Alabama, and to-day he holds in the hollow of his rough hand the destiny of this grand Republic. All this you have done for him. Is it not enough? . . . Let the negro and his rights be dismissed [from] these halls forever; and let him work out his political salvation, if not with fear and trembling, at least without any further sacrifice of the great interests of the country.[23]

According to several Democrats, desegregation was only the most recent and the most devastating campaign against the South. New Jersey Democrat John Stockton came to the aid of his Southern colleagues when he assailed the Republicans: "[You] invade every social principle without regard to distinctions of race or color; you tear away all that is worth living for in this blessed land."[24]

The policies that Stockton labeled as an invasion are best understood as the inversion of the South's caste system. Southern conservatives hated congressional Reconstruction, because it made field hands into political leaders. It inverted the order of place and difference that had sustained the South for generations. Robbins expressed the proper order of society in the following passage:

> Sir, since it is impossible for any one man to be equal to or like any other man, is it not more philosophical to say that such a thing can be no proper object of human effort or ambition? Our rights are limited by our duties, and our duties are measured by our capabilities. "To whom much is given, of him shall be much required." I lay this down as the true doctrine—that every man has the right, and is bound by the duty, to fill the sphere and move in the orbit to which God and nature have assigned him, as indicated by his peculiar natural endowments, which, being different in each individual and in each race, point out for each a different party to perform. If we could change this, and compel all to revolve in one and the same orbit, we should overthrow eternal laws and reduce the world back to chaos.[25]

No clearer enunciation of "place" exists in this congressional debate, and William Robbins was just the man to express it.

Robbins was a true son of the South. Born on a family homestead in Randolph County, North Carolina (1828), he was educated in classical studies, attended Old Trinity College, and graduated from the private Randolph-Macon College, fifteen miles outside of Richmond, Virginia. He studied law and passed the bar in 1854, moving to Eufaula, Alabama, that year. He served four years as a major in the Fourth Alabama Regiment of the Confederate Army, after which he returned to North Carolina and accepted a position as state senator. He was elected to three consecutive terms in the House of Representatives, and during the Forty-fourth Congress, he was chairman of the Committee on Expenditures for the War Department. President Cleveland appointed Robbins as the Southern commissioner on the Gettysburg Battle Field Commission in 1894, a position that he held until his death in 1905. In 1874 Robbins exemplified the respected Southern gentleman. He had been a part of the Old South and he would participate in the New. He understood the South's culture intimately; indeed, it comprised his very identity. From his perspective, his duty and privilege was to lead North Carolina and the nation. His place was to be a man among men. The idea that society should regard any African American, especially one who had been a slave, as his equal was beyond comprehension. Equality was, as he stated, a subversion of divine "eternal law." Equality's consequence was social and political "chaos."[26]

When Robbins's rhetoric is contrasted to that of Charles Sumner, it stands as the ideological opposite of the politics of equality. Recall that Sumner, reflecting the philosophy of his transcendental friends, argued for an ideal reality above the mere symbols of skin color and hair texture. From Sumner's perspective, individual difference was a distracting appearance that caused some to ignore the truer reality of human equality and the common rights of citizenship. Robbins inverts Sumner's philosophy, locating the transcendent principle of difference in the divine purpose of God. He argues that the material differences of intellect, skin, and hair reflect a sacred will that distinguishes individuals and races. Since God created each person and each race with distinct abilities, Robbins affirms that each must fulfill its own separate role in society. The politics of equality, as practiced from 1877 to Robbins's present, was an abomination, because it subverted the truth of place. Foreshadowing the thesis of Dixon's 1902 fictionalization of Reconstruction, Representative Thomas Whitehead declared, "You have not the power to make [the African American] white, and he never will be satisfied short of that. That is the trouble about the whole matter. His condition cannot be altered, and the best we can do is what we propose to do in our state—educate him, and take care of him, and do the best we can with him."[27]

Ultimately, it did not matter that the Democratic Party was in ascendancy throughout the South by 1874. It did not matter that white landowners and merchants *never* lost their economic power over black laborers. It did not matter that only South Carolina's state legislature ever had a black majority in both houses.[28] The conservatives' culture remained at risk, so long as its underlying assumptions about the *proper places* for whites and blacks continued to be a matter of national debate. Southern politicians such as Robbins felt insecure, because black representatives from South Carolina occupied the same place, quite literally, as the white congressmen of South Carolina. So long as the public sphere continued to debate the equality of black Americans, the institutional and cultural inequities of the previous era remained under siege. For politicians who believed in the ultimate righteousness of the old system, any form of attack was unacceptable. As Eldredge declared, "the white race, with its pride of blood, the memory of its achievements, the consciousness of its superiority and power, will never brook African equality or live under Africanized governments; and the sooner this truth is realized by American statesmen the sooner will the remedy for the evils that are upon us be devised."[29]

The Second Voice: The Rhetoric of Black Equality

The egalitarian claims within this nineteenth-century congressional debate are arresting. Thanks to the forceful advocacy of the black representatives, the thesis that African Americans were equal to European Americans was articulated in a way that one rarely heard in that period. Although people of color were the key advocates for black equality in this debate, several white members of Congress—Benjamin Butler and Daniel Pratt, for example—made strong statements of the same type. Although the European members of Congress expressed varying opinions, Pratt's words are representative: if the Democrats would only "forget the color of his skin, the difference between him and you would disappear."[30] The pages that follow unpack four discursive strategies used by desegregation's proponents to affirm the worth of African Americans.

Reshaping America's Public Memory

In the 1960s Lerone Bennett Jr. and Benjamin Quarles argued that American history was written from the European perspective and little credit was given to blacks who also had struggled and sacrificed for America's benefit.[31] Representations that did exist were either unflattering or portrayed African Americans in scenic terms. Historians described blacks as contexts on which others acted, and rarely were they equal agents in the progress of the nation. This historiography reflected public memory. From Fourth of July celebrations to commemorations of military sites to ceremonies that marked the continued growth of American commerce, African Americans were absent.[32] Not only did this absence reinforce the racial prejudices of the nineteenth century, but it also had political consequences. Because people of color were unimportant in the country's rituals and narratives, it was easier to relegate them to the periphery when it came to political judgments. After all, their place, or lack thereof, in public memory defined them as inconsequential for American culture and community. The texts of desegregation's advocates challenged these norms, as Republicans argued for a different vision of America's labor and military history.[33]

Black representatives did not hesitate to educate their colleagues about the history of their race. James Rapier (Alabama) argued that whatever liberty African Americans enjoyed "has been paid for over and over again by more than two hundred years of forced toil."[34] Richard Cain (South Carolina) declared: "For two hundred years the colored men of this nation have assisted in building up its commercial interests. . . . We have been identified with the interests of this country from its very foundation. The cotton crop of this country has been raised and its rice-fields have been tilled by the hands of our race. All along as the march of progress, as the march of commerce, as the development of your resources has been widening and expanding and spreading, as your vessels have gone on every sea, with the stars and stripes waving over them, and carried your commerce everywhere, there the black man's labor has gone to enrich your country and to augment the grandeur of your nationality."[35] Robert Elliott, drawing an analogy between the biblical Ruth and slavery, argued that his race had reaped others' harvests for over two centuries.[36]

These narratives contained a clear message, one that was absent from public memory: African Americans were at the heart of the slavery system, and slavery was an unavoidable aspect of American prosperity. More than victims, they were agents in an economy that had undergone tremendous growth. No doubt this was an uncomfortable argument for many members of Congress. Democrats did not express regret over slavery's demise in this debate, but they were quick to justify the institution. Robbins argued that slavery had been God's school for the edification of the slaves. Through Christianity and strict discipline, the slave owner had brought a modicum of civilization to an "originally savage race."[37] Republicans expressed their scorn for the peculiar institution, but in their condemnation they ignored important aspects of antebellum history, including Northern complicity and the importance of black labor for their own prosperity. The black representatives of this debate created a history where their race was more than the scenic backdrop for a master's will. They were an important labor force, equal to any and, as we shall see, deserving of payment.

Desegregation's advocates coupled a revised labor history with an alternative vision of America's military history. Elliott noted that blacks had participated in America's first major war: "In the events that led to the achievement of American Independence the negro was not an inactive or unconcerned spectator. He bore his part bravely upon many battle-fields, although uncheered by that certain hope of political elevation which victory would secure to the white man. . . . In the State which I have the honor in part to represent the rifle of the black man rang out against the troops of the British crown in the darkest days of the American Revolution."[38] James Rapier acknowledged the historic sacrifices of African Americans, but his speech stressed the more recent violence of the Civil War. He said:

> In every contest, from the beginning of the revolutionary struggle down to the war between the States, has he been prominent. But we all remember in our late war when the Government was so hard pressed for troops to sustain the cause of the Union, when it was so difficult to fill up the ranks that had been so fearfully decimated by disease and the bullet . . . when grave doubts as to the success of the Union arms had seized upon the minds of

> some of the most sanguine friends of the Government; when strong men took counsel of their fears; . . . when gloom and despair were wide-spread; when the last ray of hope had nearly sunk below our political horizon, how the negro then came forward and offered himself as a sacrifice in the place of the nation, made bare his breast to the steel, and in it received the thrusts of the bayonet that were aimed at the life of the nation by the soldiers of that government which the gentleman from Georgia [Alexander Stephens] figured as second officer.

Today, said Rapier, "his bones lie bleaching beside every hill and in every valley from the Potomac to the Gulf." [39]

The impassioned descriptions of these black congressmen were matched by the dramatic narrative of Benjamin F. Butler, a celebrated but controversial major general of the Union Army. Explaining how he had lost his own prejudice, Butler recalled that on 29 September 1864, he led colored soldiers across the James River to attack New Market Heights. Butler narrated:

> On that plain, when the flash of dawn was breaking, I placed a column of three thousand colored troops, in close column by divisions, right in front, with guns at "right shoulder shift." I said, "That work must be taken by the weight of your column; no shot must be fired;" and to prevent their firing I had the caps taken from the nipples of their guns. . . . As the sun rose up in the heavens the order was given, "Forward," and they marched forward, steadily as if on parade. . . . They broke a little as they forded the brook, and the column wavered. O, it was a moment of intensest [*sic*] anxiety, but they formed again, as they reached the firm ground, marching steadily on with closed ranks under the enemy's fire, until the head of the column reached the first line of abatis, some one hundred and fifty yards from the enemy's work. Then the ax-men ran to the front to cut away the heavy obstructions of defense, while one thousand men of the enemy, with their artillery concentrated, poured from the redoubt a heavy fire upon the head of the column hardly wider than the Clerk's desk.

At this point, Butler switched to the present verb tense, inviting his audience to view directly the actions he described. He said,

> The abatis resists and holds; the head of the column seems literally to melt away under the rain of shot and shell; the flags of the leading regiments go down, but a brave black hand seizes the colors; they are up again and wave their starry light over the storm of battle; again the ax-men fall, but strong hands and willing hearts seize the heavy, sharpened trees and drag them away, and the column rushes forward, and with a shout which now rings in

> my ear, go over that redoubt like a flash, and the enemy never stop running [*sic*] for four miles. [Applause on the floor and in the galleries.]

As Butler returned to the past verb tense, he reflected on the incident and how it changed his life.

> It became my painful duty, sir, to follow in the tract of that charging column, and there . . . lay the dead bodies of five hundred and forty-three of my colored comrades, slain in defense of their country, who had laid down their lives to uphold its flag and its honor as a willing sacrifice; and as I rode along among them, guiding my horse this way and that way lest he should profane with his hoofs what seemed to me the sacred dead, and as I looked on their bronzed faces upturned in the shining sun to heaven as if in a mute appeal against the wrongs of the country for which they had given their lives, and whose flag had only been to them a flag of stripes on which no star of glory had ever shone for them—feeling I had wronged them in the past and believing what was the future of my country to them—among my dead comrades there I swore to myself a solemn oath, "may my right hand forget its cunning and my tongue cleave to the roof of my mouth if I ever fail to defend the rights of these men who have given their blood for me and my country this day and for their race forever;" and, God helping me, I will keep that oath.

The chamber resounded with great applause, and Butler waited patiently until it had died down. Then he declared the final moral of his story:

> From that hour all prejudice was gone, and an old-time States-right democrat became a lover of the negro race; and as long as their rights are not equal to the rights of other men under this Government I am with them against all comers. . . . They have industry, they have temperance, they have all the good qualities of citizens, they have bravery, they have culture, they have power, they have eloquence. And who shall say that they shall not have what the Constitution gives them—equal rights?[40]

With these words, he concluded the speech.

There are a number of important qualities to the narrative of this text. One can attribute much of its significance to its performance. Karlyn Kohrs Campbell notes that well-performed narratives are one of the best means for creating virtual experience in the mind of an audience.[41] Indeed, Butler's performance involved the audience members by appealing to their own recollections of the Civil War. Many who heard his speech had experienced the conflict personally, and Butler's story recalled for them the sights, sounds, and smells of their own memory. Furthermore, the shifts in the text's verb tense moved the audience from being spectators of Butler's recollections to direct witnesses of the events he described. When Butler narrated the final climatic charge of the soldiers, he recast the audience as a collective participant in the action. This performance functioned to alter the memories of those in attendance. It invited the audience to include the bravery of these black soldiers in their own reminiscence of the great conflict. The text's imagery suggests that the United States had not included African American soldiers in its official or public memory. Recall Butler's words that these soldiers died for a flag on which "no star of glory had ever shone for them." This image is revealing, because it signals the absence of blacks from the ceremonies of national remembrance. Butler was right; America's primary icon, its symbol of national identity, excluded many who had given their lives on the battlefield and in the cotton field. Despite centuries of contribution and significant moments of heroism, there were few memorials to commemorate the sacrifices of the black race.

The discursive association between African Americans and United States military history was quite strategic. Black bravery during the Civil War already had influenced several of that era's politicians, including Abraham Lincoln. Before the war, the president had expressed no desire to extend political rights to blacks, but by March of 1864 he seemed to have shifted his position. He wrote to Governor Michael Hahn that perhaps "some of the colored people[,] . . . especially those who have fought gallantly in our ranks," should receive the elective franchise.[42] After the conflict various political factions struggled to control how Americans collectively remembered the Civil War. In *Race and Reunion,* David W. Blight argues that European Americans in the North and South romanticized the conflict. The interpretation that eventually dominated the public's memory in the years that followed emphasized national unity and reconciliation. Unfortunately, it also undermined the cause of black civil rights. The harms of slavery, how it had been the catalyst for the war, the Emancipation Proclamation, the idea that justice should accompany reconciliation, and the gallant sacrifices of black soldiers were themes that threatened the accommodationist interpretation of the past. Blight contends that these themes were suppressed.[43] In 1874, however, public memory of the war was still malleable, and desegregation's proponents tried to shape it to support black equality.

By reformulating public memory, Republican idealists associated African Americans with what was traditionally a "white" history. The Revolutionary War, the War of 1812, and even the Civil War were sacred conflicts within American folklore, and the narratives that people told about these conflicts involved white blood and sacrifice. Likewise, American prosperity was understood as the outgrowth of white ingenuity and hard work. When bill proponents retold these historical moments and included African Americans in the story, they drew several simultaneous associations. Not only did they identify the nation and its success with the courage of black soldiers and laborers, but they also implied a link between the two races. In the texts advanced by some Republicans, blacks and whites were alike because they shared important qualities, including loyalty and bravery. The "black hands," "dead bodies," and "bronze faces" of Butler's description reinforced the claim that black soldiers suffered the same pain and death as white soldiers. These narratives portrayed African Americans as the equal of European Americans, because just as both races possessed red blood, they both had shed that blood for the country's glory.

The strategy to reformulate public memory was remarkable, as well, because it established black equality on the basis of African American *activity,* not *passivity.* Remember that although Sumner argued for black equality, he grounded his arguments in American citizenship. While this logic allowed Sumner to argue for a uniformity between the races, this reasoning was linked inextricably to the Thirteenth, Fourteenth, and Fifteenth Amendments, legislation created by white politicians. While the contributions of white Republicans should not be underrated, opponents of desegregation used the authorship of the amendments to contend that blacks had done nothing to achieve their own freedom. William Robbins declared:

> Looking at what has been done for him, the negro has perhaps done less, as yet, for himself and the world than any other man in history. In his own land he has always been and still is a savage. Against his own will, the English and Yankee slavers stole him from Africa and sold him into southern servitude, and as soon as they had done so and got the money, began to roll up the white of their eyes over the sin of slavery and to plot for his freedom. Against his will, the southern master trained him to regular labor and civilized habits, and gradually fitted him for liberty. Then in a grand conflict of arms among white men, in which he took no important part, he was freed. Afterward white men, voluntarily, without any effort of his, enfranchised him, made him a voter, and empowered him to hold office.[44]

Note how this passage ascribes scenic properties to African Americans. Robbins's version of history stressed white superiority. His text made blacks the passive and undeserving recipient of citizenship. Unfortunately, even well-meaning Republicans, such as William Stowell (Virginia), sometimes articulated this perspective: "For hundreds of years the colored race was kept in chains and slavery of the most revolting and degrading character.

All generous impulses, all hope and ambition, were crushed out, and they were simply machines, subject to the will of the master. . . . But through the workings of an all-wise Providence and the disinterested patriotism and humanity of the republican party, their chains have been broken, slavery forever destroyed." Stowell's machinery metaphor may reveal more about his attitudes than he intended. Although he voted for the revised bill that passed the House on 4 February 1875, Stowell's comments reflect a blindness, the tendency to see blacks as objects on which whites exercise their will. Stowell had many reasons to be proud of himself and his party, but his well-intentioned comments reflect a troubling paternalism. "The position of the colored man in life has changed," he argued, "*We* force the duties of citizenship upon *them*" (italics added).[45]

In contrast, the rhetoric of African American congressmen and Benjamin Butler reshaped public memory to establish black power and identity on its own terms. Black sacrifice and bravery were the proof of the equality described by this discourse. The most radical idealists of 1874 and 1875 actually separated themselves from even Sumner's vision of equality. Butler, Elliott, and Rapier lauded the black race's unique contributions to American history. They focused on African American behavior, the race's willingness to proffer its lives for the country's sake; consequently, their narratives turned attention to the personal qualities of the race. Serving an epideictic function, they praised black ability and refuted the assumption that people of color suffered from inherent character flaws. In fact, this strategy implied that black Americans always had been the equal of whites; after all, they had fought and died since the Revolutionary War. Their patriotic character had existed well before the Fourteenth Amendment. The logical implication, then, was that Reconstruction's amendments did not *create* black equality; they simply *recognized* the equality that was immanent in every black person.

The physical power of the black body had been a discursive resource for some time. Black abolitionists such as Frederick Douglass and Sojourner Truth had established their own authority through narratives of physical resistance. Condit and Lucaites explain that "the ground of this Equality was the material experience of one person, like another, pitting sinew against muscle, blood against bone, mind against spirit. It thus rooted equality in the material fact that when blacks and whites face each other they must each rely on similar resources as they respond to each other from within the strikingly similar limitations of being human."[46] This empirical sameness, this sense of equality, was the unspoken argument behind Butler's tone and Rapier's word when they spoke with reverence about the black fallen dead. The Republican senator from Indiana, Daniel Pratt, made this claim explicit: "He has all the bodily faculties in the fullest perfection, the same capacity to subdue nature and supply his wants, the same appetites. . . . Is he not warmed by the same sun, does he not breathe the same air, and draw his subsistence from the same bountiful earth, which knows no distinction in the hands that till her and bring forth her fruits?"[47] In short, the daily existence of blacks is no different from that of whites.

Third and finally, this rhetorical configuration—equality through a reformulation of public memory—implied that African Americans had earned desegregation. Several of the bill's proponents, and especially black representatives, argued that the Civil Rights Bill was not a gift; it was payment for services rendered. Butler implied as much in the final moments of his narrative. Elliott said so explicitly,[48] and Cain bluntly declared that desegregation should be seen as compensation for the slave labor that had secured the nation's prosperity. He said:

> [And if] we have been hewers of wood and drawers of water; if we have made your cotton-fields blossom as the rose; if we have made your rice-fields wave with luxuriant harvests; if we have made your corn-fields rejoice; if we have sweated and toiled to build up the prosperity of the whole country by the productions of our labor . . . I submit to the nation whether it is not fair and right that we should come in and enjoy to the fullest extent our freedom and liberty. . . .
>
> I want to say that we do not come here begging for our rights. We come here clothed in the garb of American citizenship. We come demanding our rights in the name of justice. . . . We come here in the name of justice, equity, and law, in the name of our children, in the name of our country, petitioning for our rights.[49]

This rhetoric is similar to some of the claims made today for reparations. Indeed, in the minds and hearts of a significant number of black citizens, the United States has yet to pay for the years of free labor that it received.[50] Our contemporary interpretations of the slavery past are more realistic about its devastating effects, but America's sanctioned public memory has made no room for the idea of reparations.

Using the Arguments and Actions of Others

Desegregation's advocates used the words and deeds of their opponents to establish black equality. Exploiting tensions in the rhetoric and behavior of the bill's critics, advocates argued that those who opposed desegregation were hypocrites; they knew and acted as though African Americans were their equals. James Rapier began his version of this argument by dissociating European Americans into two classes: those who were ignorant and uncultured and those who were educated and refined. With the lower class of whites, Rapier associated several negative values such as prejudice, drunkenness, cowardice, and the belief of black inferiority. The higher class of whites, said Rapier, was unafraid of the Negro, while the lower class resented the potential power that blacks might wield. He said, "I have always found more prejudice existing in the breasts of men who have feeble minds and are conscious of it, than in the breasts of those who have towering intellects and are aware of it. Henry Ward Beecher reflected the feelings of the latter class when on a certain occasion he said: 'Turn the negro loose; I am not afraid to run the race of life with him.' He could afford to say this, all white men cannot."[51] These comments involved a clear distinction between two types of European Americans, and they did so by highlighting differences of class over differences of race.

Rapier then proposed that those with less ability found satisfaction in oppressing others. In Europe, Jews felt the brunt of such oppression, but in America, African Americans have been the favored target, he said. This oppression was possible because the nation sustained legislation that kept minorities from fulfilling their potential. He argued further that the experiences blacks endured were the result not of inherent inferiority, but of the dominant race's ability to keep people of color under the heel of repressive legislation. Rapier even suggested that the more restrictions a society needed to keep a race powerless, the more reason to suspect that the oppressed race possessed innate ability.[52] Speaking as a critic of society and power, he argued that those who belonged to the lower class of whites had a vested interest in keeping segregation alive: "the smaller the caliber of the white man the more frantically has he fought to prevent the intellectual and moral progress of the negro, for the simple but good reason that he has the most to fear from such a result. He does not wish to see the negro approach the high moral standard of a man and gentleman." If the freedmen and women were inherently inferior, segregation would be unnecessary. Forced to live by their own devices, African Americans would fall behind quickly. But the very fact that some European Americans wanted to prevent desegregation proved that the race was inherently equal. Rapier concluded, "By their acts, not by their words, the civilized world can and will judge how honest my opponents are in their declarations that I am naturally inferior to them. No one is surprised that this class opposes the passage of the civil-rights bill, for if the negro were allowed the same opportunities, the same rights of locomotion, the same rights to comfort in travel, how could they prove themselves better than the negro?"[53]

The significance of this strategy is threefold. First, the ideology of white superiority retained its power so long as no one examined the doctrine critically. The distinction, based upon racial heritage, assumed that every white person was superior to every nonwhite person. Rapier challenged this doctrine by offering an evaluative criterion that was grounded in class rather than race. Distinctions of class were common, and his use of such distinctions cut across racial differences to establish that not even European Americans were really equal. By emphasizing class differences, Rapier drove a wedge into the idea of a monolithic white race, and he created a context where critical questions were possible, questions such as Are mentally deficient whites still superior to all blacks? and Is the white drunkard superior to African Americans of temperance and culture? Rapier's standard was based not on color but on individual ability and character. This standard focused on particularities rather than racial generalities. Although differences of class were tied, in American culture, to racial inheritance, Rapier broke that linkage. He offered himself as living proof that if his own criterion was used, then his colleagues would have to admit that the best of the black race surpassed many European Americans. Representative Durham's claim that the poorest and humblest white person feels and knows his superiority was untrue in Rapier's framework.[54] Durham must fear his own inferiority, hence his need to maintain racial segregation.

Second, this position inverted the burdens of protection that were assigned to the desegregation measure. Critics labeled the bill an unequal exercise of special legislation. It intruded on the lives of white property owners, providing extraordinary protection to black citizens and sacrificing the normal rights of white citizens. An extreme case of positive law, its opponents characterized the bill as the worst kind of governmental intervention. Black Republicans reversed this logic. By offering alternative motives to those who argued against the measure, they implied that the current judicial system actually favored European Americans at the expense of others. Foreshadowing the contemporary arguments of critical race theorists such as Patricia J. Williams, Rapier insisted that federal and state statues were not racially neutral.[55] Segregation as a cultural practice and as a legislative policy intruded on the lives of every citizen. It sustained unearned privilege among whites, and it narrowed the opportunities of blacks.

Approached in this context, the Civil Rights Bill was a conservative measure, because it eliminated segregation laws, further narrowing the role of government in daily life. According to the Wisconsin senator Timothy Howe, "the bill imposes no burdens upon any one. It simply commands that we get off from the freedman; not partly off, but altogether off, not off his neck alone, but off his skirts as well. You are not required to lift him to his feet, but to let him get on to his feet if he can; not to lead him on his way, only not to trip him as he staggers on his way. That is all."[56] In an unpublished speech delivered in 1868, Butler had articulated a similar argument. Laying out three principles—equality of rights, equality of power, and equality in the burden of Government—he suggested that prudent policy and limited government could live side by side: "I want laws enacted, constitutions framed, society organized, so that the negro shall have a fair chance with the rest. Then, if he can beat me, so much the better for him! And, if I can beat him; so much the better for me. And we ask no more, and let me say, we will take no less."[57]

Third, Rapier's decision to use white fears to argue for black strength exploited an important tension in the opposition's rhetoric. On the one hand, the opponents of desegregation often implied and sometimes explicitly affirmed white superiority; however, they also argued that the desegregation measure would lead to the destruction of Anglo culture. Without cultural and legal restraints, blacks would oppress whites, and mixed race relationships would destroy Anglo purity. These claims attributed considerable power to people of color. For example, the Democrats' expressed concern with miscegenation was sensible only if one also believed that white men were incapable of preventing black men from overpowering white women. Moreover, the cultural habits of the former slaves must have considerable power if, as opponents argued, desegregation would result in its domination over white civilization. Republicans, especially the black members of Congress, exploited this paradox and used their opponents' rhetoric to establish their own authority. For example, on 5 January 1874 the Democrat John Harris argued that desegregation might cause the collapse of America's system of government. Later that day Alonzo Ransier responded:

> It is feared by the gentleman from Kentucky and those whom he represents in this matter of civil rights, that if we colored people are put upon a plane of civil equality with them in law—going into the same schools, hotels, and places of amusement, and into the jury-box and the cemetery—we, by virtue of our intellectual superiority and our moral and physical force, if not numbers, will absorb the race to which he and they belong. This is the

> logical deduction from the apprehensions to which he has given expression. Let me thank him, in the name of the colored people of the country, for the compliment he has, perhaps unconsciously, paid them; but I must here deny that that would necessarily follow civil equality in this country. . . . We are known, Mr. Speaker, to be too magnanimous for that. If we are powerful, we know how to be merciful.[58]

Turning his opponent's discourse against him, Ransier uncovered the inconsistencies in Harris' logic.

Equality through Enactment

Karlyn Kohrs Campbell and Kathleen Hall Jamieson contend that there is a particular form of rhetorical argument where the speaker incarnates the argument she verbally affirms.[59] In this form, which they call *enactment,* the speaker's person becomes evidence and proof for the truth of her claims.[60] Kathleen Campbell describes this strategy in detail, noting several particular instances. Barbara Jordan in her 1976 keynote address used enactment to great effect when she pointed to herself as proof that the Democratic Party reflected America's diversity. According to Kathleen Campbell, John F. Kennedy "enacted" his famous phrase, "Let them come to Berlin," because he spoke those words from that location.[61] In both cases, the orators used enactment explicitly, verbalizing the idea that they embodied or represented their arguments. Campbell notes further that an orator may use enactment without explicit self-references.[62] In other words, a speech may utilize enactment implicitly.

The African Americans of this debate used the enactment strategy to considerable effect. In part, they claimed explicitly that they represented the race that their opponents called inferior, and they challenged their opponents to argue that they were inferior. In addition, the black representatives used an oratorical style and norms of eloquence that were popular during that period. They chose to address Congress in a manner that emphasized that they were capable of reason, sustained argument, and refined expression. In the process, they demonstrated that their presence was justified not only by an election but also by the quality of their person.

James Rapier called attention to his status when he described his peculiar position to his peers. He said, "Just think that the law recognizes my right upon this floor as a law-maker, but that there is no law to secure to me any accommodations whatever while traveling here to discharge my duties as a Representative of a large and wealthy constituency. Here I am the peer of the proudest, but on a steamboat or car I am not equal to the most degraded. Is not this anomalous and ridiculous?"[63] Rapier's comments made his very presence on the floor into an illustration of segregation's discriminatory nature. His status as a representative highlighted the fact that the law recognized a level of equality that society refused to acknowledge. Republican idealists used this incongruity. Benjamin Harris, a white Republican from Massachusetts, interrupted one Virginia representative to ask whether the trains and hotels in his state had refused service to black congressmen as they traveled to Washington, D.C. Thomas Whitehead responded evasively, eventually claiming that his state did not discriminate against individuals of color. Joseph Rainey quickly stood and replied that he had been barred from a streetcar in the state's capital. Whitehead asked, "Did you tell them who you were?" to which Rainey replied, "I did not tell them who I was. It is not necessary for me to do so in order to ride in the street cars of New York or Boston." There was little that Whitehead could say in response. Personal testimony is difficult to refute, and in this debate the eyewitness accounts of black representatives became one of the more powerful dimensions to their enactment.[64] In this instance Rainey's refutation allowed his colleague, Harris, to return to the issue:

> Why, Mr. Speaker, only today, as I had occasion to remark when interrupting the gentleman from Virginia, a representative of a portion of this people my equal upon this floor [Rainey]—and it is with no feeling of shame that I confess that the gentleman who made the speech today and who made the statement to which I refer is my equal . . . declared that he, leaving the capital of his country, will be denied—(and the gentleman from Virginia did not in his reply to my question deny the truth of the statement)—will be denied the privileges which I should enjoy in the railroad train, in the hotel, in the restaurant, in any respectable refreshment-room, on his way to this southern home—he would be denied these because of his color—the privileges which I should enjoy. And yet the Constitution of his country says that he shall have all the rights of every other citizen.[65]

In this and similar instances, the presence and testimony of black representatives became evidence that the promises of Reconstruction and its constitutional amendments were unfulfilled.

The style and method of two speeches reinforced the claim that African Americans had the ability to engage in public debate. Robert Elliott and James Rapier gave strong presentations that established their oratorical excellence. One dimension of their eloquence involved the use of literary references. In his introduction, Rapier explained that he was fearful that some might view his performance as self-interested. But, at the same time, if he did not speak he might seem ungracious or uninterested in something that involved him and his race. To describe this dilemma he said, "in steering away from Scylla I may run upon Charybdis."[66] Scylla was a reference to the mythological rock or cliff off of Sicily's coast that lay across from Charybdis, an equally dangerous whirlpool. Sixteenth- and seventeenth-century literary intellectuals had used this phrase to describe a difficult or life-threatening situation. When the trope appeared, as in Francis Bacon's *Colours of Good and Evil,* the phrase implied the problem of running from one evil to encounter or invite another. Rapier's use of this analogy provided his text with a sense of refinement and intellectual authority.

In addition to classical references, Rapier and Elliott used various biblical references. Elliott's 6 January 1874, peroration reads:

> The Holy Scriptures tell us of an humble hand-maiden who long, faithfully and patiently gleaned in the rich fields of her wealthy kinsman; and we are told further that at least, in spite of her humble antecedents, she found complete favor in his sight. For over two centuries our race has "reaped down your fields." The cries and woes which we have uttered have "entered into the ears of the Lord of Sabaoth [*sic*]," and we are at last politically free. The last vestiture [*sic*] only is needed—civil rights. Having gained this, we may, with hearts overflowing with gratitude, and thankful that our prayer has been granted, repeat the prayer of Ruth: "Entreat me not to leave thee, or to return from following after thee; for whither thou goest, I will go; and where thou lodgest, I will lodge; thy people shall be my people, and thy God my God; where thou diest, will I die, and there will I be buried; the Lord do so to me, and more also, if aught but death part thee and me."[67]

Rapier, discussing how Southern railroad porters protected first-class cars from black intrusion, said, "I must do them the justice to say that they guard these sacred portals with a vigilance that would have done credit to the flaming swords at the gates of Eden."[68] In a later portion of the same speech he declared, "I could no more rejoice on that occasion in my present condition than the Jews could sing in their wonted style as they sat as captives beside the Babylonish streams."[69]

Taken together, the classical and biblical illusions of Elliott and Rapier brought their speeches into line with established norms of nineteenth-century oratory. The ability to infuse one's text with religious and classical literature signaled a person of culture. Although the norms of eloquence were changing with the advent of the industrial revolution, the Bible was still a moral authority and a means to establish identity between the speaker and the audience. Kenneth Cmiel notes in reference to criticism of late-nineteen-century philologists that the Bible's literary qualities were an important mediator between learned and popular culture.[70] A person who wished to be seen as a gentleman needed to use these topoi to establish his credentials. It is noteworthy that Elliott's use of classical and biblical references led to rumors that someone else had written the speech. His opponents could not believe that a person of his color knew of Scylla and Charybdis or how to use the reference as a persuasive illusion.[71]

Rapier and Elliott also enacted the roles of nineteenth-century gentlemen through syntactic devices that created dramatic moments within their speeches. Rapier, for example, combined *symploce* (repetition at the beginning and ending of a clause) with *erotesis* (rhetorical questions) in a passage that expressed doubt over the Democrats' desire to help blacks. He said,

"*If* [this] is so *why was it,* even after the several amendments had been officially announced to be part of the Federal Constitution, that his [Beck's] State and others refused to allow the negro to testify in their courts against a white man? *If they believed* he should be educated . . . *why was it* that his school-houses were burned down . . . *If they believe* the negro should vote . . . *why was it* that Ku-Klux Klans were organized to prevent him from exercising the right of an American citizen"[72] (italics added).

In a second instance, Rapier's text contained an anaphora to describe the Union's desperation before black soldiers entered the conflict:

> But we all remember in our late war *when* the Government was so hard pressed for troops to sustain the cause of the Union, *when* it was so difficult to fill up the ranks that had been so fearfully decimated by disease and the bullet; *when* every train that carried to the front a number of fresh soldiers brought back a corresponding number of wounded and sick ones; *when* grave doubts as to the success of the Union arms had seized upon the minds of some of the most sanguine friends of the Government; *when* strong men took counsel of their fears; *when* those who had all their lives received the fostering care of the nation were hesitating as to their duty in that trying hour, and others questioning if it were not better to allow the star of this Republic to go down and thus be blotted out from the great map of nations than to continue the bloodshed; *when* gloom and despair were wide-spread; *when* the last ray of hope had nearly sunk below our political horizon.[73] (italics added)

There was an overt sense of rhythm and drama in these instances of repetition that gave the speech an elegant tone.

Finally, these two speakers employed dramatic imagery and metaphor to demonstrate the depth and complexity of their intellect. Elliott, for example, used a powerful illness metaphor to describe the purpose of the Civil War: "The logical result of this mistake of the framers of the Constitution strengthened the cancer of slavery, which finally spread its poisonous tentacles over the southern portion of the body-politic. To arrest its growth and save the nation we have passed through the harrowing operation of intestine war, dreaded at all times, resorted to at the last extremity, like the surgeon's knife, but absolutely necessary to extirpate the disease which threatened with the life of the nation the overthrow of civil and political liberty on this continent."[74] In a vivid description of black sacrifice during the Civil War, Rapier noted that no white father ever objected to blacks "becoming food for powder" if it would save his sons from war.[75] When he remarked how slave traders once sold men and women within a stone's throw of the Capital building, he said, "[it] was so near that the shadow of the Goddess of Liberty reflected by the rising sun would fall within the slave-pen as a forcible reminder that there was no hopeful day, nothing bright in the future, for the poor slave."[76] Elliott's text mirrored the light and dark imagery of Rapier's when he declared that the "the rights contended for in this bill are among 'the sacred rights of mankind, which are not to be rummaged for among old parchments or musty records; they are written as with a sunbeam, in the whole volume of human nature, by the hand of the Divinity itself, and can never be erased or obscured by mortal power.'"[77]

These texts deserve an extended metaphorical analysis to appreciate the symbolic significance of their imagery, but for our purposes it is necessary to note only that such language enacted the speaker's equality. Elliott's speech was praised on the floor and in the press. Within the debate his rhetorical performance was used as proof of black equality. Butler declared that Elliott's speech "shows him to be the peer of any man on this floor, be he who he may." Recognizing the enactment that Elliott performed, Butler added, "I think the exhibition of yesterday showed that God has given to one of the negro race the power to be the equal, in all that makes a man, of the proudest man on this floor. And the debate has not been so far fruitless if it teaches us that God has not given to every man on this floor the power to be the equal of the colored man who spoke for his race yesterday, and such equality we cannot attain by legislation, or legislate some white men up to and some negroes down to the same level, however much we may try so to do."[78] Although Butler's words were made before Rapier's speech, Rapier's text reflects a level of eloquence that equals if not surpasses Elliott's. For both of these men, the style that they employed invited comparisons, and it demonstrated their capacity to use complex ideas, logical proofs, and pleasing language; subsequently, they came to embody the characteristics of a nineteenth-century member of Congress. Their discourse justified their presence, and it implied that similar levels of refinement were present among other African Americans.

Equality through Confrontation

Like enactment, the final rhetorical strategy involved a performance as well as an argument. African American representatives defended black equality by confronting prominent Democratic opponents. In many ways Robert Elliott's entire presentation can be seen as confrontation, because it was meant as the formal rebuttal to Alexander Stephens's speech. Stephens, who spoke on 5 January 1874, was the champion of desegregation's opponents, and Elliott was the champion for those who supported desegregation. Elliott encouraged this association, stating:

> Now, sir, recurring to the venerable and distinguished gentleman from Georgia, [Mr. Stephens,] who has added his remonstrance against the passage of this bill, permit me to say that I share in the feeling of high personal regard for that gentleman which pervades this House. His years, his ability, and his long experience in public affairs entitle him to the measure of consideration which has been accorded to him on this floor. But in this discussion I cannot and I will not forget that the welfare and rights of my whole race in this country are involved. When, therefore, the honorable gentleman from Georgia lends his voice and influence to defeat this measure, I do not shrink from saying that it is not from him that the American House of Representatives should take lessons in matters touching human rights or the joint relations of the State and national government. . . . I meet him only as an adversary; nor shall age or any other consideration restrain me from saying that he now offers this Government, which he had done his utmost to destroy, a very poor return for its magnanimous treatment."[79]

James Rapier attacked Stephens as well. He explained that Stephens had been absent from Congress for many years. When the elder statesman had been in Congress last, slave traders had practiced their profession just outside the capital building, and the presence of uniformed black soldiers would have caused a citywide panic. But now, at Stephens's return, the situation was completely different; now a black man could address the House. Because of this change, Stephens was a man out of place and time.

Using a strategic metaphor, Rapier explained, "when he comes into these Halls advocating the same old ideas after an absence of so many years, during which time we have had a conflict of arms such as the world never saw, that revolutionized the entire body-politic, he stamps himself a living, 'Rip Van Winkle.'"[80]

In both of these instances, Rapier and Elliott accomplished something that was impossible to imagine only three years before. They stood and publicly criticized one of the most prominent Southern politicians of their era. This criticism was sometimes scathing. Rapier, for example, declared that he could respect the "prejudices" of Southern men more if these men were consistent to their principles. But how, he said, could he respect a man who denounced the evil of public integration and then goes "to the arms of his colored mistress and there pour [*sic*] out his soul's complaint, tell her of the impudence of the 'damned nigger' in coming to a table where a white man was sitting"?[81] Speaking even more directly at his congressional audience, he declared: "Out of four poor unfortunate colored women who from poverty were forced to go to the lying-in branch of the Freedmen's Hospital here in the District last year three gave birth to children whose fathers were white men, and I venture to say that if they were members of this body, would vote against the civil-rights bill."[82]

The confrontations performed by these representatives sent a clear message, especially to those blacks who watched from the gallery. Here were black men, from the South, who were willing to ignore the social and rhetorical conventions of the past. Not only did they speak directly to their opponents as their equals, they condemned their behavior. Rapier and Elliott placed themselves in moral judgment of Stephens and the other Democrats who argued against desegregation. Their performances leveled the distinctions between the races, implying a relationship between rivals, between equals.

This was demonstrated ably by Alonzo Ransier. During the 1874 debate, the Virginia representative John Harris had declared that no member of Congress could claim that the colored man was created his equal. Ransier, a black member, interrupted Harris, saying "I can." Later when Harris defended racial prejudice, saying "it was born in the children of the South; born in our ancestors, and born in your ancestors in Massachusetts—that the colored man was inferior to the white," Ransier again interrupted with, "I deny that."[83] Ransier forced Harris to acknowledge his presence, and in that moment he eloquently refuted the rhetoric of place by enacting his role as an equal congressional opponent. His interruption embodied the politics of equality by asserting that blacks were equal enough to sit in Congress and equal enough to confront other representatives, regardless of their color. In addition, Ransier's behavior enacted the temporal distinction that Rapier had used to call Stephens Rip Van Winkle. Ransier represented the present, a moment of revolution, whereas Harris and the rhetoric of place were remnants of slavery. Thus Ransier's intervention caused Harris to respond: "Sit down; I am talking to white men; I am talking to gentlemen." In that moment, equality and place stood in sharp contrast, and Harris revealed his association to an inappropriate perspective and way of speaking. An utterance that would have received little notice ten years before was no longer fashionable in Congress.

The confrontational behavior of these black representatives supports the research of Cal Logue and Thurmon Garner.[84] They posit that the social relationship between Southern African and European Americans altered substantially after the war. The physical rupture represented by emancipation instantly increased the status of those who were once slaves. Blacks took advantage of this new status by speaking about their own needs in public. Some African Americans abandoned their formerly subservient rhetoric and took an assertive posture. Without a doubt, Elliott, Rapier, Ransier, and, to a lesser degree, Cain and Rainey exhibited these self-assured discursive patterns, and such behavior went a long way toward establishing their equality.

At the same time, it is important to note that the confrontational attitudes of these representatives provide an inaccurate picture of the South as a whole. The House floor has never been a good representation of general public forums. It was unlikely that House Democrats would attack physically the black representatives where they stood, but this was less true for African Americans who asserted their equality elsewhere. Immediately after the war, violence against blacks reached startling proportions, and the violence often ensued because a man or women of color had been "insolent"—that is, self-assertive. The situation remained difficult for many blacks as Reconstruction progressed. Although the Enforcement Acts of 1870 and 1871 diminished organized violence somewhat, the South was dangerous even for the black members of Congress. After Robert Elliott had spoken in favor of the 1871 Klan Act, he wrote his wife: "I write this to inform you that I shall leave for home at 7 o'clock tonight, by the Richmond and Danville R.R., and expect to reach home by the Charlotte and Columbia Rail Road on Sunday morning before day. If anything should happen to me, I have a draft on the Bank for $1,800. . . . Mr. Ordway has also a life insurance policy for my life for $10,000—which he will turn over to you. I do this, my dear, because life is uncertain." Richard Cain and his family lived in constant fear and kept their house guarded at all times.[85] One ought never forget that many African Americans of this period paid a price for direct confrontation.

The Nature of This Black Equality

Although this chapter has characterized the rhetoric of Republican idealists generally, it has emphasized the texts of African American congressmen, because their presence altered the discussion about black equality in a real and significant way. Due primarily to their presence and rhetoric, the black equality of the 1874 and 1875 civil rights debate was different from the vision offered by Charles Sumner in 1872. Sumner's equality was grounded on two premises: all humans are equal due to the Enlightenment principle of universal humanity, and African Americans are the perfect equal of European Americans because the Fourteenth Amendment has altered their status from brutes to citizens. These ideas remained salient in the debate; in fact, many white Republicans seemed to prefer them. The Senate leader Frederick Frelinghuysen declared that the principle of equality was a necessary proposition for the security of the polity, and since "there is but one idea in the bill and that is: The equality of races before the law," the Senate should pass the legislation.[86] Rapier and the speakers discussed above shared these grounds, but their emphasis was not on Reconstruction policies or even natural law. The African American speakers and, to some extent, Butler and Pratt emphasized material features such as black ability, character, and implicit power. To this extent there were two interconnected but distinct arguments for black equality in this debate.

Rapier expressed the first of these principles when he declared: "After all, this question resolves itself to this: either I am a man or I am not a man. If one, I am entitled to all the rights, privileges, and immunities common to any other class in this country; if not a man, I have no right to vote, no right to a seat here; if no right to vote, then 20 per cent of the members on this floor have no right here, but, on the contrary, hold their seats in violation of law."[87] This principled dimension of black equality was guaranteed by organic law. From that philosophical perspective Rapier declared, "nothing short of a complete acknowledgment of my manhood will satisfy me. I have no compromises to make, and shall unwillingly accept any."[88]

At the same time, the argument that African Americans were equal because of their inherent abilities was also a factor in this debate. The race had demonstrated its equality numerous times; therefore, proponents could say that the race had earned the rights that it now desired. In this second case, rights were an outgrowth of success, ability, and intellect. Based on these entailments it is important to reread Rapier's claim, "either I am a man or I am not a man," because he was not speaking only of his biological status. The entire structure of his text and the discourse of other Republican idealists implied that African Americans had achieved something more than basic manhood. Some of them, at least, were gentlemen. Whether on the battlefield or the cotton field, whether in the House of Representatives or in the nightmares of Southern whites, people of color possessed a degree of material equality and the promise for more.

These four rhetorical strategies and the substantial claims that came with them extended the era's equality politics in a new direction. Furthermore, it called for a shift in the country's assumptions about black equality, which would mean an additional alteration of the nineteenth century's racial practices. James Rapier, Robert Elliott, Benjamin Butler, and those idealists who supported civil rights seemed interested in or, at the very least, unopposed to just such a transformation. Their collective text about equality sought to recast the national community. The success of this challenge would depend on how their opponents responded. A response patterned only after the discursive habits of Eldredge and Robbins would fail, because the realities of the war and the constitutional amendments had tipped the scales against explicitly racist rhetoric. Nevertheless, even if members of Congress could no longer silence the black voice in Congress, it did not necessarily follow that the ideology of place could not be applied through subtle changes in rhetoric. A number of Democrats recognized this fact, and they sought out a more moderate position. Foner explains, "A growing number of Democratic leaders saw little point in denying the reality that blacks were voting and holding office. These advocates of a New Departure argued that their party could only return to power by putting the issues of the Civil War and Reconstruction behind them. Thus began a period in which Democrats, like Republicans, proclaimed their realism and moderation and promised to ease racial tensions."[89] Condit and Lucaites maintain that although the fire-eaters continued to express racial epitaphs, a second group spoke "an essentially elitist, romantic patriarchalism."[90] This trend among national Democratic leaders was mirrored, in part, by some Southern newspapers that argued that white citizens had to woo their former slaves from the manipulative hands of Republicans who wished to use African Americans for political gain.[91]

While the moderate Democrats replaced their overtly racist appeals, which remained popular at the state and local level, with the language of the "New South,"[92] Republicans struggled to maintain their position against the "honeyed phrases" of the Democrats. Indeed, as the rhetoric of the moderate Democrats moved toward the center, the Republican discourse sounded more and more like the claims of prewar abolitionists. As a result, the principal conflict in this debate was not a tension between the discourse of black inferiority and black equality, but between limited black equality and perfect black equality. The outcome of this battle would help to determine what definition should guide political judgments.

The Third Voice: The Moderate Democrats' Rhetoric of Place

The congressional situation in 1874 and 1875 put desegregation opponents in an awkward position. The legitimate presence of African American representatives illustrated the transformation that had transpired, and these black speakers, with their vocal support for civil rights, made traditional claims of white supremacy difficult to advocate. Though the situation merely infuriated Eldredge, Harris, Durham, Robbins, and Brown, the more moderate Democrats chose to respond with restraint and cunning. Lucius Q. C. Lamar of Mississippi justified the moderate stance as follows: "The strength and energy and will of Southern radicals are underestimated. The program which they are attempting to force upon their party is as bloody and vigorous as that of the French Jacobins, and they are backed by Grant. A few inflammatory speeches from our side would do their work for them. Never was there a more critical period in our history than the present. The only course I, in common with other Southern representatives, have to follow, is to do what we can to allay excitement between the sections, and to bring about peace and reconciliation."[93] The goal for Lamar and other moderate Democrats was to devise a rhetoric that maintained white hegemony without seeming unrepentant or extreme. As their rhetoric took shape, these Democrats constructed their own definition of black equality. They maintained that African Americans *were* entitled to equal privileges, but they sustained the fundamental belief that blacks were "other"; therefore, they occupied a distinct place in society.

Divine and Natural Racial Difference

The first rhetorical strategy that implicitly denied black equality was the claim that God had ordained natural differences between the races. Augustus Merrimon's 22 May 1874 Senate speech is instructive. According to him, God had established a natural order that humans could neither deny nor change. He said, "We know this fact, that [God] has made the races. We know this just as certainly as we know that we live or that the sun shines, or any other physical fact. We know, too, that by reason of race there are material and radical distinctions between classes of men which cannot be changed but by changing the course of nature. God has made the Caucasian race white. He has made the negro race black. . . . We know these facts—all ages have known them—just as we know that we live, and these natural facts appear to us just as the seasons, the earth, the sun and moon and stars."[94] In a strictly literal interpretation, this text does not argue for black inferiority, only for black difference. Nonetheless, Merrimon's statements had important persuasive consequences. They implied a moral obligation to maintain the differences established by a divine hand. He explained:

"Who shall dare to change, or attempt to change the course and harmony of nature? And who shall dare to blot out the distinctions of race? I ask Senators, where do they get the authority to change the color that God has blessed us with? Where can any authority be found to make my skin black and to change and corrupt my blood? . . . Show me that; and until you do show me that, let me hear no more of that false and scandalous doctrine of breaking down the distinctions among the races and blending all into one, by crowding and huddling all races together in school-houses, in inns, in railroad cars, on steamboats, in theaters, or anywhere else."[95]

To our contemporary ears, these words are recognizable as one of the basic tenets of white supremacy. At the very least, they argue for the status quo, a context in which whites exercised authority over the lives of blacks. One might add that Merrimon's text is significant, because he engages in a rhetoric that creates a powerful kind of knowledge. Resembling scientists such as Samuel Morton and Louis Agassiz, Merrimon naturalizes racial difference; consequently, difference becomes an indisputable truth. As he so eloquently explains, difference is divine; it cannot be altered and it should not be challenged. What is more, the knowledge that Merrimon creates in this text establishes racial separation as its political and social imperative. Yet despite the insights of this interpretation, it is important that one also attempt to understand Merrimon's speech from a nineteenth-century perspective. The relationships among rhetoric, power, and knowledge were not entirely clear to this audience.[96] In addition, the participants in this debate truly believed that real natural differences existed between the races. In spite of Sumner's claim to sameness, even the black Republicans acknowledged racial difference. Many of their arguments were founded on a profound sense of racial pride. My point is that while Merrimon's speech supported the ideology of white supremacy, it did not engage in the overt racism of Robbins, Brown or Eldredge. Rather, from the perspective of his white colleagues, his comments would have seemed like common sense. This, as we shall see, was an important factor in their discursive power.

The Difference of Individual Ability

Alexander Stephens argued on 5 January 1874 that it was possible to believe in equality while also acknowledging the truth of racial difference. He said, "While I do not hold the doctrine of the equality of races of men, yet I do maintain the great truth, however paradoxical it may appear to some, that all men are created equal. This great truth was first enunciated by a council of States on the 4th of July, 1776. It was then adopted and proclaimed as it came from the pen of Jefferson, the chief apostle of liberty on this continent."[97] He explained his position further:

> This truth [the Declaration] was never meant, however, in my opinion, to convey the idea that men were created equal in all respects, either in physical, mental, or moral development; but it was meant to assert the great law of nature that all men have an equal right to justice, and to stand, so far as governmental powers are concerned or exercised over them, perfectly equal before the law. This is the right of all classes of men, whether white, red, brown, or black. This American principle is as broad as our jurisdiction, and as catholic as the doctrines of Him who first announced to the world the true principle of justice; that is, "As ye would that men should do to you, do ye also to them likewise."
>
> This requires no leveling of the population of a State, either upward or downward—no equality and fraternity, as announced by the Jacobins of France—but that everyone should act toward another as that other ought, in turn, to act upon a reversal of their positions in the different and various relations of life, either socially, politically, or otherwise.[98]

In this passage, Stephens distances himself, and the moderate Democrats, from the more extreme position of William Robbins. Robbins had condemned the Declaration of Independence, saying it contained "more error and untruth" than any other statement in the English language. Alexander

Stephens embraced the Declaration, but he did so in a manner that supported racial difference.

In Stephens's text, it was possible to sustain difference and equality simultaneously, because the two ideas were not antagonistic but complementary. Equality, he said, was an ideal, an abstract or natural law that was best characterized as "justice." And how was this justice implemented? Interestingly, Stephens does not speak of laws or the Constitution; instead he offers an exemplar: "As ye would that men should do to you, do ye also to them likewise." Justice, equality before the law, was a matter of personal ethics. The logic of Stephens's text defines equality as acting "toward another as that other ought, in turn, to act upon a reversal of their positions in the different and various relations of life, either socially, politically, or otherwise." This form of equality did not alter individual differences; in fact, it was grounded in them. Equality was a personal norm of behavior, a matter of accepting the responsibilities of one's place in society.

On the basis of this logic, Stephens could conclude that equality required no "leveling of the population of a State." Differences would remain, because difference was inevitable. In many ways, it was necessary, because it gave purpose to one's life. According to Merrimon, the Republicans were correct to say that Southern whites had to help the freedmen and women. He said, "they need help from the white man in the South; they need his strong arm; they need the benefit of his advice and intelligence; they need his protecting guardianship in addition to the protection of constitutions and laws . . . they need him in all these respects, and there should be no words or causes of discord between them."[99] Merrimon's use of such terms as "guardianship" and "strong arm" suggested a paternal relationship, one in which whites were superior and blacks were helpless without them. This rhetoric had much in common with the paternalism of the antebellum and its definitions of place.[100] Coupled with the notion of equality and justice, moderate Democrats accepted a protective role that only they were capable of fulfilling.

What is remarkable about this discourse is that the Democrats chose to soften their black inferiority claims at all. Consider the following passage from Lewis Borgy, a senator from Missouri: "Mr. President, I hope the negro race will be able to achieve the high destiny that their professed friends on this floor so confidently anticipate, but I confess to some fears upon the subject. That there is a wide distinction between the two races cannot be denied. That the blacks are altogether inferior to whites I will not undertake to say. That they are human beings and justly entitled not only to recognition but to kindly treatment, we all admit. That they are capable of higher attainments and greater achievements than they have yet exhibited, I will not doubt. But that the negro race can become the full equal to the Caucasian or white race, has not yet been proved."[101] The underlying message in this passage was clearly that African Americans were, and probably would remain, inferior; yet Borgy's language is equivocal. He used qualifiers in a strategic way. He framed his comments as *personal* fears and *personal* beliefs. Making an effort not to seem heavy-handed, he did not force his audience to accept his perspective, and, leaving room for disagreement, he made his perspective seem all the more reasonable.

Social Equality

The interconnected distinctions complicated the term "equality" and led to the moderate Democrats' final strategy. They separated equality into three parts: political equality, legal equality, and social equality. Democrats argued that African Americans had been granted legal equality when the Fourteenth Amendment made them citizens. They claimed that blacks had received political equality when the Fifteenth Amendment protected their right to vote. But social equality, they said, was a new right that was granted by the Civil Rights Bill. While they could accept black political and legal equality, moderate Democrats argued that the South never could tolerate the social equality that desegregation implied.

The term social equality, though never defined clearly, entailed a consistent set of ideas. According to William Herndon (Texas), humans achieved their fullest measure of civilized perfection within society's social systems; a society's social interaction exemplified culture and higher human existence. Social equality, then, related to one's right to interact within this higher sphere as a complete equal of other participants. It meant that individuals were similar enough to enjoy the fullest, most intimate aspects of life. This included but was not limited to experiences that transpired in public accomodations. At present, said Herndon, white society could not admit the Negro because he was "unfitted for it."[102] The rationale behind Herndon's judgment related to the first two strategies discussed. According to the moderate Democrats, society's public and private relations had to reflect the natural difference that God had created. Since African and European Americans were different in abilities and physical characteristics, they belonged in separate social spheres. Hiram P. Bell, a Democrat from Georgia, explained: "This bill seeks to coerce an unnatural alliance between the races, unpleasant to them and disgusting to us, in our social relationships, it cannot be disguised that the object of this measure is to enforce social equality between the races, and that, too, by severe penalty. This is wrong in theory and impossible in practice; our social relations are controlled by laws peculiar to our social system, and independent of municipal regulations."[103] Social equality, according to this passage, was a matter of social relations. As the historian Martha Hodes recently explained, "'social equality' was a nebulous term referring largely to integration."[104]

While the moderate Democrats condemned the notion of social equality, they also insisted that African Americans were entitled to all the privileges whites enjoyed. Just moments before he condemned social equality, Bell said, "As to the right to participate in the benefits of our system of public education, they stand upon a footing of perfect equality in every respect with us."[105] For moderate Democrats, Bell's words were not in conflict. They argued extensively that everyone benefited when black children received an education. They added, however, that black children could not attend the same institutions as white children, because such a close association established social equality and denied the realities of racial difference. Segregation was necessary, they posited, to prevent the evil of miscegenation.

Hodes writes that "the issue of sex between black men and white women held a significant place in the formal political debates of Reconstruction."[106] This was particularly true when it came to desegregation. The threat of social rights was often expressed as the threat of sexual relations between the races. Sometimes coded words were used, as when Senator Eli Saulsbury (Delaware) explained the consequences of desegregation: "[The bill] proposes not, I say again, to confer any political rights upon the people of African descent, but it proposes to enforce familiarity, association, companionship between the white and the colored people of this country. Is not that true? If that is not the object and the purport and the intent of this measure, then I confess that I am incapable of understanding the force of the language used in the bill. . . . I maintain that no reason can be found other than the fact that the friends and supporters of this bill desire to enforce the intermixture, the association, and companionship between the races."[107]

Where Saulsbury used words like "intermixture" and "companionship" to imply that public contact would lead to intimacy, North Carolina representative Robert Vance was more explicit: "by placing the colored race and the white race continually together, by throwing them into social contact, the result will be more or less that the distinction between them will be broken down, and that miscegenation and an admixture of the races will follow. Sir, it must necessarily follow on such close intercommunication."[108]

At one level, the concern over miscegenation was nothing new. During the antebellum era the biracial population grew at an astounding rate. From 1850 to 1860 the number of blacks in slavery rose only 20 percent, but the number of mulattoes rose 67 percent. This presented a significant problem for the South's social order; after all, "slavery and whiteness were incompatible." Indeed, the lighter skin color of biracial children often complicated issues such as inheritances, marriage, and, most important, slavery.[109] Still, the arguments about miscegenation in the civil rights debate reveal a number of subtle changes from the antebellum era. The first is demonstrated in Merrimon's speech. According to him, when a race, black or white, perverted its blood through biracial sexual relationships, it violated nature's laws, resulting in imperfect human beings. He concluded, "a pure white man is better than a hybrid; a pure negro is better than a hybrid. The cross between the white man and the negro is the mulatto; and although I have seen some very intelligent mulattoes, I undertake to say, and to state it as a physiological fact, that a mulatto is not as perfect a man or woman, physically or intellectually, as a pure white man or a pure negro man."[110] It is important to note that this passage does not reflect the racial continuum of the antebellum period. During that era, light-skinned African Americans were accorded special privileges because they were closer to the white ideal. This was possible because the slavery system was intact, and European Americans were automatically assured that the cultural system would sustain their superiority. The "one drop" rule established a hierarchy that almost every institution protected. Even one drop of black blood was sufficient to define a person as African, subjecting that person to laws and customs that separated the races.

After the Civil War, however, the biracial population became a real dilemma for Southern conservatives. Without a formal institution to guard the superior position of whites, "mulattoes" and "quadroons" could use their whiteness to argue for parity. Conservatives responded to this threat through legislation and cultural practice. Howard Rabinowitz writes, "Nowhere was the desire to control blacks (and in this case whites as well) more evident than in the passage and enforcement of antimiscegenation laws." Several Southern states implemented them as part of their black codes. Although the Republican governments of congressional Reconstruction overturned most of these, they returned immediately as the Democrats redeemed each state.[111] Merrimon's arguments illustrate a second approach to the problem. By claiming that mulattoes were somehow flawed, he argued that the goal of both races should be to keep them separate. In other words, racial segregation was a matter of public health. Any form of social interaction might lead to private intimacy, and for the long-term health of the races, this was unwise.[112]

The discourse about social rights and miscegenation also worked an important change on the distinction between private and public spaces. Consider one angry exchange from Senator John Stockton: "do you mean or do you not mean that you propose by a compulsory system to educate the young people of different colors together, with the wish and the hope that all prejudices shall be eradicated and that they shall be one? Do you mean practical amalgamation or not? Do you mean miscegenation or not? Do you mean to degrade the white race of this country, to prostitute the power you have to degrade the white people of this country? Do you mean that or do you not mean it?"[113] Notice how quickly he moves from a discussion about public education to a discussion about private intimacy. This movement was not unusual; opponents of desegregation argued that when people of color entered public accommodations as equals, there were always consequences for private privilege. Vance warned that the Civil Rights Bill allowed blacks to intrude on private conversations: "Even if [a black man] is allowed to go into the dining-room, and is placed at a separate table because of his color, it will be a violation of this law." According to the congressman, the bill demanded that blacks be placed at the same table with whites. That, he declared, was a "social right."[114]

To appreciate the rhetorical significance of the dissociation among political, legal, and social equality, one must understand that the discourse that advanced these categorizes used the term *social equality* to collapse the public and private spheres. Every instance of integration within a public setting became a point of intrusion on the private lives of white citizens. Restaurants became locales of personal comfort and private consultation. Critics of desegregation described trains and stagecoaches as if they were the property of white passengers. Juries were not open forums for deciding legal questions, but the sanctuaries of whites, the only race with sufficient intelligence and wisdom to administer justice. Public schools were an especially private space where the character and values of innocent children had to be shielded from the other race. Put simply, that which had been seen as public in the nineteenth century was renamed social, and the newly labeled social realm became inextricably linked to the personal rights and property of white citizens. There are two important consequences of this formulation.

First, civil rights became a zero-sum game; therefore, the policy of desegregation was, by definition, an intrusion on the rights enjoyed by whites. According to John M. Glover (Missouri), "I would not elevate [blacks] by pulling down my own race. I would not widen the field of his privileges by narrowing that of the white man, who, I humbly submit, is entitled to some consideration at the hands of this Government and at the hands of his white brother."[115] Second, public accommodations became a space of private interest, because African Americans were really a contagion, a social disease. Recall the question that Merrimon posed to his colleagues: "Where can any authority be found to make my skin black and to change and *corrupt* my blood?"[116] The term corruption in this sentence is instructive. Even when Democrats refrained from calling African Americans inferior, they still argued that uncontrolled contact between the races would contaminate white civilization. According to the moderate conservatives, there was only one prudent action that Congress could follow—quarantine the problem.

Black Equality as Separate but Equal

The position of moderate Democrats developed across many texts and contexts. In each case, the distinctions between different forms of equality were minor parts of larger, more elaborate speeches that emphasized the bill's unconstitutionality or its practical consequence. As a result, the inequality theme of their discourse was more subtle than my description might indicate. The logical relationships among the distinctions made by moderate Democrats were not obvious, because the inequality thesis hid behind other themes and claims. When reading many segregation speeches together, the doctrine of black inequality is blatant, but when these rhetors gave each speech individually, they seemed to be the antithesis of the fire-eaters. Indeed, the rhetoric of the moderate Democrats was appealing and quite powerful. A decade prior, these men had chosen war rather than relinquish their belief in slavery's rectitude. Now Southern leaders applied the term equality to African Americans, and despite their narrow definition, their terms—legal, political, and social equality—seemed to vindicate the goals that Lincoln attributed to the Civil War during his "Second Inaugural Address." Indeed, a close examination of their position suggests many similarities with Lincoln's perspective.

In a study of Republican ideology prior to the Civil War, Earl Maltz argues that few in Lincoln's party cared to grant African Americans "full legal equality." Many Republicans harbored the same racist sentiments of the larger population, and they did not believe that blacks were their complete equals. Yet despite these positions, the Republicans had built their party on the theory of "limited absolute equality." "This theory," explains Maltz, "held that all men, including blacks, were entitled to a certain minimum level of rights."[117] One of the chief architects of this position had been Abraham Lincoln. In 1858, during a debate with Stephen Douglas in Ottawa, Illinois, Lincoln declared,

> I have no purpose to introduce political and social equality between the white and the black races. There is a physical difference between the two, which in my judgment will probably forever forbid their living together upon the footing of perfect equality. . . . but I hold that notwithstanding all this, there is no reason in the world why the negro is not entitled to all the natural rights enumerated in the Declaration of Independence, the right to life, liberty and the pursuit of happiness. [Loud cheers.] I hold that he is as much entitled to these as the white man. I agree with Judge Douglas he is not my equal in many respects—certainly not in color, perhaps not in moral or intellectual endowment. But in the right to eat the bread, without leave of anybody else, which his own hand earns, *he is my equal and the equal of Judge Douglas, and the equal of every living man*[italics in original].[118]

The foremost right in the theory of "limited absolute rights" was the economic right to earn wages. Indeed, this position was the cornerstone of the Republicans' attack on slavery.[119]

The arguments of moderate Democrats against desegregation coincided with limited absolute equality. Indeed, even the more extreme Southern conservatives tried to co-opt Lincoln's position. Representative Harris quoted the passage above just after he told Alonzo Ransier to sit down because he was "speaking to the white men of the House."[120] Harris's outburst probably ruined his appropriation of the president's words, but Alexander Stephens was more circumspect. His words and phrases paralleled Lincoln's; he noted the reality of racial difference, just as Lincoln had, and he made distinctions between political and social equality, just as Lincoln did. Stephens even described the purpose of the Declaration in language that mirrored the president's. In 1857 Lincoln had explained that the authors of the Declaration of Independence had "intended to include *all* men, but they did not intend to declare all men equal *in all respects*. They did not mean to say that all were equal in color, size, intellect, moral developments, or social capacity."[121]

The moderate Democrats seemed not only reasonable but also enlightened, and they worked hard to reinforce this perception. Merrimon expressed a common Democratic claim when he said, "there is no one in this

Senate who is freer from hostile feeling toward the Negro race than myself."[122] Alexander Stephens proclaimed that his opposition to the bill came from reason and not personal prejudice.[123] Henry Cooper of Tennessee, once a strong slavery proponent, said, "whatever may have been my education, whatever may have been my feelings, whatever may have been my actions in regard to the colored race, I trust I am prepared to accept as a verdict from which there can be no appeal that they are citizens, and as citizens I propose to treat them, and to treat them as equals before the law, for my equals they are before the law."[124] Allen Thurman and Eli Saulsbury both added that they had nothing but the kindest feelings toward the colored race.[125] Through a variety of assurances, the moderates distanced themselves from slavery and portrayed enlightened personae consistent with the new era and its assumptions.

Of course, with the benefit of hindsight, we understand that the equality of the moderate Democrats did not live up to even its own limited promises. Even in 1874 and 1875 their arguments did not oppose the overtly racist appeals of their more extreme colleagues, because both positions were deeply grounded in the antebellum era's notion of place. Indeed, the rhetoric of Stephens and Merrimon is best viewed as an innovative modification of the traditional rhetoric of place. Stephens was a refined and respectable version of Harris, Durham, and Eldredge. The fire-eaters offered the same distinctions as moderates, but they concluded their logic with an open and honest judgment of inequality rather than with the moderates' notion of partially equal. Historically speaking, in a context where blacks had almost no capital but their own labor—and even that was regulated by white property owners—the limited concessions of moderate Democrats meant that white superiority as a way of life remained intact. The progressive tone of their discourse became a smoke screen for the old notion of place. Indeed, this vision of equality paved the way for a new era characterized by the phrase "separate but equal."

Conclusion

The equality theme was a central issue of the 1870s civil rights controversy, because it had the greatest potential to alter the public discourse about race. The nineteenth century's popular conception of equality did not include African Americans, but at this historical moment, 1865–1875, no single definition of equality dominated the political sphere. This chapter has identified three very distinct definitions. Indeed, the very act of open congressional debate on this issue risked racism's cultural, institutional, and linguistic features. The Republicans' discourse represented a serious threat to the political culture of the South and the nation as a whole. Bond writes, "Implicit in the word 'reconstruction' lay a rebuke of the ideals that had urged southerners to leave the Union in 1861. Reconstruction meant to whites defeat on the field of battle and erosion of the social ethic's underpinnings."[126] The key to this transformation was a recategorization of the black race.

The Republicans' definition of equality was significant, because it redefined the nation's identity. Evidence for this conclusion exists in the discursive strategy of those Republicans who altered public memory. Recall Richard Cain's historical narrative in which African Americans were equal partners in the country's origin, growth, and prosperity. His discourse, like the discourse of all those who argued for black equality, demanded a reappraisal of what it meant to be an American.[127] The most revolutionary advocates of desegregation called for a *biracial* society. They advanced a vision of America where white labor, black sweat, black creativity, and white capital combined to make the country great. They actually enacted this vision by cooperating to pass the bill. This aspect of the Republicans' rhetoric went well beyond the Civil War, emancipation, and perhaps even the motives of Reconstruction's constitutional amendments.

The redefinitions offered by those who argued for complete black equality explain, in part, the response of bill opponents and the reluctance of some Republicans. Black equality was not the only concept that Democrats found disturbing; rather, the critics of desegregation and those Republicans who eventually compromised the bill wanted to sustain the identities that had existed before the war. These identities were part of the nineteenth century's culture, and they were essential components of its history and systems of privilege. Whereas several advocates of civil rights implied that America was, and perhaps always had been, broader than its white citizens, those who opposed the measure kept African Americans out of the country's identity by stressing racial differences. It is not difficult to see the physical distinctions discussed by Democrats as a more fundamental dissociation between real Americans and "other" Americans. Senator Robbins barely restrained his indignation when he argued that African Americans had hindered and not helped Southern development.[128] Contradicting Rapier and Elliott, he declared that blacks were absent from America's military history. His moderate colleagues made similar claims; they used a more polite tone. The paternal attitude taken by Merrimon and others went hand in hand with the claim that whites had built this country from the force of their own will.[129]

As a consequence of their continued racial distinctions, the moderate Democrats blunted one of the most threatening aspects of this debate—the reformulation of what "We the People" means. The egalitarian spirit of the Fourteenth Amendment opened the door for a reformulation of America's identity, but the Democrats' dissociation of legal, political, and social equality mitigated that threat by reaffirming limited black equality. Moderate Democrats moved to occupy the discursive space that Lincoln and the Republicans had held before the war; subsequently, they were able to reaffirm America's prior identity. America remained a white man's country. Moderate Democrats admitted that perhaps the freedmen and women would now prove themselves worthy of the gift of citizenship, but they also argued explicitly that Congress had to maintain many of the racial distinctions of the past. If Congress failed to sustain its political culture, then the nation would no longer be the country that it was. In a sense, they were correct. Our experiences with the Civil Rights Movement of the 1950s and 1960s suggests that if Congress's beliefs about inherited difference were removed from the process of political judgments and if the nation adopted the equality articulated by the African American representatives, then the country's very self would undergo a transformation.

5

Expediency Arguments and the Civil Rights Act of 1875

The second major fault line in the 1874 and 1875 desegregation debate involved the question of whether the policy was expedient. Charles Sumner had defended the bill's expediency by arguing that complete desegregation would help both the black populace and the nation. A national civil rights act, he said, would alleviate the harmful conditions that African Americans experienced daily, and it would raise the public mind to a new level of moral consciousness. In the debate that began two-and-a-half years later, critics and advocates split into two polar positions. Defenders of the measure—primarily Republican idealists—argued that the bill was expedient because it would eliminate the nation's racial problems and elevate the principle of equality. Those who attacked civil rights—Democrats along with a few conservative Republicans—passionately disagreed. They claimed first that the measure was unnecessary, second that it would destroy the nation's peace and stability, and third that it could not accomplish its own goals. For these reasons, they concluded that it was inexpedient and improper.

Deliberative Rhetoric and the Issue of Expediency

Congressional debates involve various types of reasoning, but perhaps the most common type involves claims about the worth of a policy given immediate circumstances and the policy's potential consequences. These argumentative forms have been the subject of theoretical speculation for some time. Sometimes translated as expedient and sometimes as advantageous or beneficial, Aristotle explains that temporally specific claims are essential to political or deliberative rhetoric.[1] Chiam Perelman and L. Olbrechts-Tyteca identify the "pragmatic argument" and describe it as a form that allows "a thing to be judged in terms of its present or its future consequences."[2] Similar to Aristotle's observations about deliberative discourse, they suggest that pragmatic arguments involve specific policies set in particular temporal contexts and circumstances.

For communication scholars, particular justifications are said to be distinct from ultimate rationales. Richard Weaver, for example, contrasts those inferences grounded in particulars against claims based on principle.[3] Aristotle juxtaposed the *telos* of the deliberative genre, the "advantageous," with forensics' outcome of justice and the epideictic's goal of the honorable. Perelman and Olbrechts-Tyteca speak at various times about absolute values, abstract values, and arguments that possess universal appeal.[4] Despite terminological differences, these theorists conceive of one argumentative type that relies on case-driven particulars while a second employs eternal, principled, or universally transcendent reasons. During the desegregation debate of late Reconstruction, the dominant term used to describe the first line of argument was expediency. In the words of Hiram P. Bell, "I invite the attention of the House to the expediency—to the question of policy involved. I approach its consideration with a profound sense of its importance."[5]

The expediency of desegregation was a contested issue in this debate, and those who argued either for or against desegregation's expediency exhibited few rhetorical subtleties. Both sides were verbal and explicit about how Congress should judge the bill. In addition, even though the Democrats and the radical Republicans took opposite positions, both sides justified their evaluations through similar topics or stasis points. They argued about whether the national situation warranted the bill, and they disputed the measure's potential consequences. These two stasis points, need and consequence, guide this chapter's analysis. This chapter reconstructs the debate's expediency theme by considering each side's answer to the following questions: What is the situation, and does it warrant desegregation? How will desegregation affect the situation, and will it work toward the nation's benefit? These questions are intended to reveal the underlying structure of each position's political judgment.

A Question of Need: Definitions of the Situation

When members of Congress discuss a measure's expediency, they usually describe those social problems that necessitate political action. The imperfections they identify, however, are not a "given." They are interpretations of material circumstances. Expediency arguments highlight certain aspects of reality, and they tend to de-emphasize other dimensions. It is crucial to understand any description of circumstances as a portrayal with inherent meanings and exclusions. For this reason, this chapter begins by recovering the "textual context" of debate participants.[6]

The Republicans' Textual Context: Slavery Continues and Justice Must Be Served

The first component in the Republicans' textual context was the argument that African Americans encountered daily prejudice and that this treatment denied their humanity and equality. Arguments of this sort were plentiful, because examples were abundant. According to James McPherson, the incidents described by Sumner in 1872 concerning Lieutenant Governor Oscar J. Dunn and Frederick Douglass were well known.[7] These examples became a staple of radical rhetoric when it pertained to Southern prejudice. The black congressmen of the 43d Congress were in a special position to speak about discrimination.

Joseph Rainey, an African American from South Carolina, provided one of the best testimonials about Southern discrimination.[8] According to him, he had experienced two examples of Southern prejudice while in Richmond, Virginia, two or three years before his 3 February 1875 speech. The first incident transpired when a city street-car conductor removed him from the car, despite the fact that Richmond had passed an official ordinance that prohibited such behavior.[9] But although Rainey found the conductor's disregard for city policy distressing, he was more distressed by the circumstances he encountered when visiting an old cemetery formerly dedicated to the city's slave population. Richmond officials had decided to build a street through the burial ground, and even though the workers had removed a few bodies, they had used some remains to fill in the low places and "mudholes." To Rainey this act symbolized continuing discrimination and its harmful effects. He declared, "Yet you talk about humanity; your kindly feeling for the colored race. Gracious Heaven! If you have no feelings for the ashes of the dead; if you have no regard for the dust of the dead slave who served you all the days of his life faithfully, honestly, well, we may have apprehensions as to the manner in which we will be treated, now that we are free and struggling for equal rights, unless we are protected by the strong arms of the law."[10] Other white and black members of Congress reported similar situations. A white Republican, William Lawrence, on 19 December 1874 described how the House's black librarian had been expelled from a railroad car.[11] Richard Cain recalled several personal examples.[12] Once while his colleague Robert Elliott traveled between Washington, D.C., and his home, a restaurant had refused to serve him. Not wanting to cause a fight when they passed through that area together, Cain and Elliott had paid to have a meal brought to their railroad car. But even in this they experienced trouble, because the railroad porters had felt that the two men were putting on airs.[13]

Cain argued that the nation's school systems evinced further examples of discrimination. Slavery's statutes had kept education from the black populace, and although the laws prohibiting black education were gone, the basic policy remained. Citing reports by state school superintendents, Cain argued that many European Americans purposefully kept black children ignorant. Using information from the California commissioner of education, he said that white prejudice was responsible for that state's educational deficiencies among colored children. He claimed as well that in Indiana and Illinois the halfhearted efforts of the few were overwhelmed by local authorities who ignored state statues and refused to educate African Americans.[14]

The significance of these examples was twofold. They demonstrated that African Americans encountered discrimination on a daily basis, and, in the process, they defined such discrimination as a problem. Opponents of desegregation admitted that these incidents did happen but denied their significance. Republicans maintained that discrimination was not neutral; it was clearly negative, because it denied the principle of equality. Segregation denied the race not only the comforts of first class, but it took their money for a first-class seat and then provided an inferior service. Rapier complained that his first-class ticket purchased him a seat in a "dirty, rough box with the drunkards, applesellers, railroad hands, and next to any dead that may be in transit regardless of how far decomposition may have progressed."[15] Although never stated, the implication in Rapier's comment was that the practice of segregation on railroad trains amounted to legalized robbery.

The significance of these stories went beyond the instances of discrimination they narrated. The issue was not simply that whites denied people of color the comforts of first-class travel or the benefits of an equal education. That fact was serious, but there was within the Republicans' context a larger issue. For them, these events represented deep sociological, moral, and legal imperfections. They reflected a repudiation of the politics of equality. Segregation denied the humanity of the black race. Benjamin Butler proclaimed: "Every man has a right to go into a public inn. Every man has a right to go into any place of public amusement or entertainment for which a license by legal authority is required. He has a right to ride in 'any line of stage-coaches, railroad, or other means of public carriage of passengers or freight,' and to be buried in any public cemetery; or he has a right in any 'other benevolent institutions or any public school supported in whole or in part at public expense or by endowment for public use'"[16] As Butler argued, every person had the fundamental right to enter any public accommodation. When restaurant owners or even church ministers prohibited African Americans from entering their establishments, they denied the rights and, thus, the humanity of the whole race. Segregation was more than a pragmatic inconvenience; it was also a very public abuse of the race's humanity. Rainey's declaration—"either I am a man or I am not a man"—was precisely the point for bill proponents.[17] By the symbolic denial of personhood, segregation re-enslaved the freedmen and women.

The Republicans did more than use examples of discrimination to describe the problems that existed in the national situation. Their collective text offered a broad temporal depiction where the immediate problems of racial discrimination were a part of the historical inequities of the old slavery system. Bill supporters implied that desegregation was necessary because the nation's problems were not only immediate but also historical. Recall Richard Cain's comments: "We have been identified with the interests of this country from its very foundation. The cotton crop of this country has been raised and its rice-fields have been tilled by the hands of our race. All along as the march of progress, and the march of commerce, as the development of your resources has been widening and expanding and spreading, as your vessels have gone on every sea, with the stars and stripes waving over them, and carried your commerce everywhere, there the black man's labor has gone to enrich your country and to augment the grandeur of your nationality."[18] The previous chapter used this text to illustrate the agency that black members of Congress attributed to those of color. Note further that Cain's narrative established the relevance of slavery within the postbellum context.

Cain created an association between the slavery past and the Reconstruction present first through the verb tense that he employed. Throughout the passage above, Cain used the present perfect tense to describe a complex temporal relationship where the contributions of African Americans had no definitive conclusion. He said: "We have been identified," the cotton crop "has been raised" by blacks, and that our labor "has gone to enrich your country." Cain could have said, "we had been identified," or that the cotton crop "had been raised by blacks." This past perfect tense would have suggested a clear conclusion to black action, and it would have created a distinction between the past and the present. Instead, Cain's present perfect verb tense gave the passage a sense of openness and possibility; it allowed for additional claims, such as "blacks continue to grow the nation's cotton" and "our labor continues to enrich your country." His present perfect tense also denied any clear separation between the past and the present, and this denial was the first step toward an overt argumentative link between two historical eras.

In the same speech, Cain declared, "Inasmuch as we have toiled with you in building up this nation; inasmuch as we have suffered side by side with you in the war; inasmuch as we have together passed through affliction and pestilence, let there be now a fulfillment of the sublime thought of our fathers—let all men enjoy equal liberty and equal rights."[19] In this sentence, Cain directly associated the past and the present. He argued that blacks had been an integral part of the nation and that their service demanded the fulfillment of some sort of historical transaction. At an economic level, his words implied a wage system where the labor of slaves would be paid by equal inclusion in American society. At a more abstract level, Cain implied that the presence of African Americans and their shared history with whites required their inclusion in the nation's glory. In both cases, the past necessitated present action—a national desegregation policy. As Cain conflated the past and the present, his text established a broad situational perspective. His answer to the question of whether circumstances warranted the Civil Rights Bill was a resounding yes, and he argued that the bill was expedient in part because the historical dimensions of the present situation made it necessary. Not only was the bill's expediency a matter of immediate concern, but it also involved a struggle to right past wrongs and pay overdue debts. His view of the present connected it with broader issues such as slave labor, unjust gain, and years of wrongful oppression.

The proponents of desegregation were not satisfied only to identify prewar instances of injustice. Just as Sumner had, they argued that the immoral prejudice that characterized the antebellum South continued. William Purman, a white representative from Florida, reminded everyone that after the war the South had sought to re-enslave the freedmen and women. As proof, he pointed to the black codes that many Southern states instituted shortly after 1865.[20] He recalled that Georgia's state legislature had declared that local officials could label as a vagrant any colored person found in idleness and without property. This individual could be fined, imprisoned, or bound to a white man for a period of service. Congress had struck down every one of these immoral statues, because, according to Purman, it had recognized that the Democrats could not be trusted to protect black interests. As Representative William H. H. Stowell (Virginia) affirmed the day before, "the democratic party has persistently and brutally opposed every measure tending to ameliorate and advance the condition of the colored man, and he can only rely in the future, as in the past, upon the republican party to recognize his claims to justice."[21]

Because the past and the present merged for the advocates of civil rights, they were able to argue that individual acts of discrimination were really systemic failures. Put another way, their "now" was defined by their "then." To the Republicans, these more recent instances of injustice indicated a persistent prejudice that went back to slavery. George Edmunds of Vermont declared in the final speech of the entire debate that, despite the Democrats' "honeyed phrases," the country understood that the South maintained the same distinctions and beliefs as it had during the slavery era.[22] On 3 February 1875 Cain expressed a similar thought: "No, Mr. Speaker, it [the problem] is a damnable prejudice, the result of the old cursed system of slavery. It is that which brought about this prejudice and has caused it to overshadow the whole land. Slavery has left the poison still in their minds."[23] Thus the Republicans aligned the slavery past and the postbellum present to form an expanded description of the national situation. From their perspective, one could understand the attitudes of Southern whites, whether they were political leaders or poor laborers, only within a context that included slavery and its foundation—black inequality. There was for these men a direct ideological stream that began in the antebellum era, flowed through the Civil War, and continued after the conflict to their present day. The situation that they defined encompassed this entire period, and based on this depiction, they identified a great evil that would not die.

Of course, desegregation's opponents interpreted the national situation very differently. They answered the question of whether the situation warranted the Civil Rights Bill with a resounding no. According to the Democrats' collective text, the situation in 1874 and 1875 was without significant racial problems. The only tension that did exist was the result of the Republican Party. Goodwill and tranquillity existed between the races, and opponents argued that this peace would expand if only the North would refrain from agitating everyone's emotions and prejudices.[24]

The Opponents' Textual Context: Bury the Past and Harmony Will Prevail

One might think that the Democrats and Southern conservatives would avoid the topic of slavery, but that was not the case. As he narrated a chronology of U.S. history, Merrimon declared, "From the foundation of our Government, as I have shown, the negro race in this country were held in a state of bondage, in a state of servitude; they were slaves." Eventually, he explained, a good portion of the American people came to "dislike" this institution, because "they believed that no human being had a right to hold another human being in bondage." Nevertheless, the South thought that slavery benefited both races, and, said he, it believed that the institution was not only practical but morally proper.[25]

Merrimon's description of slavery is drastically different from Cain's depiction. Cain had described slavery as a relevant concern; Merrimon discussed slavery as part of a historical era removed from the present context. Merrimon used past tense verbs. He said, "the negro race in this country *were held* in a state of bondage" and "they *were* slaves." He discussed the era with neither nostalgia nor condemnation. Rather, like a neutral observer, he seemed to stand in the present, observing events in the distant past. Merrimon maintained this distance even when he described the Civil War. According to him, when the North "made war" upon the South, the Southern states had reacted to defend slavery, and, as a result, "these two aggressive spirits came together, first in moral, then in political conflict, and finally conflict of arms. That conflict resulted in the absolute destruction of that institution by force . . . that civil war resulted in its abolition, in its destruction, in its absolute overthrow."[26]

Several aspects of this rhetoric are significant. Merrimon's depiction of slavery assumed a tone of detachment and objectivity. He presented himself as uninfluenced by the old slavery system, which is remarkable when one considers that the myth of the Old South, a rhetoric that valorized the antebellum, was gaining strength among Southern communities.[27] A detached observer, Merrimon stood in the present and observed events in the distant past. His version of history almost avoided the actual conflict completely, as it emphasized how the war had destroyed slavery. Other moderate Democrats also highlighted the effects of the war rather than its actual events. Alexander Stephens declared, "This thorn in the flesh, so long the cause of irritation between the States, is now out for all time to come."[28] William Robbins said on 24 January 1874, "The old system of negro slavery, as once existing in all the States, is forever dead and buried, and I have no tears to shed over its grave."[29]

The bill's opponents articulated a temporal perspective marked by four distinct stages. In the beginning was the mythic period of the founders. Democrats constructed this time as an idyllic moment in U.S. history. Subsequently, the benign institution of slavery turned malignant, resulting in geographic and ideological division. Critics of desegregation failed to explain why or how this transpired but argued instead that strife and conflict marked this period. Eventually the conflict escalated into the Civil War, which, in Stephens's terms, removed the thorn of slavery from the national body. For Democrats, the war became an epochal rupture that divided time and textual contexts. Stephens's corporeal metaphor of slavery as a thorn in America's flesh illustrates this divide. Prior to the war, Southern politicians characterized the nation as a set of sovereign states joined by *contractual* relationships. In 1874 Stephens chose to portray the United States as a single organic whole, a significant choice that constructed a context in which the states were interdependent and unified. This metaphor helped to establish a temporal disjunction: the United States as an injured body and the United States as a healing organism. Such images existed in a "then" and "now" frame. Then, before the war, the nation suffered from the "thorn" of slavery, but now, Stephens assures his audience, "the passions and prejudices which attended the conflict are fast subsiding and passing away, the period has now come for the descendants of a common ancestry, in all the States and sections of the country, to return to the original principles of their fathers."[30]

The "now" or present circumstances of bill opponents suggested that a new sensibility guided their behavior. Not only had they abandoned their principled defense of slavery, but they had embraced a new perspective illustrated by a desire to reconcile regional differences. Representative Harris declared, "The passions of the war have subsided, or are rapidly subsiding. Let us control our actions uninfluenced by those passions. The country is now being pacified and reunited in sentiment as well as in fact. The people of my own State are exhibiting this sentiment in their public actions. May we not expect it to be reciprocated here, and to have a manly response to manly overtures for peace?"[31] Hiram P. Bell said that it would be most unfortunate to disturb the "good feeling and harmony now existing between the races" throughout the South.[32]

In this context, stability and "good feelings" became the norm. If anyone was to blame for continued tension between the North and the South, then, it was the North. A number of the more extreme Democrats chided the Republicans for their attitude. Senator Eli Saulsbury, for instance, said that he was deeply disturbed by the Republicans' continued use of the terms "rebels" and "traitors." According to Saulsbury, this rhetoric proved that the party was unable to put the war's animosity behind it.[33] Lewis Bogy proclaimed that thanks to the Republicans, the Southern states were full of "bold, unscrupulous, selfish demagogues who have gone there for no better purpose than to make tools of the colored voters and induce them to lend their assistance to the accomplishment of the most nefarious and destructive schemes—schemes that look only to the enrichment of the demagogues and the impoverishment of the people, both white and black."[34] According to the Democrats, the South had moved forward while the North remained trapped in the animosity of the Civil War.

The North's agitation was especially unfortunate, argued bill opponents, because present circumstances actually benefited African Americans. Moderate Democrats argued that they had moved to protect and provide for the former slaves. "The white people of Georgia," declared Bell, "are now earnestly engaged in an effort to solve the great problem of free labor which emancipation thrust upon them."[35] The South had addressed the issues of safety and political rights as well, Democrats claimed. In fact, civil rights' critics argued that since the war African Americans enjoyed privileges equal to, if not surpassing, those of whites. Durham said, "[blacks] are protected in their lives, liberties, and in the pursuit of happiness at the expense of the white people. They are protected in all their political rights without the payment of one farthing to secure that protection."[36] The most important of these privileges, claimed Democrats, was an education. According to Allen Thurman, 999 out of every 1,000 dollars in Ohio's taxes came from whites, "yet [Ohio] gives to the negro child per capita precisely the same amount for his education that she does to the child of the white parent."[37] Senator John Johnson affirmed that Virginia landowners were taxing themselves to further black education, and that: "[Virginia's] system provides that the schools of the white and colored people shall be kept separate; but except in that particular they are the same. They employ good teachers in both. They give the same proportion of public money to each. They build the same sort of school-houses for both, and the colored people are provided to the same degree precisely by this common-school system that the white people are."[38]

At this point the implications of the Democrats' depiction are quite clear. First, they distinguished between the past and the present. This strategy undermined the Republicans' sense of continuity, which they established through their claim that desegregation was a proper response to the inequities of slavery. Moreover, the Democrats' dissociation allowed them to emphasize those increased privileges that blacks enjoyed in 1874 and 1875. With slavery and its entailment of oppression "killed" by the war's outcome, they discussed the present context almost as if African Americans enjoyed a utopia. This second strategy was crucial because it refuted the bill's expediency. If African Americans enjoyed so many privileges and such protection, desegregation was unnecessary. To reinforce this basic premise, the Democrats supplied a third component to their textual context—the generosity of Southern whites.

According to them, the Southern people possessed only goodwill toward blacks; Southerners were interested in helping African Americans succeed. Senator John Johnson of Virginia said, "Some Senators seem to think that the southern whites are inflamed with hatred of the colored people, that they desire nothing so much as to destroy them, deprive them of every right, impose upon them every burden. Mr. President, there can be no greater mistake than that. . . . The southern people have every desire to treat them with the last degree of justice, and to give them every opportunity of attaining the highest civilization possible for them to reach."[39] Thurman added that he had no doubt that every man in his state wanted to see the colored race educated.[40]

The persuasive force of this argument strengthened the Democrats' major thesis that the bill was unnecessary and therefore inexpedient, but simultaneously it shifted the focus of attention from institutional and governmental policy to *individual action*. Benjamin Butler and other Republican idealists described the situation as if racial discrimination was a social and institutional phenomenon. When the Democrats described race relations, they focused not on corporate or state policy but on personal prejudice, on the individual feelings of Southerners. They emphasized the attitudes of specific people. This shift in focus was apparent especially when various Democrats compared their own behavior with that of white Northerners.

Alexander Stephens proclaimed, "there is not a colored man in Georgia who knows me (and my acquaintance with that class is not very limited) who would not come to me for a personal favor, or personal counsel, or in case of real grievance for a redress of personal wrongs, with more confidence in my having justice secured him than to any 'carpet-bagger' in the State."[41] Thomas Whitehead argued that he was a good example of the men in his state, and yet he was willing to have Congress judge whether his character was not equal to Benjamin Butler's.[42] Using Butler's own words against him, Whitehead said that he was no more an "assassin" or "horse-thief" than the Massachusetts congressman. The North could be assured that he would protect and defend the freedmen just as surely as Butler might.

Facilitated by a textual context that separated historical considerations from the present, opponents shifted attention from the formal aspects of prejudice to the standard of personal behavior. The testimony of Stephens and Whitehead was significant, because it construed race relations as the proper management of one's interpersonal behavior. Appropriate behavior in this case did not involve the consideration of ideology, cultural practice, or legal statues. According to this pattern of judgment, decorous action was a matter of virtue. Most Southerners possessed the necessary character to treat African Americans honorably, they argued. Stephens and Whitehead used themselves as exemplars; they became synecdoches for Southern whites. Because these men would treat blacks well, the North could expect the same behavior from the South generally.

The significance of this rhetoric for Congress's political judgment was intense. This discourse depoliticized the practice of racial discrimination by transplanting race relations into the private realm of personal ethics. By emphasizing feelings and interpersonal relationships, moderate Democrats offered an alternative to the formal requirements of a new civil rights law. The consequence of this position is clear: discrimination in public accommodations was not a problem that demanded a legal solution, especially if that solution came from the federal government. Using this context, the bill's critics offered a negative evaluation of the measure. In the internal logic of their discourse, the Republican's desegregation policy was an inappropriately formal reaction to circumstances that were personal. They offered many reasons why the policy was inexpedient, but the primary thrust of their textual context implied that the South's racial problems resulted from weaknesses of character, not from structural inequities. For opponents, a prudent decision in this debate required a calculation based not on some abstract ideal, but on the concrete feelings of the Southern people and the local history of each community.

Evaluating the Bill's Consequences

Both Democrats and Republicans agreed that they had to judge the Civil Rights Bill according to its potential consequences. This consensus, however, was the only point of agreement between the two sides, because they differed greatly in how they thought the bill would affect situational realities. Most Republicans argued that the bill would secure justice, protect the nation's future, and usher in a new age of progress and civilization. Democrats, along with a few Republicans, claimed that the bill would destroy the nation's stability and its schools, and that it would create conflict between the races.

A Bill to Secure Justice and Protect National Prosperity

Whatever their private thoughts, Republicans argued publicly that desegregation would solve the multiple imperfections that they believed to exist. An excellent example of their faith was expressed by Purman, who said, "pass this bill, and the tyranny of prejudice, violence, and error against this class of citizens will disappear like the miasma of night before the morning sun."[43] The optimism Purman affirmed seemed unqualified and sure, but although he said that the bill would stop segregation and perhaps eliminate prejudice, the Republicans' perspective was more complex than this affirmation implied. A close examination of their arguments reveals that desegregation's proponents argued that the bill would cause an immediate change in the public arena and a slower but certain change in the private beliefs of individual citizens. On that basis Senator Henry Pease (Mississippi) declared, "Believing that we have the constitutional right to enact this bill, there is but one other phase of the question to be considered, and that is the question of expediency. I believe that it is expedient for the Congress of the United States now to fix a remedy for existing evils and settle forever the question of the rights, privileges, and immunities of American citizens."[44]

The most obvious and direct consequence of the Civil Rights Bill would be the elimination of all public segregation, affirmed the proponents of civil rights. This, after all, was the bill's substance, and those who supported it never questioned, publicly on the floor, whether its provisions were sufficient to safeguard desegregation.[45] Instead the Republicans continuously repeated their claim that desegregation was necessary and that the bill would accomplish its stated goals. Again, according to Pease, "when this question is settled I want every college and every institution of learning in this broad land to be open to every citizen, that there shall be no discrimination. I want Harvard to throw open her doors; I want Dartmouth to do the same thing."[46] But the texts in this debate suggest that desegregation of public accommodations was only the first step. Many Republicans expressed some hope that this bill would set in motion a series of corollary effects.

James Monroe of Ohio offered one interesting explanation of the benefits of desegregation. He suggested that democracies remained strong only when their citizens were loyal and patriotic. The Civil Rights Bill, he argued, was a necessary measure not only because it eliminated discrimination—a worthy goal in and of itself—but also because it would create a patriotic allegiance in the hearts of former slaves for their adopted country. As citizens, blacks had to believe that their interests were protected. Without the bill, they would feel vulnerable, and, said Monroe, they might become disillusioned. No country could prosper with five million citizens so disenchanted, he concluded.[47]

A second benefit of desegregation was that it would affirm equality as the country's most sacred principle and allow the nation to move beyond the antebellum era. Once the bill became law, James Rapier said, his legal "manhood" would be complete and his citizenship would be perfect.[48] He proposed further that the measure's passage would inscribe Jefferson's ideals into the law once and for all. Robert Elliott of South Carolina agreed. Calling the bill the "cap-stone" to the temple of liberty, he argued that the bill would guarantee equal access and reaffirm equality's truth for every citizen.[49] Advancing a closely related point, Republicans argued that the elevation of equality within the polity would allow the country to move forward. Several Republicans implied that America stood at an epochal crossroads. "It seems to me that we have again reached a critical point in the politics of this country. Step by step a great party has insisted that the

Declaration of Independence instead of being a glittering generality shall be made a practical verity. This is another step in that march," argued Ellis H. Roberts (New York).[50] Charles Williams of Wisconsin declared, "settle this question right now, and the color line falls out of politics. Settle it wrong, and it will come to plague you again. It may cause temporary strife, but better this than that growing prejudice and growing hate should rend and distract this country ever again."[51]

When the advocates of desegregation spoke of moving on, they meant more than just an immediate change of circumstances. For some, like the black representative Josiah Walls, desegregation was linked to historical progress. He stated, "Let equity, founded in justice, honesty, and right—the souls and spirit of the law—be prescribed by the superior power of the Government, and the inferior compelled to obey. It is the duty of the men of to-day, in whose hands is intrusted the destiny of the Republic, to remove from the path of its upward progress every obstacle which may impede its advance in the future."[52] A higher form of civilization was the stated purpose of some of the Republican idealists.

Clearly these comments reflect the Enlightenment's faith in progressive history. What is significant about the idea of progress as it was articulated here is that humans were in partnership with history. History as an agent or force was not omnipotent. Congress could help or hinder the nation's development, depending upon its action on the bill. If evaluated correctly, in the light of human equality and civilization, then Congress would pass the bill as an expedient policy for civilized development. But if it decided to ignore the bill's consequences, at least as the Republicans perceived them, then the nation would not evolve to the next stage. Inaction would mean that the country had not risen to the challenge of that era, and, therefore, it would stall in the process of achieving its own potential.

As the Republicans discussed the consequences of desegregation, they had to deal with a particularly powerful counterargument—that the bill would lead to "social equality" and private intimacy between the races. It is important to note that Republicans of either race denied this allegation. John Lynch, the first African American to deliver a keynote speech at a party's national convention, tried to use the force of deductive logic to allay his colleagues' fears.[53] He said:

> That the passage of this bill can in any manner affect the social status of any one seems to me to be absurd and ridiculous. I have never believed for a moment that social equality could be brought about even between persons of the same race. I have always believed that social distinctions existed

> among white people the same as among colored people. But those who contend that the passage of this bill will have a tendency to bring about social equality between the races virtually and substantially admit that there are no social distinctions among white people whatever, but that all white persons, regardless of their moral character, are the social equals of each other; for if by conferring upon colored people the same rights and privileges that are now exercised and enjoyed by whites indiscriminately will result in bringing about social equality between the races, then the same process of reasoning must necessarily bring us to the conclusion that there are no social distinctions among whites, because all white persons, regardless of their social standing, are permitted to enjoy these rights. See then how unreasonable, unjust, and false is the assertion that social equality is involved in this legislation.[54]

According to bill proponents, desegregation would not institute social equality, because the policy affected only public space. Social equality, they argued, involved the right of one person to choose her or his friends and intimate relations.[55] All social (that is, personal) relationships were regulated by the mutual and social recognition of individuals, and such recognition could not be regulated by governmental authority. Therefore, they maintained that the bill was concerned only with public issues. Again, Lynch argued, "No, Mr. Speaker, it is not social rights that we desire. We have enough of that already. What we ask is protection in the enjoyment of public rights. Rights which are or should be accorded to every citizen alike."[56]

In effect, the Republicans tried to separate the private and the public, just as the Democrats' discourse conflated these concepts. Black Republicans seemed to stress the private/public distinction most vigorously. Richard Cain, on 3 February 1875, said that he had no intention of intruding where he was not wanted. Moreover, he affirmed that personal autonomy in private relationships was important to African as well as European Americans. He said:

> "I regret exceedingly gentlemen talk of social equality [*sic*]. That seems to be their great bugaboo. O, if you put colored men upon an equality before the law they will want social equality! I do not believe a word of it. Do you suppose I would introduce into my family a class of white men I see in this country? Do you suppose for one moment I would do it? No, sir; for there are men even who have positions upon this floor, and for whom I have respect, but of whom I should be careful how I introduced them into my family."[57]

Rainey added to Cain's comments, "Now, gentlemen, let me say the negro is not asking [for] social equality. . . . I prefer to choose my own associates, and all my colleagues here and the whole race I belong to prefer to make that choice."[58]

Celeste Condit and John Lucaites suggest that the distinction between the public and private spheres was an important aspect of African American rhetoric during the Reconstruction era: "[blacks] wished to draw a line between Social Equality, which the government could not and should not regulate, and 'public rights,' which the government should insure for all."[59] This distinction was more than a matter of political philosophy for black leaders. For years Southern white men had taken advantage of African American women, and the black community wished to end this sexual exploitation. Cain explained that he dared not introduce his family to some of his colleagues because he "should be afraid indeed [that] their old habits acquired beyond Mason and Dixon's line might return."[60] Nevertheless, the separation between "social" and "public" rights was not an easy distinction to make. One black politician, Pinckney Pinchback, offered a particularly interesting dissociation that facilitated this division.

Pinckney Pinchback was the son of a wealthy plantation owner, Major William Pinchback, and a female slave.[61] During the Reconstruction era, Pinckney Pinchback was involved heavily in state politics; not only did he serve as a state senator, but he also was elected twice to the Senate and once to the House. Due to election irregularities and accusations of bribery, he was never seated; therefore, he did not participate in the congressional debate.[62] Fortunately, the Moorland-Spingarn archives at Howard University contain a speech he gave on the subject in June of 1874.[63] Pinchback argued that public discrimination against freedmen and women was both a matter of state law and social custom. He said further that men who argued that segregation was only a limited intrusion into the lives of African Americans forgot that the practice violated the Declaration of Independence. Jefferson's creed existed "not only as a philosophical but substantial truth, out of which the political and civil rights of the people have sprung." Desegregation was nothing more than the practical outcome of that truth. It did not create social equality, but, stated Pinchback, it provided African Americans with the "right to stand on the same *civil social* plane with our fellows."[64] Dissociating social equality from "civil social" equality, he concluded: "Civil liberty is nothing but the liberty of the individual regulated in its relations to society by just and equal laws."[65]

The dissociation of social equality into civil liberties and social liberties was important for the advocates of desegregation, because it allowed them to deny the most pernicious consequence that the Democrats attributed to the bill—miscegenation. Civil liberties were part of the public sphere, whereas social liberties involved the intimate elements of a person's life. According to this logic, societies sustained two levels of interaction, one public and the other private. But, at the same time, the public/private distinction that the bill's advocates created undermined another aspect of their argument. The Republicans affirmed that the bill would eliminate racial prejudice, but they claimed, as well, that prejudice was an *attitude* that stemmed from the flawed belief system sponsored by slavery. If the bill only affected the public or civil sphere as they proposed, how could they hope to alter those prejudices that existed as attitudes and beliefs within the minds of whites? If the bill had no effect on the private sphere, that place where beliefs existed, then perhaps their opponents were correct—the bill could not achieve the very aims that it intended.

A fascinating answer to this dilemma emerged within the discourse of the bill's most extreme proponents. According to one white Republican, desegregation would transform the public school system and help to eliminate prejudice. Not only would the teachers instruct students about basic human equality, the students would experience that equality firsthand. The radical Senator George Boutwell of Massachusetts explained, "The public school is an epitome of life, and in it children are taught so that they understand those relations and conditions of life which, if not acquired in childhood and youth, are not likely afterward to be gained."[66] This unique environment provided a unique opportunity: "I do expect by having children of different races and different colors educated in the same school, that this prejudice against race and color will be removed and the idea of universal human equality as the basis, in my judgment, of republican institutions will be substituted in place of this unnatural and unjust prejudice."[67] Boutwell's text resolved the paradox between the demise of personal prejudice and the Republicans' private/public distinction, because it suggested that changes within the public sphere could eventually transform that which was private. The bill, he argued, would integrate the school systems, a consequence in the public sphere; subsequently, this integration would eliminate the private belief in inequality. Viewed in this manner, the bill itself never intruded directly into the private realm; rather, it created a situation where private belief was transformed, owing to changes in public policy.

This idea—private transformation as a consequence of public interaction—reveals why the school desegregation clause was so important and so controversial. The innocence of school children provided, for the more extreme desegregationists, a context where the new morality of equality could take seed. It was a place where, as James L. Alcorn put it, contact would remove racial prejudice.[68] At the same time, the measure's school clause was the greatest threat to white hegemony. It is no accident that the Democrats attacked the public school clause most directly. It also is understandable that this provision made the moderate Republicans the most nervous, since they were not immune to the prejudices of the mid-nineteenth century. Perhaps the opponenets of desegregation feared that white children might not find black children as offensive as members of Congress found black adults.

A Bill to Create Conflict and Increase Prejudice

Whereas the Republicans were willing to accept the consequences of desegregation, Democrats were not. According to Whitehead, "The men who vote and speak here should carefully look into its expediency. If it were constitutional, it is not expedient. Saint Paul said that all things were lawful, but that all things were not expedient. As legislators it is as much your duty to look to the expediency of a law in reference to your constituents as to look to its constitutionality."[69] Part of the reason why the bill was inexpedient was that it could not accomplish its stated purpose. It would not help those of color. According to Charles Eldredge's speech of 4 February 1875:

> To make the colored citizen feel that he is the pet, the especial favorite of the law, will only feed and pander to that conceit and self-consequence which is now his weakest and perhaps most offensive characteristic. If he be made to feel that extraordinary provisions of law are enacted in his favor because of his weakness or feebleness as a man, the very fact weakens and enfeebles him. The consciousness that there is necessity for such legislation and protection for him must necessarily humiliate and degrade him. Such laws, too, are a constant reminder to him that he is inferior to the white race. They not only remind him of his inferiority and the superiority of the white race in its not requiring these special enactments, but they naturally and necessarily awaken in him a feeling of bitterness and unfriendliness toward the white race.[70]

Driving to the heart of the Republicans' position, Eldredge argued that the measure would have the opposite effect intended. It would create dependency, damage the self-esteem of black citizens, and increase their jealousy of European Americans. Of particular interest is that Eldredge also affirmed that these negative consequences would transpire without diminishing the prejudices of the Southern people. Articulating a position that would be heard over and over again in the twentieth century, he said that no amount of legislation could ever rub away personal prejudice. Whether prejudice was the result of slavery or the will of God, law could not remove it from the hearts of whites everywhere.[71]

The critics of desegregation were not content to argue that the bill would fail to accomplish its purpose. Repeatedly and consistently, they used strong images and destructive terminology to describe the bill's interaction with the circumstances they had represented. Senator Saulsbury said, "you have no right to afflict the white people of this country in order to make party capital and secure the negro vote."[72] Thomas Whitehead suggested that the bill was part of a larger conspiracy: "We are not going to have any bayonets down our way; you may as well understand that. I know that this bill is intended to stir up bad blood, to mix the two races in the schools, so that the children may first get to fighting and then the parents, and then instantly there will be a call for bayonets. . . . You have started this thing; and whether gentlemen here personally believe it or not, it is in *somebody's* mind to keep up this disturbance, to keep up this difficulty, until it ends in somebody's political benefit."[73] Even the more moderate Merrimon characterized the bill as an act of "aggression."[74]

The terms "aggression," "afflict," and "disturb" carried a host of negative ramifications and one central claim that worked against desegregation's expediency. By mixing the two races in theaters, in hotels, on transportation facilities, and in schools, Democrats proposed that desegregation would cause rather than eliminate racial conflict. Thurman, for instance, argued that the bill would injure African Americans by increasing hostile feelings, leading "to acts of oppression or violence."[75] Democratic Senator T. F. Bayard said in 1875, "I can see only new and increased heart-burnings and unkindnesses between those races whom every good man must wish to see at peace with each other in their relative spheres of life and usefulness . . . I fear this bill will create causes of collision, of unkindness, and misunderstanding, in which pecuniary loss must occur to the white, with no benefit whatever to the black."[76] The conservative Republican Simeon Chittenden declared that the bill would "breed mischief, prejudice, and cruelty" for African Americans across the South.[77]

Opponents contrasted the bill's negative consequences with the peace and tranquillity they attributed to the existing national scene. To use a metaphor, the Democrats' arguments portrayed the South as a tranquil pond, and desegregation became a large rock hurled at its center. This was made perfectly clear by Hiram P. Bell, who argued that "the great mass of the colored people in the South are quiet and contented; they neither know nor care anything about the provisions of this bill . . . it is unfortunate and unwise in the extreme, by this agitation, to disturb the good feeling and harmony now existing between the races."[78]

A few fire-eaters went so far as to suggest that the American people, especially the Southern population, would not allow a travesty so great as desegregation. Eli Saulsbury declared that the bill would create serious anger among Southerners.[79] In thinly veiled threats John Stockton of New Jersey claimed that the people would not allow Congress to enact this legislation, and, referring to the Civil War, Harris warned that history often repeated itself.[80] The threats of discord offered by these opponents were powerful not because the North feared another armed conflict, but primarily because Americans were tired of the entire issue. It was logistically impossible for the South to wage another war of the same magnitude, but it could and did resist. Despite almost ten years of Republican legislation, many of the old problems remained; moreover, Reconstruction was losing ground, and some Northerners began to blame African Americans for its failures.[81] Taking advantage of the North's frustration, the Democrats described in detail how the measure would create additional strife rather than peace.[82]

In the school desegregation provision, bill opponents found their most powerful argument about the bill's negative consequences.[83] The Democrats claimed that the former slaves already received a quality education at the expense of white taxpayers, but this generosity had its limits. According to Thurman, the South's prejudice would overcome its generosity if the Republicans insisted on the bill: "The result will be that schools will not be established; the taxes will not be laid; the laws for the common-school system will be repealed or rendered nugatory; and the consequence will be that both the negro children and the poor white children too will go without education. There never was so fatal a blow aimed at the common-school system, never so fatal a blow aimed at the education and elevation of the children of this colored race, conceived by the mind of man as this civil-rights bill."[84] Representative Herndon declared that the bill would "crush" the Southern public school system.[85] John Bright said on the same day, "should Congress attempt to drive the Southern States, having separate common schools, to the wall, and attempt to force their tastes, and, if you please, their natural and conventional repugnance to color and race, into social contact, they will refuse to tax themselves for the support of such an educational system."[86] These claims were powerful, and they cut across both parties.[87]

Among the Republicans there was little unity about how to approach the school clause, and the tension that had always existed between idealists and moderates was obvious when it came to this issue. Several Republicans claimed that the Democrats were bluffing. John Lynch, one representative among the dwindling few who supported the clause in 1875, said that in those Southern states controlled by the party of the Union, similar provisions had passed and whites had not abandoned the schools.[88] Senator Henry Pease agreed and declared that all men were governed by self-interest; therefore, the South could not abandon the school system, as such action would harm the region.[89] Others were less certain. A few, including the former slave owner James Alcorn and eventually Benjamin Butler, backed away from the clause, even while they endorsed its principles. Both speakers explained that the bill was never meant to establish mixed schools. They assured their colleagues that African Americans could, and probably would, choose to attend separate institutions. Alcorn argued, "there is no mixing in this bill. . . . You have a right to send your child to any school you choose. That is the citizen's right; but it is simply a right that the colored people exercise by sending their children to the colored school; it is a right that the white people enjoy by sending their children to the white school."[90]

Through such strained logic, the Republicans hoped to accomplish two things. First, idealists tried to shore up the support of those conservatives who were uncomfortable with the school provision. Second, every advocate hoped to remain a champion of civil rights without alienating his white constituency. According to Gillette, "Republican Senators, it seemed, were attempting to please all groups by endorsing educational equality in principle and through statutes to satisfy the blacks, while, to placate the whites, they were pointing out the narrow reach of the law and suggesting possibilities of circumventing it."[91] These tactics were not entirely successful, and several Republicans, such as James Sener, expressed their own opposition to civil rights with reference to the school clause. These men argued that they could not in good conscience vote for the bill out of concern for the South's children.[92] Open defections such as this were few;

most moderates and conservatives preferred to keep their dissatisfaction out of the *Congressional Record;* nevertheless, the issue remained controversial, and eventually the Republicans removed the school clause entirely. Although one could argue that they removed the clause for political reasons and not from a genuine fear of Southern reprisals, the Democrats' threats about the destruction of common schools put them on the defensive. These threats forced the Republicans to justify the measure, and when the Democrats tried to destroy the bill through a filibuster in 1875, Republican leaders eliminated the controversial provision.

When the Democrats argued that Southern prejudice would not allow black and white children to attend the same school, they created a tension within their own rhetoric. They had argued extensively that Southern whites were interested in the welfare of black Americans, but now they acknowledged that racial prejudice existed throughout the South, and they affirmed that Congress ought to respect these prejudices. If prejudice existed, how could the nation expect Southern whites to act as benevolently as the Democrats claimed they would? The answer to this apparent conflict revolved around the definition of prejudice offered by Southern congressmen.

Merrimon acknowledged that although he had only kind feelings toward African Americans, prejudice existed within the heart of every Southerner. He said, "there is this natural antipathy between the races. Whatever you may say about the corruption of man, there is still something that lingers and lives within his bosom and whispers to him of that law of his nature which he shall not contravene, and wherever you find him, however corrupted and degenerate, you find that whispering of conscience within him. You cannot strike it down." He said further, "I believe [prejudice] is inherent in the nature of the white man; I believe it is inherent in the nature of the black man everywhere. Naturally, those of one race like their own best, until they are corrupted and brought in close contact with another, when the evil consequences I adverted to a while ago are brought on."[93]

Merrimon's explanation of prejudicial feelings expressed a common opinion among the Democrats. They distinguished between unkind feelings and prejudicial feelings.[94] From their perspective, prejudice was an internal attitude that facilitated the natural separations that God had intended. Prejudice was not a negative attitude of hatred or anger; instead, it was an internal guide to help one locate one's place in society. Prejudice reinforced separation, not oppression. According to Democratic discourse, such prejudice did not necessarily position white against black; it simply kept the two races distinct.

One can see in this definition an essential linguistic and ideological difference between the Republicans and the Democrats. The Republicans discussed prejudice as a negative emotion or attitude just as we ordinarily do today. For them it was a poisonous legacy of slavery—a pernicious attitude that contradicted the politics of equality. The Democrats, however, said that prejudice was a positive attribute because it helped to maintain the world's natural order. The difference that separated Republicans and Democrats could not have been plainer, and this difference separated opponents and advocates more clearly than any geographical boundary.

The Substantial Patterns of Place versus the Formal Patterns of Equality

From a distance, the claims of Republican and Democrats seem to display a high degree of deliberation. Both sides spoke about the same issues, both sides discussed the need for the bill and its consequences, and almost everyone argued over particulars such as black education. But despite these common points of dispute, the debate's participants spoke past one another. The degree of interaction that seemed to transpire is actually deceptive, because participants used very different standards of judgment, grounded in fundamentally different value types. James Jasinski's analysis of the Constitution's ratification helps to illustrate this point.

Building on Ronald Beiner's distinction between formal and substantial schemes,[95] Jasinski argues that the anti-Federalists expressed a "substantial" pattern of judgment that placed relational virtues over procedural standards.[96] He notes that substantial standards highlight personal feelings and shared experiences. They are based on empathy and common sense, and they prioritize particular values (for example, friendship, loyalty, individual liberty, and expediency) above abstract or institutionalized modes of policy evaluation. In the 1870s contest over civil rights, the notion of place directed desegregation's opponents to substantial patterns of judgment. In contrast, the discourse of Republicans, which was grounded in the politics of equality, reflected a "formal" pattern of judgment. Formal schemes are not tied to particular moments. They transcend individual cases, and they promote social stability through methods that apply a culture's abstract ideals (for example, representation, freedom, justice, and equality) consistently. Either side in the civil rights debate advanced a different principle to guide political judgment, and these principles constrained the talk about the bill's expediency.

The debate exhibits several examples of each pattern of judgment, but two moments relate directly to my point. Barbour Lewis of Tennessee declared, "Mr. Speaker, I am in favor of this bill in a modified form, because it is just and right, and is therefore of the highest expediency. The Government owes its protection to every citizen. . . . We must carry out our principles and make the immortal Declaration of Independence a living reality. Equality before the law—legal, not social equality—is the cardinal, inspiring principle of republican institutions."[97] The Republican Aaron Sargent of California disagreed. He argued that his colleagues were *too* concerned about principles and not concerned enough about the actual situation. He said, "We ought to legislate here as statesmen, having in view not merely abstract ideas or theoretical principles or sublimated ideas, but to observe the condition of the times and know whether by any law which we may pass here we inflict an injury upon the country. . . . We may insist that we are led in a certain direction by our principles and should disregard all prudence in order to follow them; but that is not wise statesmanship."[98] Such direct declarations were the exception rather than the rule; however, when one examines the debate as a whole, and when one considers the arguments described thus far, consistent and divergent patterns of judgment are obvious. The criteria expressed by Sargent and Lewis did reflect the rhetorical tendencies of their respective positions. A brief summary of the rhetoric discussed supports this hypothesis.

When the Republicans discussed segregation, they did not claim only that such behavior kept African Americans from nourishing their bodies, conducting their business, or enjoying a happy life. Although these concerns—which represent concrete considerations—were present in their text, their discourse expressed a more overt concern for black *rights* as defined by the Declaration of Independence and Reconstruction's equality politics. They explicitly argued that segregation denied the basic humanity of African Americans, and these arguments were tied to abstract ideals. In addition, one might observe that their representation of the situation invoked a grand moral drama. When Cain discussed slavery, when Butler argued about black soldiers, and when Purman described the evils of the black codes, their examples created a moral narrative that was much larger than the illustrations they employed. In their story, one class of individuals had held another class in the immoral bonds of slavery, but despite this condition, the oppressed class had contributed immensely to the nation's welfare. Furthermore, a great war had destroyed the economic arm of this immoral institution, but the feelings, attitudes, and effects of the previous age remained; consequently, one final redemptive act was necessary to right past wrongs.[99] The Republicans proposed that desegregation was this final act, and in the process of telling this moral story, they demanded justice based upon an abstract set of values.

Those who opposed desegregation used evaluative criteria firmly grounded in concrete values, the most prominent of which were social peace and individual feeling. Avoiding any grand moral drama, Democrats such as Merrimon described the nation's history as an amoral unfolding of both positive and negative events. They argued that the Southern people currently held only positive feelings toward the former slaves, and, as proof, they noted that whites had taxed themselves to benefit the colored race. Throughout the South, peace and social stability would prevail only if the federal government refrained from intruding into Southern life. All of these claims emphasized the particulars of the Southern situation, and Democrats stressed the unique circumstances that existed in that region. The present realities, they argued, did not justify federal assistance for African Americans. Merrimon explained, "The plans suggested are not practical; they are not just; they indicate a total ignorance of what is necessary to be done for the best interests of the negro race and the people of all races and the whole country. Rights are practical things; governments are practical things, and they must be upheld and sustained in a practical way and by practical means. Fancy theories will not do, and whoever thinks so is not wise."[100]

The fundamental differences in patterns of judgment extended beyond each side's situational interpretation and to their respective discussions of the bill's consequences. Specifically, opponents employed the concrete value of social stability by emphasizing the bill's immediate effects. They claimed that desegregation would produce violence and anger. Moreover, their concern for the unique prejudice of Southerners caused them to label the measure unwise, and their standard was so narrowly pragmatic that they held that any disturbance of the Southern schools or social system was sufficient to condemn the bill. The consequences that the Republicans foresaw followed from the abstract values that they had implied in their own interpretation of the situation. They proposed that the bill would be the "cap-stone" of liberty. According to the bill's advocates, the immediate racial tensions caused by desegregation was unimportant, because the bill renewed the nation's commitment to the Declaration of Independence.

The long-term effects of affirming the equal rights of all—i.e., an enhanced form of civilization—far outweighed the short-term discomfort of some white citizens.

Perhaps the most interesting and complex expression of the difference between concrete and abstract modes of evaluation was evident in the temporal perspectives of each side.[101] The Republican idealists combined the past and the present to create an enlarged situation. This formulation worked against a narrow focus that attended only to the circumstances of 1874 or 1875. When discussing the bill's consequences, proponents often emphasized not an immediate future but an ultimate future. They spoke in terms of a new age realized through progressive enlightenment; they perceived the Civil Rights Bill as one component among many in this development. In contrast, the opponents' discourse repeatedly emphasized a narrow temporal context. Their concerns for the bill's consequences were immediate. They separated the slavery past from the civil rights present. Whether desegregation could work in the long term was never considered; rather, the bill's immediate effects dominated their discourse.

Conclusion

In Reconstruction politics, it is easy to see the divide between Democrats and Republicans. The partisan nature of that era is legendary, and this debate illustrates how inflammatory the conflict could become. What is less obvious, however, is that there was an important difference between those who advanced the policies of Reconstruction and those who opposed them. At one level, the expediency arguments of the debate involved a political exchange over whether desegregation would harm or help the public. Those who spoke against the measure used concrete and substantial values to support their judgment that desegregation was inexpedient. Through the temporal dissociation of the slavery past and the utopian present, they suggested that Congress should allow the burgeoning peace to continue. As Bell argued, "It is unfortunate and unwise in the extreme, by this agitation [desegregation], to disturb the good feeling and harmony now existing between the races."[102] In contrast, the discourse of civil rights advocates used a pattern of judgment that highlighted abstract values and formal systems of justice. Sumner argued that the bill was necessary and that no "equivalent," such as separate but equal facilities, would suffice. He justified the bill further by claiming that it would direct the public mind toward virtue.[103] An enlightened civilization was one of the goals of House

Republicans in 1874 and 1875. Simultaneously, they argued that desegregation would solve existing racial injustice.[104] Any short-term pain that desegregation might inflict was secondary to the larger progress that they believed was possible.

At a second level, the debate over the bill's expediency was a struggle over different notions of what constituted prudent political judgment and social interaction. The discourse expressed by desegregation's critics established an ethic grounded in place. When Alexander Stephens explained his position in regard to the Declaration of Independence, he reformulated its equality ideal within a very personal ethic. He said, "everyone should act toward another as that other ought, in turn, to act upon a reversal of their positions in the different and various relations of life, either socially, politically, or otherwise."[105] This was the essence of place for the Southern conservatives. Good race relations were a matter of individual character and personal relationships.[106] Decorous public action, they maintained, was a function of each person's willingness to balance the unique needs of each context against the place that they held in society. Individual Southerners, white and black, knew one another well enough to make the necessary adjustments that interracial relationships required. There was no immediate place for the federal government in this scheme. According to the discursive patterns of judgment established by those who opposed desegregation, only a social ethic grounded in personal feeling, attitude, and sensibility would lead to good race relations.

In contrast, the advocates of desegregation enunciated an ethic that called not for passive healing but for aggressive treatment, regardless of the pain that might initially result. With abstract principles and formal evaluative criteria as their guide, the Republicans forwarded norms that made individuality less important than a community dedicated to ideals that transcended particular circumstances.[107] The individual sensibilities of a citizen should be subject to the law, which acted without feeling, attitude, or prejudice. This perspective advanced an ethic based on rules, not individuals or relationships, and this model had implications for congressional action and the general public. Under the Republicans mode of prudence, individuals such as Representative Harris had no right to silence a fellow congressmen simply because his color differed from Harris's own. When it came to the public sphere, they argued that principle, not feeling, should guide the interactions between the races.

Thus, at a fundamental level, each side articulated a different set of norms, values, and evaluative criteria, one based in equality, the other in place. This difference exacerbated the political conflicts, making consensus impossible and even compromise difficult. Consider, finally, the issue of public education. Both Republicans and Democrats said that they wanted to provide African Americans with an education. What this chapter suggests, however, is that each side approached the issue with different modes of judgment. Those who advocated desegregated public schools saw the issue in universal terms. Black students deserved the same education received by white students. Knowledge was not particular, and it certainly did not correspond to racial distinctions. From this perspective, it was reasonable to educate black children to be doctors, lawyers, and college professors; indeed, black professionals would legitimate the Republicans' argument that African Americans had the same potential as European Americans. Opponents of desegregated schools approached the issue in particular, substantial terms. They were worried about the effects of integration on their children, but their perspective also reflected a belief that black students did not require the same knowledge as white students. Knowledge should be specific to one's place in society, and it was wrong to education white and black alike, because it would only complicate future racial interactions. Until the Republicans gave in to the demands of desegregation's critics and the conservatives within their own party, the school provision sparked some of the most heated exchanges in this debate.

[illegible]. This difference accounts for the political conflict, making consensus impossible and even compromise difficult. Consensus about the issue of public education: both Republicans and Democrats said that they wanted to provide African Americans with an education. What this chapter suggests, however, is that each party pursued this issue with different modes of judgment. Those who advocated desegregated public schools saw the situation in [illegible] terms ([illegible] students deserved the same education as [illegible] white students; knowledge was the same thing, and it certainly [illegible]. From this perspective, it was [illegible] able to [illegible] children to [illegible] and [illegible] [illegible] would [illegible] the Republicans [illegible] that African Americans had the same potential as whites and [illegible] [illegible] about the effects of the [illegible] belief that black students [illegible] the same knowledge as white students [illegible] could [illegible] place in society and [illegible] to [illegible] would only complicate [illegible] Republicans [illegible] to the demands of desegregation [illegible] than their own party, [illegible] some of the [illegible].

6

Constitutional Arguments and the Civil Rights Act of 1875

This chapter analyzes the debate's constitutional arguments about desegregation, and, in the process, it implicates a larger controversy over the Thirteenth and Fourteenth Amendments. Two broad and conflicting interpretations of Reconstruction constitutionalism exist today. A minority position holds that the Republicans who passed the Thirteenth through Fifteenth Amendments intended a constitutional revolution. According to scholars such as Robert Kaczorowski, the philosophies of American federalism and states' rights were overthrown by a nationalist perspective of universal human rights and a liberal ideal of centralized governmental authority.[1] Michael McConnell extends this claim, arguing that the Fourteenth Amendment was intended not only as a drastic departure, but also as a means to make segregation unconstitutional.[2] The more widely accepted interpretation of this period holds that the Republicans were a loose amalgamation of radicals, moderates, and conservatives. According to Earl Maltz, maintaining party unity was difficult; consequently, the Republicans were forced to compromise on Reconstruction's amendments.[3] Their policies sustained the conservative philosophies of federalism and limited black equality, and the Thirteenth and Fourteenth Amendments were never intended to justify desegregation, especially in public education.[4]

The Civil Rights Act of 1875 is situated in the middle of this controversy; extended debates have appeared in the *Virginia Law Review* (1995) and *Constitutional Commentary* (1996) that feature the act as a means for deciphering the Fourteenth Amendment's original intent.[5] This chapter does not attempt to privilege one interpretation over the other; neither does it try to reconcile the two. Rather, it uses both sides in the controversy to tease out the significant constitutional issues at play in the civil rights debate. Approached from a rhetorical perspective, this debate suggests that the motive behind the Fourteenth Amendment was not fixed. The intent of its framers was in flux, first because the Fourteenth Amendment, like all amendments, was a discursive and political construction, a compromise between differing philosophies and agendas. Second, this chapter contends that the experiences of Reconstruction had made the Republicans of 1875 more willing to pass radical legislation. Several of the Republicans who championed desegregation insisted that the Fourteenth Amendment legitimized desegregation, but this evidence is not definitive proof. Likewise, the fact that Republicans passed the bill only *after* their political power was threatened does not mean that their claims for its constitutionality were disingenuous. This debate demonstrates only a moment in the evolution of constitutional interpretation of the Thirteenth through Fifteenth Amendments, and even that moment is not decisive.

Reconstruction Constitutional Politics: Setting the Stage for Desegregation

To understand the constitutional arguments surrounding desegregation, one must appreciate that Reconstruction's amendments were created within a tumultuous political environment. When Congress passed the 1875 Civil Rights Act, the Republicans had been influenced by over ten years of political struggle in which partisan politics and principle were indistinguishable. On 3 March 1865, a month before his death, Lincoln signed a measure that created the nation's first regulatory and social welfare agency to supervise abandoned lands and manage issues relating to those who were once slaves.[6] The Freedmen's Bureau was responsible for overseeing the freed slaves, particularly those who had followed the Union armies as they swept across the South. Its funding came from the War Department, and it had the power to divide abandoned and confiscated land into forty-acre plots, first for lease, then for eventual sale to African Americans and white refugees. Lincoln's measure was remarkable, as well, because it established the principle that certain forms of racial discrimination were morally and legally wrong. Even conservative politicians supported this idea, because they hoped to provide the former slaves with enough capital to fend for themselves; Congress, then, could avoid additional responsibility. In contrast, radical politicians, Thomas D. Eliot and Charles Sumner in particular, saw the measure and the bureau as agencies to guide the daily lives of the freedmen and women.[7] They envisioned an expanded federal role in the regulation of civil rights.

In January of 1866 Lyman Trumbull, chairman of the Joint Committee on Reconstruction, introduced a bill to extend and expand the Freedmen's Bureau. The measure provided better funding, and it gave bureau agents jurisdiction over court cases involving African Americans. Trumbull was a moderate Republican with ties to Johnson. To him, the bureau bill modified presidential Reconstruction in only minor ways, but, again, the radicals in Congress had other intentions. They hoped that the bill indicated a new direction for reconstruction policy.[8] Because the bill's language justified both of these perspectives, it passed almost unanimously, and Congress expected no resistance from the president. To its surprise, on 19 February Johnson exercised his veto power. According to President Johnson, Congress never had authorized public money to assist whites; therefore, it could not justify such expenditures for blacks. He implied further that the measure would make the former slaves lazy, creating permanent dependence. Dependency, he argued, was wrong, because the Emancipation Proclamation was meant to make African Americans free and self-sustaining.[9] Three days after his veto, 22 February 1866, Johnson told a crowd gathered to celebrate George Washington's birthday that he had stood against the traitors of the South and now he was standing against the traitors of the North. He declared that Thaddeus Stevens, Wendell Phillips, and Charles Sumner were "opposed to the fundamental principles of this government," and that the radicals in Congress wanted to destroy his administration.[10] Stunned by the president's decision and his inflammatory comments, Congress tried but failed to override the veto.

When Trumbull reported the Freedmen's Bureau Bill, he also reported the first national measure specifically designed to define black civil rights. The 1866 Civil Rights Bill declared "that there shall be no discrimination in civil rights or immunities among the inhabitants of any State or Territory of the United States on account of race, color, or previous condition of slavery." Furthermore, it stipulated that African Americans had the right to "make and enforce contracts, to sue, be parties and give evidence, to inherit, purchase, lease, sell, hold, and convey real and personal property, and to full and equal benefit of all laws and proceedings for the security of persons and property and shall be subject to like punishment, pains and penalties, and to none other."[11] Anyone who suppressed these fundamental rights through state law could be fined or jailed.

The bill's provisions focused on two forms of rights: those economic liberties that were necessary in a free labor system and protections by and from governmental authority. On 2 February the bill passed the Senate by a vote of thirty-three to twelve; only three Republicans voted with the Democratic opposition. When it came to the House, congressional representatives referred it to the Judiciary Committee. Moderates, concerned about the bill's constitutionality, wanted to ensure that the measure did not infringe the individual rights of white citizens. The committee made the bill a prohibition against state law, not individual action, and it restructured some of the bill's language to appease conservative Republicans and Democrats.[12] When it returned to the House, it passed on 13 March. The Senate followed the House's lead on 15 March. Again Congress looked to the president, and again, on 27 March, the president went his own way.

Johnson's veto came despite the lobbying efforts of his Republican friends.[13] Jacob D. Cox, the Republican governor of Ohio, had written the president: "The *bark* of the law would, I think, be infinitely worse than its *bite,* and it seems to me that sensible Southerners could easily be brought to see this, and to see further that in yielding to this measure, all conservative Union men at the North would gain vantage ground with the people which will make us far more powerful for good in other matters & other directions."[14] Furthermore, the bill presented Johnson with an important opportunity. Johnson could have isolated the leaders of the radical faction—Charles Sumner, Thaddeus Stevens, Salmon P. Chase, and Carl Schurz—by aligning himself with the bill's moderate architects, Trumbull and William P. Fessenden. Questioned by Democrats and conservative Republicans, Trumbull and James Wilson, chairman of the Judiciary Committee, stated explicitly that the terms "civil rights" did not entail political rights and the desegregation of public schools. According to the moderate Republicans, "civil rights and immunities" meant only the economic and natural rights that were enumerated within the bill.[15] If Johnson had signed the measure, he would have implemented an equality that several Republicans defined in narrow economic terms. Instead, Johnson ignored this advice and justified his veto, arguing that slavery had made African Americans incapable of citizenship. He declared further that Congress did not have the right to legislate any civil rights policy that might interrupt state statute. Raising the inflammatory issue of miscegenation, he said that if Congress had the authority to pass civil rights legislation, then perhaps it had the authority to enforce romantic relationships between the races.[16]

Republicans were stunned. Brooks Simpson writes, "many Republicans had warned him that a veto would destroy any real hope of cooperation. Angry moderates believed the president had deceived them. Radicals cheered, for Johnson's messages had helped unite Republicans against a common enemy."[17] Congress had failed to override Johnson's veto of the Freedman Bureau measure, but the president's stubbornness in the face of friendly advice altered the minds of several moderates. Republicans quickly overrode his veto of the 1866 Civil Rights Bill; it was the first time that Congress had overridden a president's veto on such an important piece of legislation. With the passage of the 1866 Civil Rights Act, a crack opened between the two branches of government. It only widened in the coming months. Still, it would be inaccurate to view the subsequent conflict between Johnson and Congress as a simple agonistic relationship. One of the more striking aspects of this period is the degree to which moderate Republicans tried to bring about reconciliation. Even though moderates became increasingly alarmed over the policies of President Johnson, the Republican Party never united behind the equalitarian principles of the radicals. Indeed, the party seemed incapable of sustaining a single agenda. Taking every rumor as an encouraging sign from the president, moderates worked against the radicals for the sake of compromise. Their efforts often limited the politics of equality during this period. For example, the idea of providing confiscated land to African Americans never moved beyond the fringes of congressional acceptance. The Civil Rights Act of 1866 was far less extreme than it might have been. Finally, like much of the legislation from 1865 to 1867, the Fourteenth Amendment also involved a series of compromises. These compromises were necessary, because without them the Republicans could not obtain a two-thirds majority.[18]

By mid-April 1866 Congress began to seek its own solutions to the twin problems of Southern reconciliation and black civil rights. The president seemed uninterested in compromise, and his Reconstruction policies failed to please even many moderates. While the controversy surrounding the Civil Rights Bill (1866) occurred, the Joint Committee on Reconstruction discussed several constitutional amendments designed to readmit the

Southern governments and to determine the "full" rights and immunities of the freedmen and women. Thaddeus Stevens introduced a measure that would have based representation in Congress on the number of qualified voters within a state. John A. Bingham offered a bill that gave Congress the power "to make all laws which shall be necessary and proper to secure to the citizens of each State all privileges and immunities of citizens in the several States; and to all persons in the several States equal protection in the rights of life, liberty and property." Both of these proposals were defeated, either because they were too radical or not radical enough.[19] The future of a Fourteenth Amendment was murky when Robert Dale Owen, the abolitionist and reformer, approached Republicans with a comprehensive plan. The first step involved a constitutional amendment that guaranteed black civil rights; that required black suffrage by 4 July 1876; that denied complete representation in Congress to any state that refused black suffrage prior to 1876; that repudiated the Confederate debt; and that provided Congress with the authority to enact this legislation. In contrast to the earlier amendment proposals, "there was something in [the Owen plan] for everyone."[20] With this amendment as a prototype, Congress began the work of revision.

The Joint Committee on Reconstruction altered several key sections of Owen's plan. Most notably it eliminated the provision in favor of black suffrage. The version reported to Congress on 30 April 1866 prohibited states from denying the equal rights of African Americans. It reduced congressional representation in proportion to the number of male citizens denied suffrage. It denied suffrage, until 1870, to those who had aided the Confederacy voluntarily, and it prohibited payment of the Confederate debt. These changes satisfied the House (one hundred twenty-eight to thirty-seven), but Senate moderates suggested additional modifications. Rather than deny suffrage to all Confederates, the Senate barred from national or state office anyone who had repudiated an oath of allegiance to the Constitution by joining the Confederacy. The changes implemented by Republicans to the Fourteenth Amendment were motivated by at least two factors. First, its architects understood that the amendment must contain language that two-thirds of the Republicans would accept. This was not easy, and it required some amount of strategic ambiguity. Second, radical Republicans were concerned that too many of the former Confederates retained control of local and state politics. Thaddeus Stevens declared that he did not want "yelling secessionists and hissing copperheads" in the House, at least not while he was alive. Senate Republicans were less willing to disenfranchise everyone who had served the Confederacy; after all, who would be left? Compromise finally led to a thirty-three to eleven outcome in the Senate. On 13 June the House approved the Senate version (one hundred twenty to thirty-two), and the Fourteenth Amendment was sent to the states.[21]

Several incidents late in 1866 and early in 1867 changed the course of Reconstruction forever. Between October and January, all of the Southern legislatures that considered the Fourteenth Amendment rejected it; of the governments reorganized by either Johnson or Lincoln, only Tennessee ratified the amendment.[22] The message of that repudiation was heightened by race riots in Memphis and New Orleans that left a number of African Americans dead. Then in January, President Johnson vetoed a measure that granted suffrage to African American males in the District of Columbia. With a strong two-thirds majority in the Senate and House, Republicans overturned the veto, but by now Congress had moved toward a more radical implementation of the politics of equality. Congress believed that neither the president nor the South had any intention of establishing civil rights for people of color. Citing these incidents, Thaddeus Stevens argued for a new approach to the issue. He demanded universal black suffrage. He suggested that the Southern governments be abolished, and he called for new state constitutions determined by white *and* black delegates.[23] Only then, he claimed, would African Americans obtain the rights that Congress intended.

The passage of the 1866 Civil Rights Act and the Fourteenth Amendment constitute the primary battleground for scholars who argue over Reconstruction constitutionalism. According to Maltz, the 1866 Civil Rights Act and the Fourteenth Amendment were conservative measures. The Republicans of the Thirty-ninth Congress believed that the state governments were still the primary arbiters of fundamental rights, and they understood that the federal government could intervene only when the states failed to live up to their responsibilities to guard the rights and privileges of state citizens.[24] Maltz states that Lyman Trumbull, the driving force behind the 1866 Civil Rights Act and the Fourteenth Amendment, "clearly contemplated that the federal government would be involved only where the states failed in their obligation to protect the fundamental rights of free blacks."[25] Kaczorowski sharply disagrees. He argues that a majority of Republicans, *including* Lyman Trumbull, wanted the 1866 Civil Rights Act and the Fourteenth Amendment to enlarge the federal government's ability to protect freedmen and women. The Republicans interpreted the Thirteenth

Amendment as more than a negative injunction, he contends; they believed that the Thirteenth Amendment entailed a positive duty for Congress to guarantee the complete freedom of black Americans. Thus Congress had the right to pass intrusive legislation to secure that freedom.[26] Kaczorowski states: "The scope of [congressional] authority was potentially destructive of American federalism. If Congress chose, it could legislate criminal and civil codes that displaced those of the states. Furthermore, Congress could confer upon the federal courts jurisdiction over ordinary crimes and civil disputes that supplanted the jurisdiction of state courts. In short, the supremacy of national sovereignty so centralized power in the national government that the states as separate and autonomous political entities could have been destroyed."[27] Kaczorowski admits that the Republicans chose not to destroy the states as "separate political entities," but he affirms that they still intended a shift in the relationship between the states and the federal government. Federal jurists understood this fact, and they began to interpret the Constitution not from a traditional federalist perspective, but from a new nationalist perspective.

Without reaching a judgment about the full intent of the 1866 Civil Rights Act and the Fourteenth Amendment's framers, two conclusions can be drawn from this history. First, the 1866 Civil Rights Act and the Fourteenth Amendment departed from the policies of the antebellum. The Republicans enacted a "politics of equality"; that is, they insisted that people of color deserved "equality before the law." Furthermore, the Republicans gave the federal government a role in protecting the civil rights of the newly freed slaves. The extent of this role and the meaning of equality before the law continue to be matters of interpretation to this day, however. Second, the 1866 Civil Rights Act and the Fourteenth Amendment were enacted within a political environment that fused principle and pragmatism. To obtain the two-thirds majority necessary to override the president's veto or to pass a constitutional amendment, Republicans needed the support of the radicals who abhorred segregation and the conservatives who abhorred integration. Furthermore, Johnson's vetoes and the South's resistance to even moderate proposals motivated the Republicans to put aside their differences. In Michael Klarman's view, the Fourteenth Amendment's core provisions "are best understood as Republican responses to political exigencies having little to do with constitutional principle." Klarman underestimates the importance of Republican idealism, but he is correct that policies which were unlikely based solely on principle became possible because of the hostility of President Johnson and the Southern governments.[28]

The 1870s Civil Rights Debate: Two Versions of the Constitution

One can become hopelessly entangled among the various constitutional arguments of the civil rights debate; consequently, attention to the speech texts of Alexander Stephens and Robert Elliott may lend clarity to the analysis. These two texts are useful places to begin for several reasons. First, each speaker discussed extensively the constitutional question of this controversy: Did Congress have the authority to pass the measure and enforce desegregation through federal intervention? Second, within the context of the House 1874 debate, these speakers were paired—one representing the antebellum past and the other a reconstructed future. Third, the discourse of Stephens and Elliott displays the divergent modes of constitutional interpretation used by their respective positions. Thus, while the constitutional arguments of these representatives are a point of entry, the analysis also includes the texts of other congressmen.

Constitutional Continuity: American Federalism and States' Rights

The primary thesis of desegregation opponents was that Congress did not have the authority to pass and enforce the measure because it infringed upon the power of state governments to determine their citizens' rights.[29] To build this case, Alexander Stephens focused his attention on that section of the Constitution used by the Republicans to justify the bill. The Republicans, he said, had declared that the first and fifth sections of the Fourteenth Amendment authorized the desegregation measure:

> I. All persons born or naturalized in the United States, and subject to the jurisdiction thereof, are citizens of the United States and of the State wherein they reside. No state shall make or enforce any law which shall abridge the privileges or immunities of citizens of the United States; nor shall any State deprive any person of life, liberty, or property, without due process of law; nor deny to any person within its jurisdiction the equal protection of the laws.[30]
>
> V. The Congress shall have power to enforce, by appropriate legislation, the provisions of this article.[31]

However, Stephens argued, the Republicans were incorrect to suppose that these passages justified the measure. As he interpreted its words, the Fourteenth Amendment had two primary goals: "It made the Colored race citizens of the United States, and it prohibited the states from denying to the

Negro the same privileges, immunities, and civil rights which were secured to the 'citizens of the several States, respectively, and of the United States, by the Constitution *as it stood before citizenship to the colored race was declared by this amendment'"* (italics added).[32] Note the italicized words; they reveal the key assumption of antidesegregation forces. Based on a close examination of the Fourteenth Amendment's language, opponents of desegregation contended that the system of federalism remained unchanged.

The prevailing theory of government both before and during the Civil War entailed a notion of shared authority between the states and the national government.[33] This governmental structure, typically termed American federalism, ensured that both systems of government worked independently of each other, and while neither government was responsible to the other, the system effectively protected state officials from federal intervention. Within this broadly accepted philosophy two variations existed. Those who eventually became Confederates advocated a version of federalism similar to John C. Calhoun's, which held that the states possessed ultimate sovereignty and that the federal government exercised authority only as an agent of the states.[34] According to them, the Constitution was a state-created compact; consequently, the states could undo that which they had made. Another group, comprised of Whigs, some Democrats, and eventually the Republicans, believed in divided and equal authority. They maintained that no state possessed the right to leave the Union or to determine a law's constitutional worth.[35] Despite these differences, both sides agreed on one fundamental assumption. The Constitution granted only limited and expressed authority to the federal government, while it gave power over civil matters—including civil rights—to the states. When it came to the rights of citizens, the states possessed absolute authority to delegate and protect as they pleased. Desegregation's critics insisted that this system was still in force.

Southern conservatives gained additional legitimacy for their constitutional position from the Supreme Court's *Slaughter-House Cases* decision.[36] On 8 March 1869 the state of Louisiana had granted the Crescent City Live-Stock Landing and Slaughter-House Company a twenty-five year monopoly. The restriction was intended to protect the public health, and, according to Michael A. Ross, the public's health needed protection: "Over 300,000 animals were slaughtered in New Orleans each year, and the conditions surrounding this operation were ghastly." Animals were killed in locations throughout the city, and the waste from the process typically ended up in the streets or the Mississippi River. According to the law, all butchers in New Orleans were required to use the newly built slaughterhouse that sat on the opposite bank of the Mississippi river. Butchers had to pay to use the facility, and all of the meat that was produced had to be inspected by health officials before it could leave the premises. For the butchers who had experienced little regulation until that moment, the law was unacceptable; several groups sued the state, arguing that the monopoly deprived them of their civil rights. Ironically, the butchers, who were white, used the Thirteenth and Fourteenth Amendments to defend their position. In effect, the white butchers used Reconstruction's amendments to argue against a monopoly that assisted people of color to enter the livestock trade. Under the monopoly, the slaughter of animals could proceed only by renting space at the Livestock Company; subsequently, butchers no longer needed their own facility. This policy was a boon to African Americans, because they did not have to raise capital to build or purchase their own slaughterhouse.[37]

The Supreme Court decided against the butchers on 14 April 1873, five to four. The majority opinion was written by Justice Samuel F. Miller, a staunch Republican and the leader of the court's "liberal wing." Writing for the majority, he held that Louisiana's police powers gave it the right to protect public health through the monopoly. He also ruled that the white butchers were in error, because the rights that they demanded were not covered under the Fourteenth Amendment. According to the decision, the Fourteenth Amendment *had not* destroyed the distinction between state and national citizenship. Federalism remained intact, and the states retained the power to regulate certain rights, while other rights belonged to national citizenship.[38] State authority, Miller explained, still protected the fundamental privileges of most citizens, while national citizenship assured only specific narrow rights.[39] In summary, Miller's opinion argued that the Fourteenth Amendment's "privileges or immunities clause" *did not* give the federal government authority over the Bill of Rights.[40]

The Democrats and conservative Republicans who opposed desegregation saw the *Slaughter-House* decision as a serious blow to the Republican idealists, and they seized on Justice Miller's opinion.[41] Stephens, for example, cited Miller to establish the premise that the federal government had not possessed the right to determine the civil rights of any citizen prior to 1866. He quoted: "the entire domain of the privileges and immunities of citizens of the States, as above defined, lay within the constitutional and legislative power of the States, and without that of the Federal Government."[42] After he established this historical premise, Stephens used the justice's opinion to ask the following question: "Was it the purpose of the Fourteenth Amendment, by the simple declaration that no State should make or enforce any law which shall abridge the privileges and immunities of citizens of the United States, to transfer the security and protection of all the civil rights which we have mentioned, from the States to the Federal Government?"[43] In the *Slaughter-House Cases,* Miller had answered this question with a firm negative. His audience knew the justice's conclusion, so Stephens offered the following passage from the decision: "Under the pressure of all the excited feeling growing out of the war, our statesmen have still believed that the existence of the States with powers for domestic and local government, including the regulation of civil rights—the rights of person and of property—was essential to the perfect working of our complex form of government, though they have thought proper to impress additional limitations on the States, and to confer additional power on that of the Nation."[44] Stephens then concluded in his own words, "it is here judicially affirmed that all the essential features of our original complex federal system are still preserved. In substance it amounts to this, that these amendments (whether rightfully or wrongfully incorporated into the Constitution) do not change the nature and character of the Government."[45] Continuity, not rupture, was the result of the Thirteenth, Fourteenth, and Fifteenth Amendments.

Stephens's use of the Miller opinion is interesting on several levels. First, he hoped to capitalize on the growing authority of the Supreme Court as the final arbiter of constitutional meaning. He was not alone. A good number of the bill's critics discussed the *Slaughter-House* decision at length. Milton Southard, for example, quoted from the decision to argue that the rights of blacks "are fundamental in their character, and have no relation to the peculiar and special privileges comprehended in the bill before the House."[46] Second, Stephens and the critics of desegregation used the *Slaughter-House* decision to capitalize on the antebellum era's constitutional tradition. Note that the extended quotation above ends with the words, "though they [the statesmen who drafted Reconstruction's amendments] have thought [it] proper to impress additional limitations on the States, and to confer additional power on that of the Nation." The opponents of desegregation denied that the new constitutional amendments granted the federal government any additional power. According to Stephens, "the exercise of no new power was conferred by either of these new amendments."[47] He declared instead that the Fourteenth Amendment's fifth section—"The Congress shall have power to enforce, by appropriate legislation, the provisions of this article"—simply confirmed that the federal government could protect the colored race, just as it had protected the rights of white citizens before the war. Stephens's colleagues agreed. Representative William Finck, on 3 February 1875, argued that the fifth section provided no new powers to Congress. Robert Hale, a moderate Republican from New York who voted for the measure, asked Finck, "Then the gentleman gives no effect whatever to this section?" Finck replied, "No effect, whatever. It does not confer upon Congress one particle of additional power. I maintain that this fifth section of the amendment confers no power upon Congress which it did not already possess."[48]

These arguments frustrated the politicians who supported desegregation. What had been the purpose of Reconstruction's amendments if they did not give the federal government additional power, asked the Republican majority? Stephens had a ready answer: the Fourteenth Amendment's only real innovation pertained not to the federal government but to the *states.* The states were now prohibited from enacting laws that discriminated against the civil rights of its citizens. But, Stephens cautioned, "the denial of the exercise of any number of powers by the United States, severally, does not, most certainly, confer its exercise upon the Congress of the States. Neither of these amendments confer, bestow, or even declare, any rights at all to the citizens of the United States, or to any class whatever."[49]

Although Stephens's interpretations of the *Slaughter-House Cases* and the Fourteenth Amendment were limiting, his discourse was more generous than some of his Democratic colleagues. Stephens argued that the states maintained their original authority, but he also acknowledged that the Fourteenth Amendment prohibited the unequal regulation of citizens' rights. He declared that Reconstruction's amendments prohibited unequal state action: "Whatever rights they grant to other citizens shall not be denied to the colored race as a class."[50] One way to read this argument is to conclude that Stephens supported the separate but equal doctrine. In spaces controlled or licensed by state authority, the state was required, according to Stephens's interpretive framework, to provide equal accommodations for the races. A number of Democrats did not grant Reconstruction's amendments even this power. Senator John Stockton of New Jersey said, "Mr. Justice Miller, in delivering the opinion of the court, declares that it is too clear for argument that the clause in the Fourteenth Amendment on which the bill before us was drawn was not intended to protect a citizen of a State against the legislative power of his own state."[51] According to his reading, the Fourteenth Amendment prohibited state authorities from legislating unequally only those rights protected by *national citizenship.* These rights included only interstate travel, diplomatic protection abroad, use of U.S. waters, and the right to obtain a writ of habeas corpus.

The key feature of Miller's *Slaughter-House* opinion that strengthened the position of desegregation's opponents was its emphasis on dual citizenship, which seemed to argue for the continuation of antebellum legal philosophy. A passage from Senator Thomas Norwood of Georgia illustrates this point well:

> The Supreme Court, including the three dissenting justices, say in the Slaughter-house cases that the fourteenth amendment declares, if it does not create, a citizenship of the United States separate from that of a State. The necessary sequence to this proposition is, that there must be privileges and immunities of a citizen of the United States different from those which belong to a citizen of a State. For if there be two citizenships, there must be also two classes of duties and obligations imposed on the citizens of the respective governments. . . . But the governments being separate and distinct, the objects of either being separate and different, the powers of one being the complement of the powers of the other, and these powers being different, it must also follow that the privileges and immunities of a citizen of the State . . . must be different from his privileges and immunities as a citizen of the United States, which are the result of the Constitution and laws pursuant thereto. And it must also be true, *that the protection of the privileges and immunities derived from citizenship must be given by the government from which they are derived; for it would be manifestly absurd to say, that the rights derived by a citizen from one government are under the protection of another* (italics added).[52]

Miller's opinion allowed the opponents of desegregation to argue that the system of American federalism remained intact. Since state citizenship still guaranteed the rights afforded by the Bill of Rights, the Fourteenth Amendment did not authorize a national desegregation policy. Representative Finck warned that the Civil Rights Bill entered into the states to regulate "the local affairs and concerns of the people of the States. It proposes to go into the State and say how its school system shall be conducted. It proposes to define and regulate how a hotel within a state shall be conducted. It proposes also to regulate the rights of citizens who enter theaters, places of public amusement, and public conveyances." This was an intrusion on states' rights; therefore, Finck concluded that the bill was unconstitutional.[53] Allen Thurman agreed. He said that the Fourteenth Amendment was only a limitation on state power to protect the privileges and immunities of national citizenship.[54] Those rights determined by state authority could be managed as the states saw fit, equally or otherwise.

The opponents' constitutional arguments are significant not only for their substance, but also for the interpretive strategy that they employed. The critics of desegregation shared a common hermeneutic: they focused on the literal language of the Constitution and its amendments. This interpretive stance is evident when Stephens declared, "as to the first section of the Fourteenth, all I have to say here is that it very clearly appears from its *words* that it has but two objects" (italics added).[55] Not only did Stephens focus on the words of the first section, but he also focused quite narrowly on the literal text of every constitutional passage he examined. Likewise, one of the more vocal Republicans to oppose desegregation, Matthew Carpenter, gave a speech that examined in detail the precise language of the Fourteenth Amendment. A section of his text reads as follows:

> If this bill can be maintained at all, it must be under the second clause [of the Fourteenth Amendment]: No state shall make or enforce any law which shall abridge the privileges or immunities of citizens of the United States. The phraseology of this section of the amendment merits critical examination. It provides that—All persons born or naturalized in the United States, and subject to the jurisdiction thereof, are citizens of the United States *and of the State wherein they reside* [emphasis his]. The phraseology of the next clause is essentially different: No state shall make or enforce any law which shall abridge the privileges or immunities of *citizens of the United States* [emphasis his]. It will be seen that this amendment does not, in words, forbid States to abridge the privileges or immunities of citizens of the State. To make the two clauses equally comprehensive, the latter should read thus: No State shall make or enforce any law which shall abridge the privileges or immunities of citizens of the United States, *or of such State*. But the words "or of such State" are not found in the second clause, and the variation in phraseology is so material that it must be considered intentional.[56]

Carpenter's emphasis on the "phraseology" of the Fourteenth Amendment is significant. It facilitated a number of careful distinctions, including his claim that the Fourteenth Amendment did not prevent the states from restricting the civil rights of their citizens. As an interpretive strategy, Carpenter's narrow focus had its own persuasive function.

The opponents' emphasis on the literal words and phrases of Reconstruction's amendments resulted in a constitutional interpretation that ignored the complex political and social context that necessitated the amendments. The original intent of the Fourteenth Amendment with respect to desegregation remains a contentious issue to this day; nevertheless, one must recall that the Republicans decided to amend the

Constitution, because they believed that the South might not protect black rights and privileges. They also believed that the federal government was responsible, at least in some fashion, for the race's welfare, and these politicians must have assumed that their goal—to protect African Americans—was possible only through the drastic step of a constitutional amendment. As is true of all amendments, the framers wanted the Fourteenth Amendment to stand as a broad statement of principle that would alter the nation permanently.[57]

Because the opponents' constitutional hermeneutic concentrated on the "words" of Reconstruction's amendments and refrained from any discussion of the bill's history, critics of the bill were able to ignore the amendments' most powerful dimensions—their character as abstract statements of principle. Opponents treated the amendments as if they were distinct from the charged and chaotic context of their origin; subsequently, opponents implied that the amendments were *stable* texts, amenable to a literal interpretation grounded in the actual words as recorded. This was not the case. The amendments, like the Constitution itself, were naturally ambiguous. The outcome of compromises between radical and moderate forces in Congress, they were open to multiple interpretations from their very inception. Indeed, their most enduring aspect has been their presence as abstract confirmations of equality, freedom, and liberty. In 1874 and 1875 the opponents of desegregation used an interpretive strategy that ignored these elements. Their strategy narrowed the scope and ramifications of Reconstruction's amendments, and, without their egalitarian ideals, the amendments' potential as catalysts for significant social transformation diminished.

Constitutional Transformation: Rescuing the Slaughter–House Decision

When Robert Elliott addressed the House on 6 January 1874, he faced a difficult task. His opponents were using the *Slaughter-House* decision to undermine his party's authority to pass the Civil Rights Bill. Stephens's reputation as a statesman also overshadowed Elliot's own limited experience in Congress. But Elliott, to his credit, did not shrink from this task. He began his speech boldly: "But, sir, we are told by the distinguished gentleman from Georgia [Mr. Stephens] that Congress has no power under the Constitution to pass such a law, and that the passage of such an act is in direct contravention of the rights of the States. I cannot assent to any such proposition."[58] The Thirteenth through Fifteenth Amendments invest Congress, "in positive words," with the authority to protect citizen's civil and political rights. Those who claim otherwise, said he, have an inaccurate understanding of the Constitution, its amendments, and the intent of the amendments' framers. After this bold statement Elliott attacked the most damaging aspect of the opponents' proof—the *Slaughter-House* decision. He stated:

> I venture to say here in the presence of the gentleman from Kentucky [Representative Durham], and the gentleman from Georgia [Representative Stephens], and in the presence of the whole country, that there is not a line or word, not a thought or dictum even, in the decision of the Supreme Court in the great *Slaughter-house* cases which casts a shadow of doubt on the right of Congress to pass the pending bill, or to adopt such other legislation as it may judge proper and necessary to secure perfect equality before the law to every citizen of the Republic. Sir, I protest against the dishonor now cast upon our Supreme Court. . . . The Supreme Court of to-day is a tribunal as true to freedom as any department of this Government, and I am honored with the opportunity of repelling a deep disgrace which the gentleman from Kentucky, backed and sustained as he is by the gentleman from Georgia, seeks to put upon it.[59]

How could Elliott make this claim? The answer is twofold: first, the *Slaughter-House* decision was *not* a repudiation of the politics of equality. Second, Elliott's rhetorical skills were sufficient to "rescue" the decision from the interpretation offered by the critics of desegregation.

Michael Ross writes that in "the *Slaughter-House Cases* the Supreme Court began to limit the positive effects that the Fourteenth Amendment might have had upon the lives of African Americans. Specifically, the Court narrowly interpreted the Fourteenth Amendment's privileges or immunities clause." At the same time, Ross posits that one must look beyond the court's commentary about federalism. For example, one might note that the legislature that passed the sustained Louisiana statute was extremely unpopular because it was biracial. Ross argues that racial prejudice among New Orleans's white population is the best explanation for why the city's citizens supported the lawsuit. Furthermore, the butchers who filed the suit disliked its regulations, but they also were incensed that it opened up their trade to blacks. Finally, the actual language of Miller's opinion also suggests that the decision was not clear-cut. The decision mirrored the position of Charles Sumner, in part. Like Sumner, Miller stated explicitly that the cause of the Civil War had been slavery; furthermore, the purpose of the Fourteenth Amendment was to *destroy* slavery's last vestiges. According to the decision, the Fourteenth Amendment *did* justify federal intervention in cases where states created biased legislation that was racially discriminatory. Its equal protection clause, Miller explained, was a guarantee to the freedmen and women. In summary, when one considers the political and economic contexts that surrounded this decision and the actual language of the opinion, it is possible to view the *Slaughter-House Cases* as a progressive judgment that affirmed black rights and congressional authority. Elliott and the other supporters of desegregation used the *Slaughter-House* opinion exactly in that manner.[60]

According to Elliott, the *Slaughter-House Cases* involved two primary issues: Louisiana's police powers and the economic rights of white butchers. The questions before Congress in 1874 were quite different, he declared. The Civil Rights Bill did not infringe on a state's duty to protect its citizens, and desegregation was a policy designed to ameliorate the racial discrimination experienced by African Americans. Elliott argued that Stephens and the Democrats were wrong to link Miller's opinion and the Civil Rights Bill, because they had failed to adhere to a basic requirement of legal interpretation. One must always interpret any judicial decision in light of the facts of the case. He explained: "It thus appears from a simple statement of the case that the question which was before the court was not whether a State law which denied to a particular portion of her citizens the rights conferred on her citizens generally, on account of race, color, or previous condition of servitude, was unconstitutional because in conflict with the recent amendments, but whether an act which conferred on certain citizens exclusive privileges for police purposes was in conflict therewith."[61] Racial discrimination and segregation were not dimensions of the case; therefore, the outcome of the Supreme Court's decision was not directly applicable. Approached from the proper legal perspective, said Elliott, Miller's opinion was instructive but not prescriptive when it came to black rights.

Elliott argued that Miller's opinion contained two conclusions that Congress should consider as it debated desegregation. First, he agreed with Justice Miller that Louisiana had protected its community appropriately with its butchering monopoly. He added that "the only ground upon which the grant of exclusive privileges to a portion of the community is ever defended is that the substantial good of all is promoted."[62] Second, Elliott expressed his approval of Miller's claim that the Fourteenth Amendment did not apply to the butchers, because, as Miller said, "the leading and comprehensive purpose of the Thirteenth, Fourteenth, and Fifteenth amendments was to secure the complete freedom of the race, which, by the events of the war, had been wrested from the unwilling grasp of their owners."[63] Note that these two aspects of Miller's decision not only distanced the opinion from the desegregation issue, they supported the idea that Congress had passed Reconstruction's amendments to assist people of color. If that had been the intent of the amendments' framers, then perhaps the amendments applied to blacks in a way that they did not apply to Louisiana's butchers.

Elliott's interpretation of the *Slaughter-House* decision was possible because of the opinion's dual nature. The case syllabus clearly affirmed that the second clause of the Fourteenth Amendment protected the rights of "citizens of the United States as distinguished from the privileges and immunities of citizens of the States." Yet also in reference to the Fourteenth Amendment, the syllabus affirmed, "the clause which forbids a State to deny to any person the equal protection of the laws was clearly intended to prevent the hostile discrimination against the negro race so familiar in the States where he had been a slave, and for this purpose the clause confers ample power in Congress to secure his rights and his equality before the law."[64] Elliott emphasized those aspects of the opinion that supported desegregation. Miller's opinion contained an extensive discussion about the origins of the Thirteenth through Fifteenth Amendments, and the Republicans used this section to their advantage. Elliott claimed that any interpretation of the recent amendments had to recognize the purpose and "pervading spirit" that guided them. Furthermore, he employed Stephens's strategy from the day before, quoting from Miller's opinion to support his position that the amendments' creators intended to secure black freedom and to protect the race from an unfriendly Southern populace.[65] After quoting from the opinion, Elliott concluded in his own words: "These amendments, one and all, are thus declared to have as their all-pervading design and end the security to [*sic*] the recently enslaved race, not only their nominal freedom, but their complete protection from those who had formerly exercised unlimited dominion over them. It is in this broad light that all these amendments must be read, the purpose to secure the perfect equality before the law of all citizens of the United States."[66] Relying on the *Slaughter-House* decision, Frederick Frelinghuysen argued that Reconstruction politicians had created the amendments "to wipe out every consequence of [slavery]; to prevent State legislation of every kind that discriminated on account of race, color &c., and make the race formerly in servitude equal in all respects to other citizens."[67] Representative William Lawrence reminded the House of its decision to pass the 1866 Civil Rights Act, and reinterpreting what he and his colleagues had done, Lawrence concluded that there as well Congress had intended to secure a broad equality for all citizens.[68]

Lawrence's comments and the position of desegregation's advocates generally support an expansive interpretation of Reconstruction history. According to this rhetoric, the Civil War had altered the balance of power between federal and state governments. The Union government, under Lincoln's direction during the war, had expanded its authority beyond previous bounds.[69] As the war concluded, many wondered whether the national government would or should relinquish the control it had established. Some Republicans and abolitionists saw opportunity in extended federal power, and they embraced the wartime expansion, arguing that a vast "reconstruction" was necessary not just to rebuild the South's ravaged infrastructure, but also its morals, beliefs, and institutions. According to Foner, this view became one of the defining characteristics that distinguished the radicals from moderate Republicans, who were leery of an enlarged role for the executive, judicial, and legislative branches.[70] Those who supported desegregation in 1874 and 1875 differed from opponents most directly by arguing that the Constitution was no longer the same document it had been. Where the Democrats saw constitutional continuity, the Republicans argued for constitutional change, a shift that had altered the nation's legal system. Elliott expressed this change when he said, "equality before the law is now the broad, universal, glorious rule and mandate of the Republic."[71] Robert Hale alluded to the transformation when he reminded his colleagues that he alone among House Republicans had opposed the Fourteenth Amendment, because its fifth clause "was to a certain extent a revolution of our form of government in giving Congress a control of matters which had hitherto been confined exclusively to State control."[72] Senator Timothy Howe, a self proclaimed "strict constructionist," admitted that before the amendments the bill would have been unconstitutional, but now, he said, "the Constitution has been changed. . . . Some prerogatives have been withdrawn from the States; some new faculties or powers have been given to the Government of the United States. Three whole chapters have been added to the organic law."[73] A proper view of the Constitution's history meant rupture, not continuity, according to the bill's advocates.

Just as the opponents of desegregation utilized a constitutional hermeneutic that strengthened their liberal claims, bill proponents approached the Constitution with an interpretive strategy that supported their position. Specifically, Republican idealists emphasized the very social and political context that the Democrats ignored. According to proponents,

Reconstruction's amendments had been a response to black oppression. The Thirteenth Amendment was a response to slavery. The Fourteenth Amendment was a reaction to the South's repudiation of the 1866 Civil Rights Act. The Fifteenth Amendment was an answer to the violence and discrimination that had continued against freedmen and women. Furthermore, those who advanced the Civil Rights Bill argued that Congress must decide its constitutionality in light of the Constitution's spirit as well as its exact phrasing. They treated the Fourteenth Amendment, in particular, as a statement of principle. For them the Constitution was not just a procedural document, but a broad and living declaration of principle. Their position caused Thurman to react, "The Senator from Vermont [George Edmunds] has with infinite skill dealt in generalities. He points out no clause of the Constitution that authorizes this provision in the bill. He deals simply in generalities, speaks about equality, that the Constitution secures equality before the law."[74] For Edmunds, the generalities that Thurman so easily dismissed were the reasons that the Civil War was fought. He declared, "The Constitution of the United States, as was stated in an opinion of the Supreme Court once by an eminent democratic judge, is a bill of rights for the people of all the States." This bill of rights included the right to be protected against discrimination and racial prejudice.[75]

Although the Republicans were creative in their interpretation of Miller's opinion, the *Slaughter-House Cases* remained a problem. Several Supreme Court justices had signed a minority opinion that stated that the majority had misconstrued the intent of the Fourteenth Amendment. The opinion, written by Justice Stephen J. Field, declared that Louisiana had exceeded its authority by prohibiting the butchers from pursuing their trade. He declared that the Thirteenth and Fourteenth Amendments were not limited to individuals of African descent, and he argued that the amendments had altered the nature of everyone's citizenship. He stated:

> A citizen of a State is now only a citizen of the United States residing in that State. The fundamental rights, privileges, and immunities which belong to him as a free man and a free citizen, now belong to him as a citizen of the United States, and are not dependent upon his citizenship of any State. The exercise of these rights and privileges, and the degree of enjoyment received from such exercise, are always more or less affected by the condition and the local institutions of the State, or city, or town where he resides. . . . But in no other way can they be affected by the action of the State, or by the residence of the citizen therein. They do not derive their existence from its legislation, and cannot be destroyed by its power.[76]

Returning to the Civil Rights Act of 1866 for evidence, Justice Field argued that national citizenship protected a person's civil right to pursue economic gain without undo governmental intrusion. When these rights were combined with the power of the Fourteenth Amendment, Field declared that the "privileges and immunities" designated in the fourth article of the Constitution became a part of national citizenship.

This was a profound declaration; it foreshadowed contemporary jurisprudence. At the same time, it also complicated the position taken by the Republicans. Their strategy did not directly contradict Field's opinion, but it called into question how the Republicans and the dissenting justices could view the majority opinion so differently. Did Miller's opinion support a new civil rights initiative as the Republicans claimed, or was Field correct that the opinion removed the heart from the Fourteenth Amendment? Senator George Boutwell, a Republican from Massachusetts, admitted on 21 May 1874 that the Supreme Court had made a "great mistake" when it had sustained the dual citizenship doctrine.[77] The next day, Wisconsin Republican Timothy Howe argued that the court's comments about federalism were not central to the judgment and thus not binding. They were *obiter dicta:* "Mr. President, I am glad to feel authorized to say that that is not the conclusion of the court. I understand [Miller's comments about state and federal citizenship] to be a part of the argument simply by which the justice who delivered the opinion of the majority undertook to defend the judgment of the court."[78] The comments of these two men and a general unease among the moderate Republicans when they discussed the case suggest that no matter how one approached the decision, Miller's opinion had narrowed the scope of Reconstruction's amendments. Robert Palmer interprets Miller's opinion as a wise "middle course, defined and revised in response to vigorous criticism" from Fields, Bradley, and Swayne.[79] Though this view is accurate, the fact that the majority opinion supported both federalism and black rights made it a discursive resource for both critics and advocates of desegregation.

The Discursive Structure of Constitutional Meaning

For historians of the Constitution and legal theory, how one interprets this civil rights debate is more than a question of historical perspective, it is an indication of one's position regarding constitutional hermeneutics. For legal scholars who appreciate the judicial decisions of the Warren court but remain committed to historicism and original intent, the Reconstruction era is extremely attractive. Egalitarian statements can be found throughout the congressional discourse of the period, providing contemporary scholars with both a sense of social justice and a conservative jurisprudence. The Republican rhetoric during the 1875 civil rights debate is a case in point. Based on an extensive analysis of the congressional debate, McConnell argues that the framers of the Fourteenth Amendment *intended* to desegregate public schools. Citing the texts that are analyzed throughout this book, he argues that many of Republicans who voted for desegregation in 1872, 1874, and 1875 had also passed the Fourteenth Amendment. The Republicans' support for school desegregation in 1874 signals, for McConnell, the Republicans' intent to desegregate schools back when they drafted the Fourteenth Amendment.

McConnell has his critics, however. Specifically, Maltz and Klarman applaud McConnell's detailed scholarship, but they argue that his conclusions are flawed. According to Klarman, McConnell provides no reason for why the "intent" of the Fourteenth Amendment should rest with the Republicans in Congress and not with the state legislators who ratified the measure. The ratifying states certainly did not support widespread desegregation in the 1860s. Maltz and Klarman both contend that the Republicans in 1875 were of a different mind than in 1866. Despite a growing lack of interest in the greater populace, Republicans were embracing stronger and stronger civil rights policies to protect the Republican Party in the South. Maltz adds historical evidence to this position. He notes that Republicans in 1866 explicitly denied the claim that juries could be desegregated under the Fourteenth Amendment; nevertheless, by 1872 they were using the Fourteenth Amendment to support that policy. Furthermore, although McConnell is correct that the Republicans in 1874 and 1875 rejected amendments to create "separate but equal" public schools, it is also true that the bill became a law only *after* its school clause had been removed. McConnell, of course, offers logical counterarguments to the objections of Maltz and Klarman, but the most reasonable conclusion that one can make is that this debate fails to provide definitive proof for the Fourteenth Amendment's original intent.[80]

The complexities of passing legislation and the discursive norms of the congressional process make it impossible to determine a single motive for political judgments. Did Reconstruction's Republicans intend to enlarge federal authority and disrupt federalism when they created and passed Reconstruction's constitutional amendments is an interesting question, but it is inevitably unanswerable. The rhetoric, voting record, and history of the 1875 Civil Rights Act does not provide definitive proof of any originalist interpretation. A better question would start by approaching this debate as a moment in the *evolution* of constitutional rhetoric and thought. How did Republicans use the Constitution to create arguments that supported their political judgment is a more viable question. Clearly the egalitarian rhetoric of the 1870s debate implied a strong role for the federal government in the protection of African American rights.

The Democratic Position: To Preserve State Authority

A cursory examination of this debate might lead one to believe that federalism was the central constitutional issue, because it was such an important aspect of the Democrats' rhetoric and the primary explanation for their objections. For example, after Alexander Stephens declared that the amendment did not enlarge the powers of the federal government, he argued that it would not matter even if the Fourteenth Amendment stated clearly that Congress could legislate the civil rights of citizens against a state's wishes. The bill would remain unconstitutional, because it destroyed the nation's basic system of government. He said, "if there is one truth which stands out prominently above all others in the history of these States, it is that the germinal and seminal principle of American constitutional liberty is the absolute unrestricted right of State self-government in all purely internal municipal affairs." The Civil Rights Bill deviated from this principle, and it presented the nation with a clear choice between two different types of governments, he said. Either it could degenerate into "centralism" or it could choose to continue along the path of "constitutionalism."[81]

The dichotomy that Stephens created contrasted a strong national government with a federal government where the states maintained their traditional authority. But note the actual terms that Stephens used to create this comparison. Instead of using a "centralism-federalism" ratio, Stephens used a "centralism-constitutionalism" ratio. He aligned the Democratic-Republican notion of limited federal power so closely to the original Constitution that, despite the new amendments, he saw no difference between his philosophy and the meaning of the document. From his perspective, federalism *was* the Constitution, and Stephens promised to defend the union's sacred text against what he believed to be a serious deviation from its essentials. As he made this promise, he invoked one of the most powerful myths of his era.

The mythic origin of the United States was a crucial aspect of public memory. According to this story, much of America's success related to the way in which the founders combined principle and procedure in the Constitution. America was unique and powerful because its framers had struck a balance between state powers and a national government. As a result, the country functioned efficiently while individual liberties remained protected—something that was unique in world history. The opponents of desegregation tapped into this myth of America's unique heritage and origin. More than that, men such as Stephens and his colleagues became the defenders of that heritage. He declared, "the old Jeffersonian democratic republican principles are not dead, and will never die so long as a true devotee of liberty lives."[82] Other Democrats were quick to accept this responsibility as well. John J. Davis of West Virginia declared: "Shall not a halt be called, and that pernicious species of contruction, which enlarges the powers of the Federal Government to the destruction of the whole system, be excluded and forever abandoned? Let us preserve religiously the Constitution, which forms the key-stone that binds together the well-constructed arch of the Union, and in so doing we shall secure good government and liberty to all."[83] As long as Stephens and his colleagues defended federalism and opposed desegregation, liberty would flourish.

The Republican Position: To Ensure Black Equality

One might have expected Elliott to counter Stephens's arguments with the claim that the Constitution's transformation and the Declaration of Independence granted the national government all the authority it needed. This idea was a staple of Sumner's constitutional arguments, and several of the bill's proponents followed this line of reasoning. Elliott, however, refused to dwell on Stephens's concern that the bill established a centralized government. He focused on a different dichotomy to justify its constitutionality. This dichotomy posited black humanity against black inhumanity or subhumanity. Elliott argued that the *Slaughter-House* decision was instructive, because it outlined the necessary conditions for limiting the civil rights of citizens. Governments, state or federal, could restrict someone's liberties only when those liberties threatened the public welfare. For example, the *Slaughter-House* case would be applicable to desegregation, according to Elliott, if the Democrats were willing to classify African Americans as "unwholesome" or analogous to "large and offensive collections of animals." Louisiana rightfully had controlled the butchering of livestock to protect the public's health. Elliott inferred, then, that his opponents had two choices. They could argue openly that African Americans were less than fully human and, therefore, a threat to the public. He challenged: "Does the gentleman from Kentucky [Durham] say that my good is promoted when I am excluded from the public inn? Is the health or safety of the community promoted? Doubtless his prejudice is gratified. Doubtless his democratic instincts are pleased; but will he or his able coadjutor [Stephens] say that such exclusion is a lawful exercise of the police power of the state, or that it is not a denial to me of the equal protection of the laws?"[84] If, however, Elliot's opponents were unwilling to take this position openly, then they should honestly admit that blacks were human and that the bill was constitutional.[85]

At one level, Elliott's arguments were a creative appropriation of the *Slaughter-House* decision. At a second level, his text confronted the audience with the implications of his opponent's temporal scheme. If America's constitutional system really was unchanged by Reconstruction's amendments, as the Democrats claimed, then Elliott asked whether African Americans were still three-fifths human. Unlike Stephens, Elliott interpreted the Constitution's origins as a tragic rather than a triumphant event. The founders had made a grave mistake by affirming that those of color were not fully human. This "short-sighted policy" led, he said, to "the cancer of slavery" and the war for its removal.[86] Reversing Stephens's historical narrative, Elliott argued that Congress faced a clear choice. It could return to the constitutional principles of the antebellum, in which case it would reinstate the failed framework of the past, or it could respect the new principles established by Reconstruction's amendments, in which case the mistakes of the founders would be redeemed. His black colleague, Joseph Rainey, explained it this way: Article 4, section 2 of the Constitution—"The citizens of each State shall be entitled to all privileges and immunities of citizens in the several States"—was now applicable to blacks. "It must be remembered that we are not dealing with the past, but with the immediate present and for the future," Rainey said.[87] The nation's future as well as its political soul was at stake.

What is especially remarkable about the black humanity-black inhumanity dichotomy that Elliott articulated was that it made the issue of federalism inconsequential. The logic of Elliott's text suggested that it did not matter whether civil rights were derived from state or national citizenship. Elliott took the conservative position that the states could continue to administer all fundamental rights so long as everyone received equal treatment and protection under the law. He said, "All discrimination is forbidden; and while the rights of citizens of a State as such are not defined or conferred by the Constitution of the United States, yet all discrimination, all denial of equality before the law, all denial of the equal protection of the laws, whether State or national laws is forbidden."[88] The logic of his discourse meant that the Fourteenth Amendment established black citizenship, period. The location of this citizenship did not matter so long as it maintained the race's complete humanity and its right to equal protection and administration of the law. A second black congressman, John Lynch, agreed with Elliott's position. Lynch argued: "Any State can, without violating the fourteenth or fifteenth amendments and the provisions of this bill, prohibit any one from voting, holding office, or serving on juries in their respective States, who cannot read and write, or who does not own a certain amount of property, or who shall not have resided in the State for a certain number of months, days, or years. The only thing these amendments prevents them from doing in this respect is making the color of a person or the race with which any person may be identified a ground of disqualification from the enjoyment of any of these privileges."[89] The Fourteenth Amendment was not, according to these black Republicans, a repudiation of state authority, but it most certainly was a restriction of state power where it concerned issues of race and the history of slavery.

Revisiting Originalism and Constitutional Intent

Our contemporary dispute over whether Reconstruction's members of Congress intended a constitutional revolution obscures two deeper issues that are not tied to the minds or intent of those statesmen. First, the political conflict between those who supported desegregation and those who opposed it helps to explain the egalitarian rhetoric of some civil rights proponents. Clearly the Republican idealists were motivated by their principles, but for the regular Republicans who were less certain about the bill's wisdom, the continued resistance of the Southern conservatives helped to justify the measure's passage. As this chapter has illustrated, Reconstruction's equality politics evolved in direct correlation to the South's resistance. The black codes in 1866, the vetoes of President Johnson, the initial rejection of the Fourteenth Amendment, the violence of the Ku Klux Klan, and, finally, the stunning victory of the Democrats in the 1874 election moved the Republicans toward stronger and stronger policies. The Fifteenth Amendment is one example. A majority in Congress was opposed to black suffrage in 1866, yet the Republicans needed black voters in 1867 and 1868 to create new Southern governments that excluded Confederate leaders. In 1869 the Fifteenth Amendment was passed not only because of Republican principles but also because of the need to protect black suffrage from judicial review. One need not interpret the Republicans' evolution as solely partisan or vengeful; instead, Southern resistance was a stimulus to the party's general commitment to black civil rights. The policies of that era became increasingly radical because it seemed as though nothing else could secure even a limited approach to equality.

Second, the ideological principles of Reconstruction's amendments sustained their own trajectory, regardless of the framers' motivations. Even if it were possible to prove that the Fourteenth Amendment was never intended to affirm a complete racial equality or to make segregation unconstitutional, it would not end the discussion. The history of Jefferson's Declaration teaches that statements of principle, especially statements that promise legitimacy and authority to those who have none, cannot be contained by the original intent of their framers. Once rhetoric enters the public sphere it takes on a life of its own. Constitutional declarations always become a discursive resource for those who would interpret their meaning for progressive ends. Susan B. Anthony's use of the Fourteenth Amendment to argue for women's suffrage in 1872 and 1873 is a case in point.[90] This debate provides another example. For the advocates of desegregation, Reconstruction's amendments were a key resource that they could use to justify their political judgment.

The Constitution is one of the most important resources for political judgments. It is the ultimate repository for jurisprudence, and it acts as the sacred text for America's political culture. How one proceeds to interpret it is a significant epistemological issue. Politicians offer divergent interpretations of its meaning, because its rhetorical nature—as a strategic compromise that utilizes sometimes ambiguous language—makes multiple interpretations possible. Furthermore, the act of interpretation is significant not only because it provides evidence for political judgments, but also because the very structure of such knowledge establishes systems of power. Knowledge has a direct relationship to power, and in the case of the Constitution this is particularly evident, because the meaning of the Constitution has a profound effect on what counts as a reasonable argument in any given political culture.[91] For example, the political rhetoric of the antebellum period helped to sanction slavery as a constitutionally protected institution. Antislavery politicians such as Abraham Lincoln argued that they had no right to interfere with slavery in the Southern states. Legislation such as the Wilmot-Proviso inhibited slavery's growth in the territories, but the prevailing interpretations of the Constitution gave Congress no authority to effect slavery in the South. Of course, the votes of Southern Whigs and Democrats ensured that the federal government had no authority over slavery, but men such as John C. Calhoun also limited the government's role by sustaining the constitutional doctrine of federalism in their rhetoric.

In 1874 and 1875 moderate Democrats fought desegregation by adopting an interpretive stance that was both conservative and traditional. Their hermeneutic emphasized continuity, limited national government, and it literally interpreted the Constitution's "real meaning." Moderate Democrats and conservative Republicans portrayed themselves as the caretakers of the founder's promises. America's experiment in government would only succeed, they argued, if the country maintained the past's interpretive understandings. Their rhetoric implied that slavery could be removed as a consideration in constitutional hermeneutics without altering the political and legal cultures that had brought the nation to that point. According to Stephens, "in substance it amounts to this, that these amendments . . . do not change the nature and character of the Government."[92] The Constitution was the same, and the nation's political culture need not change. For them, the continuation of American federalism preserved the traditional systems of power *and* the separate and distinct places of the federal and state governments. In short, desegregation's critics found the rhetoric of place within the Constitution. Democrats argued that federal and state governments had distinct and unique roles with respect to public policy.

This position conflicted with the implications of the Republicans' constitutional discourse. They did not expressly herald a consolidation of power; nevertheless, their hermeneutic facilitated such a shift. Desegregation's proponents contended that the Civil War and Reconstruction had transformed the Constitution. In response to Stephens, Elliott declared, "equality before the law is now the broad, universal, glorious rule and mandate of the Republic."[93] For the Republicans, then, proper interpretation involved a broad perspective. "The constitution," concluded Elliott, "ought always to be construed in favor of human rights."[94] The larger implications of the Republicans' position were twofold. First, it contradicted the Democrats' methodology. No longer a simple matter of searching through the Constitution's literal words, correct interpretation involved a broader investigation of society and abstract ideals. A limited interpretation of the text was insufficient because that orientation could not account for the document's principles or the government's duty to protect those principles. Second, the Republicans' rhetoric legitimized a shift that favored the federal government over the states. If Congress had the constitutional authority to protect every citizen in all of his civil rights, the power of the federal government would increase tremendously. While in the short run, the states would recapture some of their former glory, those who argued for desegregation did foreshadow a transformation that would lead to a national authority that superseded state control. The struggle over states' rights would continue, of course. It continues to this day. Yet the transfer from state to federal authority had begun and would continue on several fronts, even while race relations remained a state concern.

Conclusion

Thurgood Marshall, in a 1987 speech reproduced by the *Harvard Law Review,* declared that the government devised by the Constitution's framers was "defective from the start." It had led to several amendments and a Civil War. He stated: "While the Union survived the civil war, the Constitution did not. In its place arose a new, more promising basis for justice and equality, the fourteenth amendment, ensuring protection of the life, liberty, and property of all persons against deprivations without due process, and guaranteeing equal protection of the laws. And yet almost another century would pass before any significant recognition was obtained of the rights of black Americans to share equally even in such basic opportunities as education, housing, and employment, and to have their votes counted, and counted equally."[95] Marshall's comments reflect our contemporary interpretation of the Fourteenth Amendment, but, more important, they reveal how the historical context of any particular scholar or critic influences his or her interpretation of the Constitution. Today we see Reconstruction's amendments as a dividing line, and although legal scholars continue to argue over the validity of that perspective, the general public understands the Fourteenth Amendment in a manner that reflects the arguments of Robert Elliott, Benjamin Butler, and William Lawrence. Regardless of the original intent behind that period's amendments, the Republicans' rhetoric articulated the type of jurisprudence that Thurgood Marshall and the NAACP helped to bring about. The vision of Reconstruction as the dawning of a new age is revealed in Marshall's eloquent comments. According to the arguments of desegregation advocates, Reconstruction's politics of equality guaranteed that the words "We the People" encompassed all Americans.

Unfortunately, the constitutional interpretations of desegregation's critics were not the norms adopted by the nineteenth-century Supreme Court. On 15 October 1883 the Supreme Court decided that the 1875 Civil Rights Act was unconstitutional.[96] It concluded that the denial of equal accommodations in inns, public conveyances, and places of public amusement were not badges of slavery; therefore, the Thirteenth Amendment did not authorize the legislation. Furthermore, the court argued that the Fourteenth Amendment existed only as a prohibition against state activity. Justice Joseph Bradley, writing the majority opinion, explained: "Individual invasion of individual rights is not the subject-matter of the amendment. . . . It nullifies and makes void all State legislation, and State action of every kind, which impairs the privileges and immunities of citizens of the United States. . . . It does not invest Congress with power to legislate upon subjects which are within the domain of State legislation; but to provide modes of relief against State legislation, or State action, of the kind referred to. It does not authorize Congress to create a code of municipal law for the regulation of private rights; but to provide modes of redress against the operation of State laws."[97]

In short, the Fourteenth Amendment provided Congress with the power to take corrective action against specific state statutes, but it did not give Congress the right to act preemptively, establishing the rights of African Americans.

Bradley's opinion had a subtle but sure effect on the system of American federalism and the issue of segregation. The *Civil Rights Cases* did not legitimize segregation, per se. As McConnell notes, the decision only stipulated that Congress lacked "the power to protect against discrimination at the hands of private parties *if the laws of the state provide equal protection for all persons without regard to race*" (emphasis his). Put differently, the court argued that Congress did not have the authority to interfere with the laws of every state but only with those states that *refused* to protect black rights.[98] Nevertheless, by attributing only "corrective" powers to Congress, Bradley placed a significant burden on the federal government to demonstrate that its interference was necessary. The decision affirmed every state's right to determine and legislate the civil rights of its citizens. In a sense, the Supreme Court had adopted Stephens's moderate position. With *The Civil Rights Cases,* the court upheld states' rights without really discussing what constituted "equal protection," but in *Plessy v. Ferguson* (1896), the court corrected its oversight. Separate but equal accommodations were a sufficient implementation of equality before the law.

7

The Triumph of Place over Equality

Emancipations are deceptive, even paradoxical phenomena. In many western cultures, the emancipation of a slave population is a defining moment in the evolution of that society. Historical narratives characterize it as a moment when freedom triumphed over greed and avarice. Through rituals of remembrance, societies elevate the "emancipation moment" to an iconic status, and in public memory it is transformed into proof that a culture was willing to exorcise a great evil and seek redemption. Unfortunately, the facts of emancipations are often quite different; rarely do they eliminate the systems of domination that characterized the past.[1] Emancipations are better understood as a point of disruption, a moment that opens the door to the possibly of freedom *and* the likelihood of massive resistance. Whether and how a society changes depends on what follows from the controversy emancipation creates. The participants of the 1874-1875 debate over civil rights were aware of this paradox; they explicitly argued that a decision either for or against desegregation would have consequences beyond the bill itself. This chapter interprets the debate as a larger struggle to control the extent of America's emancipation. Although the civil rights measure became a law, the real victory in this controversy belonged to the moderate Democrats who refined the notion of place into a new discourse that sustained the conservatives' regional power.

The Reconstruction of America's Political Culture

In 1962 Lucian Pye argued that political judgments arise out of the beliefs, values, and attitudes of a particular political culture.[2] Today, after more than three decades of study, the idea of a political culture is multifaceted. Influenced by anthropological theories as well as the quantitative methods of political science, studies of political culture enact various methodologies—the empirical analysis of voting records and public opinion, the comparative study of countries, and the study of political communication, to name a few.[3] This book constitutes yet another study in the relationship between politics and culture. It has operated from the assumption that the norms and beliefs of political cultures exist within a linguistic context that governs communicative action and legislative judgment; moreover, political cultures are determined by a system of symbols and meanings, shared values, ideologies, and performative conventions specific to a community and temporal location. Agents, both within and without the official political system, usually take the norms of their culture for granted; nevertheless, these norms are always present, and they constrain policy decisions. Who gets to talk, what counts as reasonable proof, what discursive behavior is decorous, and how one defines the relevant issues uncover a great deal about a culture and its modes of political judgment.[4] Fortunately for the evolution of societies, political cultures are not permanent.

In moments of controversy, political cultures may evolve in drastic ways. Every generation involves itself in the task of reproducing language and assimilating meaning into "the linguistically defined and animated social constitution of human relationships."[5] Yet revolutions in technology, incommensurate ideologies, economic hardship, war, and disaster may shift the discursive norms of a society. When a public debate arises about the rules of rational discussion and policy formation, political cultures undergo a transformation.[6] Such moments are revealing for what is at issue in those times and places, and they are generative of new rhetorics that provide a vision that departs from the past. There seems to be little doubt that the politics of the Reconstruction era constituted just such a controversy. From 1863 to 1875 the politics of equality seemed to transform the halls of Congress. This analysis is instructive, however, because it reveals that innovative rhetoric need not be politically, culturally, or socially progressive. In the words of Thomas Wentworth Higginson, "Revolutions may go backward."[7] The Reconstruction era did reshape the political and legal structures of the United States, but the egalitarian vision of its politics did not last. Whereas the Republican idealists quickly slipped from the national stage, first after the fall elections of 1874 and then again in 1877, the moderate Democrats were more successful.

The most innovative discourse of this controversy arose not to challenge the assumptions of the mid-nineteenth century but to sustain them. Historians and rhetorical scholars have noted the rhetorical transformation that certain Democrats, especially at the national level, underwent. The "paternalistic" rhetoric noted by Celeste Condit and John Lucaites, the "accommodation" arguments identified by Cal Logue, and the "New South" rhetoric discussed by Waldo Braden all reflected the same rhetorical form based on a revised ideology of place.[8] The conciliatory remarks of Lucius Lamar at Sumner's death reached their perfection in Henry Grady's "New South,"[9] but Alexander Stephens and the Southern conservatives who opposed desegregation offered one of the first complete explorations of a rhetorical form that combined the antebellum era's notion of place with the language of equality.

The modified rhetoric of place that came out of this debate sustained several argumentative claims. First, it affirmed that physical racial differences signified deeper intellectual and spiritual differences that kept the races forever separate. These differences were established by God and nature, and they constituted a social order in which each person, as well as each race, occupied a unique position. Humans might choose to ignore the order, but they could not change it. Furthermore, each person's location implied specific duties, and each role entailed a code of conduct. Everyone, African and European Americans alike, was subject to this order and the implications of its class hierarchy. Some, like the landowners and merchants of the South, were intended to be the "heads" of society. This prestige came with responsibility. As August Merrimon explained, the freedmen and women need "help from the white man in the South; they need his strong arm; they need the benefit of its advice and intelligence; they need his protecting guardianship in addition to the protection of constitutions and laws."[10] While Merrimon was meant to be a leader, others, African Americans in particular, were destined to be laborers.

Second, the rhetoric of place affirmed that even though different roles existed for each race and person, that fact *did not* nullify the general idea of equality. Recall Stephens's comment that while he believed in the

Declaration of Independence, he did not believe in the equality of the races. Equality, argued the moderate Democrats, was a complex and varied notion. Just as there were different forms of equality—political, legal, and social—it was possible to apportion civil rights in different ways, all without undermining the Declaration. More precisely, it was necessary to distinguish a person's rights on the basis of her or his place. Equality was no longer a binary, either-or proposition. The rhetoric of place established that it came in various shades and colors.

Third, prudent action, especially where it related to race, was the direct result of respecting the dictates of place. Each person had a moral duty to understand his or her unique place and how the location of that place related to others. This maxim applied to governmental authorities as well as individuals. So long as a person, administration, or organization followed the norms of conduct that pertained to his, her, or its place, racial and social harmony continued. But when individuals or groups ignored their place or attempted to redefine it, they violated the natural order, making "harmony" impossible. The Republicans had committed this particular sin, and Representative Robert Vance admonished them, "Let the people of the South alone, and this thing will adjust itself. It will come out all right . . . but if you undertake to coerce society before it is ready, you will damage the colored man in all his interests, and at the same time do damage to the white race."[11]

To appreciate the practical consequence of this discourse, one need only consider an 1879 debate sponsored by the *North American Review.* Among the speakers that attended the symposium were James Blaine, James Garfield, Wendell Phillips, and Lucius Q. C. Lamar. Lamar was an important figure among the Southern conservatives and one of the architects of the modified rhetoric of place. When asked whether Southern conservatives had used force to limit black suffrage and reestablish white control of Southern politics, Lamar answered quickly, no. Then, in a revealing moment, he backed away from his denials to ask a hypothetical question: Would it have been wrong if whites had manipulated Southern politics to regain control of the South? He answered his own question in the negative. Reconstruction's constitutional amendments did not prohibit white domination; rather, they were only meant as a shield to protect a free *laboring class.* Southern whites had a divine responsibility to lead society, he said, and it made no sense to interpret the Constitution as a restriction of their duties. He concluded, "is free labor anywhere on earth more firmly established, more fully developed, or more absolute in its demands . . .

than in the South? In all respects, negro freedom and negro equality before the law, security of person and property, are ample and complete."[12]

Lamar's comments are revealing, because they illustrate how the post-Reconstruction view of place constrained black civil rights. Recall that the moderate Democrats in Congress had used the notion of place to refine the Republican notion of limited absolute equality. According to them, a person's rights were determined by the needs of her or his place. Whites possessed those rights that were necessary to lead society. African Americans, in Lamar's terminology, were a "prosperous laboring population," an extensive resource for industry and agriculture; therefore, they were entitled to a different set of rights. According to Lamar, the Constitution guaranteed them only those rights that were necessary to fulfill their role as an economic resource. Lamar concluded that since blacks possessed their economic freedom, it logically followed that they possessed their constitutional rights.[13] The genius of the modified rhetoric of place was that it effectively co-opted the politics of equality articulated by desegregation's proponents.

Describing the conclusion of the civil rights congressional debate, William Gillette quotes a Baltimore correspondent: "whites of both parties simply refused to be taken in by the 'tinsel tattle' of Radical orators, by appeals to the Declaration of Independence, and all that muck-mammocky rot about liberty and equality and 'the philosophy of first principles'; in which the Senators indulged."[14] The implications of this observation are significant. If the reporter's feelings are applied to the historical consequences of the 1875 Civil Rights Act, then somehow the failures of this policy relate to the rhetorical effectiveness of its advocates. Bertram Wyatt-Brown and Gillette concur, explaining that despite the bill's passage, the policy failed because the act was compromised by the Republicans' latent hypocrisy. Though the idealists and a few moderate Republicans spoke of black equality, they did not themselves believe it; therefore, they removed the clause to desegregate public schools, and they failed to provide a sufficient enforcement mechanism to ensure desegregation's success.[15] W. R. Brock offers a slightly more charitable explanation when he explains the bill's failure by positing that the radicals' ideology was too abstract and general to sustain a broad coalition among moderate and conservative Republicans.[16]

Whether the Republicans "believed" in the politics of equality is irrelevant. The history of Reconstruction demonstrates that they were motivated by high ideals and low politics, by principle and expediency. The bigger issue is that regardless of their motives, the Republicans' rhetoric conflicted with the material circumstances of late Reconstruction. Historians tend to agree that by 1875 the general public had tired of political activism. When the Democrats won the fall elections of 1874 by a landslide, constituents sent a clear message that desegregation was unwelcome. A weary Northern populace still wanted protection for the former slaves, but they also preferred to trust existing legal statutes rather than engage in a protracted effort to change Southern attitudes from Washington, D.C.[17] Southern and Democratic newspapers always had been hostile to desegregation, but support for the Civil Rights Bill began to wane in Republican papers such as the *New York Times* and the *Chicago Tribune* even before the bill became law. In 1875, for example, the *Times* published only the comments of senators who opposed the bill. Editorials and news items that appeared in the paper suggested that the bill, if enacted, would cause more trouble than good for blacks and the Republican Party. David Domke argues that the press's framing of language, news, and opinion reveals a diminishing support for black civil rights between 1865 and 1869. Although there were exceptions, mainstream newspapers quickly abandoned the idea of aggressive federal civil rights enforcement.[18] Furthermore, the depression of 1873 and 1874 shifted the country's attention from continued violence against people of color to the problems of economic survival.[19]

Wary of a prolonged public dialogue about race, rights, and equality and diverted by interests closer to home, most Americans wanted stability rather than additional change. The Republicans' rhetoric promised agitation, not stability; it demanded a social and cultural transformation. As Frederick Douglass argued in 1883, the act's symbolic meaning demanded that the citizens of every region reevaluate their own prejudices.[20] The nation was neither prepared for nor interested in such extended critical reflection. When the Civil Rights Act became law, some proprietors accepted the change, but a majority in the North and the South resisted it. Individual patrons avoided public places where African Americans had entered. Business owners closed or converted to private rather than public institutions. Theater owners still refused to allow entry, and hotels employed "no vacancy" signs to avoid confrontations. There seemed to be little relationship between the progressive discourse of those who favored desegregation and the public's attitudes and feelings. Still, the lack of cohesion between Republican idealism and public sentiment does not explain fully the implications and causes of the bill's defeat. There is a second half to this equation.[21]

The Republicans' liberal discourse was not the only option; a more responsive and attractive rhetoric existed. Indeed, the modified rhetoric of place seemed more attuned to the external circumstances of late Reconstruction. Those members of Congress who imitated Alexander Stephens combined convention and divergence to address several social exigencies. Two parts conservatism and one part innovation, their constitutional arguments provided stability and a means for the North to extract itself from the difficulties of protecting black rights. The modified rhetoric of place was also significant, because it disavowed the slavery past and enacted a limited vision of equality politics. When moderate Democrats argued that African Americans deserved legal and political equality, they created a space for themselves within the postbellum context. In fact, they seemed to have adopted the very perspective articulated by Lincoln in 1858 and by the Republicans in 1865. This change, from a Northern perspective, amounted to a confession of sin. Such rhetoric eroded the barriers of distrust and fear, and it gave the nation an excuse to accept the moderates' reassurances. Furthermore, because a number of the Democrats refused to embrace this accommodationist stance, the modified rhetoric of place gained additional legitimacy. The voices of John T. Harris, William Robbins, and John Brown represented the unrepentant South. In the immediate context of the congressional debate, the tone and style of the fire-eaters galvanized Republican support for civil rights. On the larger public stage, however, the fire-eaters' claims made the moderate Democrats seem extremely reasonable. Only the moderate Democrats in this debate offered a discourse that promised stability rather than upheaval. In the post-Reconstruction era, a new generation of Republican leaders found this discourse compelling.

One prominent Republican began adopting the rhetoric of place as early as 1877. Touring the South that fall, the new president, Rutherford B. Hayes, proclaimed that most Southern whites had "no desire to invade the rights of the colored people." To a biracial gathering in Atlanta, Hayes stated:

> What troubles our people at the North, what has troubled them, was that they feared that these colored people, who had been made freemen by the war, would not be safe in their rights and interests in the South unless it was by the interference of the general Government. Many good people had that idea. I had given that matter some consideration, and now, my colored friends, who have thought, or who have been told, that I was turning my back upon the men whom I fought for, now, listen! After thinking over it, I believed that your rights and interests would be safer if this great mass of

> intelligent white men were let alone by the general Government. [Immense enthusiasm and cheering for several minutes.] And now, my colored friends, let me say another thing. We have been trying it for these six months, and, in my opinion, in no six months since the war have there been so few outrages and invasions of your rights, nor you so secure in your rights, persons, and homes, as in the last six months.[22]

Hayes's intentions were honest; he likely believed that his "let alone" policy would reconcile the races and the nation.[23] Southern conservatives, however, were only too pleased to hear their own arguments coming from a Republican president. Throughout the civil rights debate, they had argued that desegregation would lead to unnecessary hostility.

In 1877 President Hayes seemed to agree, and by 1880 the Republican president had embraced the ideal of place completely. On 20 May he gave a speech at the anniversary of the Hampton Institute, where he made the following pronouncement: "We would not undertake to violate the laws of nature, we do not wish to change the purpose of God in making these differences of nature. We are willing to have these elements of our population separate as the fingers are, but we require to see them united for every good work, for national defense, one, as the hand. And that good work is Hampton doing."[24] The hand metaphor that Hayes articulated became famous fifteen years later when Booker T. Washington used it as a central theme in his famous "Atlanta Exposition Address." Washington was working at Hampton when the president spoke, and it seems likely that he would have attended the address.[25] The metaphor expressed by both men reflects the rhetoric of place extremely well. Just as each finger is separate, each "element of [the] population" is discrete. No two fingers have the same length, and each serves a distinctive purpose. Furthermore, the passage suggests that divine law, not human institutions, created these differences. Individual citizens, regardless of race, could cooperate together for "every good work," but that association did not undermine distinctions of person or position. In short, each citizen had his or her place, and it was government's responsibility to respect and protect the natural order.

Booker T. Washington's role during the post-Reconstruction era raises an important issue when considering the triumph of place. Washington's accommodationist stance provided the Tuskegee Institute with resources and autonomy, but Southern conservatives and Northern politicians also used Washington as proof that African Americans would embrace a subservient place. Presidents Cleveland, McKinley, and Roosevelt maintained close ties to Washington, while they ignored other leaders in the black community who continued to agitate for equal rights. When McKinley traveled through the South in December of 1898, he went to Tuskegee to lavish praise on Washington. He stated, "Patience, moderation, self-control, knowledge, character will surely win you victories and realize the best aspirations of your people. An evidence of the soundness of the purposes of this institution is that those in charge of its management evidently do not believe in attempting the unattainable, and their instruction in self-reliance and practical industry is most valuable."[26] By "attempting the unattainable," McKinley was referring to the policies of W. E. B. Du Bois, George A. Towns, William Monroe Trotter, and John Hope, who declared: "I regard it as cowardly and dishonest for any of our colored men to tell white people that we are not struggling for equality. . . . If we cannot do what other free men do, then we are not free. Yes, my friends, I want equality. Nothing less. . . . If equality, political, economic and social, is the boon of other men in this great country of ours, of *ours,* then equality, political, economic and social, is what we demand.[27]

In all fairness, it is crucial to note that the idea of separation was an important dimension of black thought throughout the nineteenth century. Early black nationalists, such as Martin Delany and Bishop Henry Turner, argued that people of color would never receive justice in America; emigration to Africa or Haiti was preferable to second-class status in the United States.[28] African Americans that rejected emigration often still embraced separation. Many former slaves left the white churches of the South to build their own congregations. Rather than continue the labor practices of slavery, blacks moved out of the slave quarters, away from the master's house, and into the field where they farmed small plots of land, sharing the profits with the landowner and merchant. This move was both practical and symbolic. Distance ensured some autonomy in daily life, but it was also an important statement of independence. Likewise, African Americans in the South often embraced segregated schools. People of color accepted these institutions because they believed that there was no other option, but a few blacks argued that separate institutions provided more autonomy and a better environment for the race's development.[29]

It would be a mistake to equate the voluntary separation of blacks from whites with the rhetoric of place. Place implied more than just separation. One might speak abstractly of political or legal equality, but place insisted that these were ideals to be defined by a white elite. Moderate Democrats argued that the "reality" of race was difference, and that difference must be recognized in law and local custom. Furthermore, as place was enacted as a norm for political judgment, it reinforced the ideology of white supremacy. This was not the kind of separation desired by most African Americans. John Lynch, the black representative from Mississippi, provides an insightful look at the difference between separation and place. He said:

> The colored people in asking the passage of this bill just as it passed the Senate do not thereby admit that their children can be better educated in white than in colored schools; nor that white teachers because they are white are better qualified to teach than colored ones. But they recognize the fact that the distinction when made and tolerated by law is an unjust and odious proscription; that you make their color a ground of object, and consequently a crime. That is what we most earnestly protest against. Let us confer upon all citizens, then, the rights to which they are entitled under the Constitution; and then if they choose to have their own children educated in separate schools, as they do in my own State, then both races will be satisfied, because they will know that the separation is their own voluntary act and not legislative compulsion.[30]

Lynch saw a difference between black separation and the practice of accommodation. The politics of equality demanded that both races have the opportunity of access. Separation under that condition was not an accommodation but an exercise of personal autonomy.

Much of Booker T. Washington's philosophy was articulated by others in the nineteenth century, but it was Washington who failed to recognize that his vision for the black community was being co-opted by those who used the rhetoric of place to affirm black inferiority as well as separation. C. Vann Woodward concludes that "in proposing the virtual retirement of the mass of Negroes from the political life of the South and in stressing the humble and menial role that the race was to play, [Washington] would seem unwittingly to have smoothed the path to proscription."[31] Yet perhaps it was not Washington's program per se, but the political culture of the post-Reconstruction era that made the Tuskegee approach so debilitating. Washington's program, which was both racially conservative and accommodating, had been negotiated with the Southern conservatives who were of an older elite class of Southern agrarians. In the final decade of the nineteenth century, new Southerners were rising to power based on the industrial revolution and an explicit affirmation of white supremacy. These Southerners, the radicals, argued that freedom had caused people of color to regress into barbarism. White supremacy was the natural order, they argued, and even minor expressions of black autonomy needed to be controlled. The radicals found a receptive audience among white urban laborers who long had seen people of color as a potential threat. In this changing political and economic environment, Washington's accommodations only encouraged a legal and extralegal campaign to put blacks in the inferior places that they deserved.[32]

The Triumph of the Rhetoric of Place

Although the rhetoric of place gained momentum after the Compromise of 1877, it is not true that the politics of equality disappeared immediately or completely. Equality continued to be an important constraint on political judgment at the state level. During the 1870s almost every state in the Northeast desegregated its public schools, and a number of Midwestern states followed during the 1880s. After the Supreme Court overturned the 1875 Civil Rights Act, eighteen Northern, Midwestern, and Western states passed desegregation measures.[33] The changes begun during the Reconstruction era were not confined to the North. The first Democratic president in twenty-four years, Grover Cleveland, appointed leading black Democrats to six federal offices. Southern states continued to send African Americans to Congress through 1901; from 1873 to 1901 every Congress except the Fiftieth contained a black representative or senator. Robert Smalls, John M. Langston, James O'Hara, and George Henry White were among a group of black politicians who refused to be intimidated when the federal troops withdrew from the South in 1877. James O'Hara of North Carolina is a good example of this group. He served first in state politics as the chairman of the Halifax Board of Commissioners. He had personally desegregated the main saloon of a local steamer ship immediately after the 1875 Civil Rights Act was passed. Due to his political activism, local newspapers characterized him as a "living, foul-mouthed libel on honor, decency and truth," who "inflamed the worst passions" of his race. In 1878 he ran for Congress but lost because of election fraud. He ran again, winning in 1882 and serving from 1883 to 1887. His most prominent moment came when he introduced a constitutional amendment to secure equal access to all public accommodations.[34]

The egalitarian rhetoric of the Reconstruction era did not vanish, either. In the same speech where Hayes described his "let alone" policy, he also declared, "I believe, further, that it is the duty of the Government to regard alike and equally the rights and interests of all classes of citizens. [Cheers.] That covers the whole matter. That wipes out in the future in our politics the section line forever. [Cheers.] Let us wipe out in our politics the color line forever. [Cheers.]"[35] As late as 1890 President Benjamin Harrison affirmed the need to protect black civil rights and equal participation. In his first annual message, he wrote:

> The colored people did not intrude themselves on us. They were brought here in chains and held in communities, where they are now chiefly found, by a cruel slave code. . . . If it be said that these [Southern communities] must work out this problem for themselves we have a right to ask whether they are at work upon it. Do they suggest any solution? When and under what conditions is the black man to have a free ballot? When is he in fact to have those full civil rights which have so long been his in law? When is that equality of influence which our form of government was intended to secure the electors to be restored? This generation should courageously face these grave questions, and not leave them as a heritage of woe to the next.[36]

Harrison was even willing to put his words into action. Between 1889 and 1892 he lobbied Congress to pass another civil rights act protecting black voters from violence.

Yet the problem of racial violence during the post-Reconstruction era reveals the ultimate triumph of the rhetoric of place. With the exception of Harrison, the post-Reconstruction presidents acted in accordance with the South's wishes; they were silent about the escalation in violence. Violence was a problem during the Reconstruction era, but in the final decade of the nineteenth century, Williamson writes that "lynching became a special Southern occurrence in which black men were the special victims." This violence was initiated by the Southern radicals who argued that African Americans were beasts that preyed on the purity of white women. White Southerners accepted even the rumor of an assault, and in an explosion of violence that peaked in 1892, they hunted down the black men that seemed to represent their darkest fears. From 1889 to 1899 an average of one person was lynched every other day; 88 percent of these victims were African Americans. Even as incidents of lynching declined, urban race riots increased, with major outbreaks in 1898, 1900, and 1905. With the exception of Harrison, the presidents said little and did even less in response to this terror. President Cleveland made no public statements about lynching during his second term in office (1893–1897). President McKinley offered a single brief statement in his inaugural address. "Lynchings," he said, "must not be tolerated in a great and civilized country like the United States."[37]

In December of 1889 there was some hope that Congress might involve itself. Henry Cabot Lodge drafted a bill to protect black voting rights. The measure gave federal circuit court judges supervision of all congressional races, and since most of these judges were Republican, both parties assumed that Lodge's measure would be used to protect black voters. The House debate over the bill was acrimonious; the extreme language used by both sides had not been heard since the debate over the 1875 Civil Rights Act. Opponents decried the "Force Bill," proclaiming that it constituted a return to the tragic period of Reconstruction. Over the Democrats' objections, on 2 July 1890 the House passed the bill by a narrow margin, one hundred fifty-five to one hundred forty-nine. It never went further. A filibuster prevented its consideration in the Senate. Republicans were more worried about the Sherman Antitrust Act and the Sherman Silver Purchase Act. Although they promised to get to the Civil Rights Bill, they never did. The process of retreat that began with the 1877 Compromise culminated in the Republicans' failure to pass the Federal Elections Bill. Congress would not consider another civil rights measure until the 1930s.[38]

In retrospect, one begins to wonder whether the decline and failure of the Reconstruction era resulted, in part, from the political discourse of its final years. The economic depression of 1874, the redemption of the Southern states, and the Grant administration's ineptitude, political corruption, and racial prejudice all contributed to Reconstruction's demise, but the attractiveness of the "place" rhetoric also hastened this trend. Put simply, Benjamin Butler and the other Republican idealists failed to find a viable political rhetoric that could encompass the entire nation. The moderate Democrats succeeded where the Republicans failed. Less than a month after the Supreme Court struck down the 1875 Civil Rights Act, the *Chicago Tribune* ran an article entitled "Civil v. Social Rights." The *Tribune* had been one of the most consistent supporters of desegregation from 1871 to 1875, but in 1883 the paper had changed its position. According to the *Tribune*, "The right to occupy a berth on a sleeping car, to sit at a hotel table, or to secure a place at a theatrical performance is of a social character, because it involves the personal comfort or preference of those occupying adjoining seats or berths." These kinds of relations "will always be regulated by *unwritten laws outside of statutes*" (italics added).[39] These were precisely the arguments advanced by Alexander Stephens and the Southern conservatives in 1874 and 1875. The man who was once the Confederacy's vice president had led a second charge against the forces of equality and freedom; subsequently, much of what the Southern Democrats lost in the war they regained with rhetoric. Not only did the conservatives reestablish regional power and control, but white Republicans in the North adopted many of their assumptions about place and race. Thus the rhetoric of place became the real legacy of the 1870s civil rights debate.

Epilogue

Eric Foner writes, in a 1993 issue of *The Nation*, that America needs a third Reconstruction. According to him, the successes and failures of the Reconstruction era and the Civil Rights Movement (that is, the second Reconstruction) are remarkably similar. Both periods had the same goal: to create an interracial democracy. Unfortunately, both periods were followed by a conservative backlash that led to retrenchment. Today, he argues, separate but equal is still the law of the land.[1] It seems plain that race remains a perplexing problem for America. Exactly one week after the O. J. Simpson verdict, a trial with racial ramifications that has outlived the relevance of its participants, the *New York Times* ran an article entitled, "Blacks look at Simpson in the Context of the Past." The article was remarkable not because it noted how black and white citizens seemed polarized as to whether Simpson actually killed his white wife. The article was striking because those African Americans whom it quoted saw the trial within the wider context of continued racial animosity directed at them. Indeed, one woman was so convinced of overwhelming white hatred that she was fearful of discussing the verdict with her white coworkers. She admitted, "I haven't met one [white] person I can sit down and have a conversation with. . . . When will that be? I don't think I'll ever trust a white person."[2] Why does such distrust exist, and how is it that racism not only persists, but remains a debilitating force that prevents interracial communication?

The history and rhetoric surrounding the Civil Rights Act of 1875 provide some answers. I began this book with an 1883 speech by Frederick Douglass in which he described the fall of Act as "a studied purpose to degrade and stamp out the liberties of a race. It is the old spirit of slavery, and nothing else."[3] The United States has reached its current position through a complex drama in which the "spirit of slavery" has continued to dominate race relations. The demise of the 1875 act was one scene in a broader play that African Americans know well. To use a metaphor popularized by Dr. Martin Luther King Jr., people of color believe that America has a habit of writing bad checks. The promises in the Declaration of Independence were not applied to African Americans, either in the North or the South. The new hope of the Reconstruction era was slowly destroyed by a compromise with Southern whites. A persistent attack on the self-esteem of black women and men has undermined civil rights philosophies in the twentieth century, be they founded on integration or black nationalism. Currently, the race's aspirations are destroyed by an economic and social system that views blacks as a liability to be made over or arrested.

To be sure, race relations in this country are not now, nor have they ever been, this simple. I have argued throughout this text that the history of segregation in the nineteenth century was extremely complex. Nevertheless, the truth or fiction of racism in the United States can never be determined by the factual accuracy of our histories. Rather, it is the structure of our collective memory and public discourse that makes racism a persistent problem. Andrew Hacker writes: "Being 'black' in America bears the mark of slavery. Even after emancipation, citizens who had been slaves still found themselves consigned to a subordinate status. Put most simply, the ideology that had provided the rationale for slavery by no means disappeared. Blacks continued to be seen as an inferior species, not only unsuited for equality but not even meriting a chance to show their worth. Immigrants only hours off the boat, while subjected to scorn, were—and still are—allowed to assert their superiority to black Americans."[4] Where Hacker states, "being 'black' in America bears the mark of slavery," I would argue that being black in America implicates the *rhetoric of place*. It is not the material history of bondage that African Americans feel so much as it is the "spirit" of slavery, represented in a discourse that symbolically sustains a racial caste system. People of color are learned observers when it comes to America's racial policies, and, despite some exceptions, the majority believe that their equality has been undermined by deeply held prejudices that even well-meaning whites fail to appreciate.[5]

Memories of the past and their rhetoric are sometimes conscious but *always* subconscious regulators of African American language and reason. For example, the current campaign against "preferential treatment" typically involves assurances that the critics of affirmative action are not racist and that opportunities will continue for those *individuals* who have the ability. What many conservatives, white and black, fail to appreciate is that the larger community of color understands this rhetoric in relation to the past's failures. It is easy for people of color to believe that the opponents of affirmative action do not want to enforce the Fourteenth Amendment for all citizens but desire, instead, to keep blacks in their place. Segregation and prejudice continue to haunt the minds and the lives of African Americans, because the language used by today's conservatives sounds remarkably similar to the claims of Alexander Stephens and Augustus Merrimon. Arguments about personal responsibility and ability are perfectly reasonable, but a good portion of the black community believes that this discourse is an attempt to depoliticize problems such as crime, poverty, and disparate educational opportunities. Today, African Americans continue to turn a suspicious eye on such arguments, just as blacks did when Reconstruction Democrats declared their kindly feelings toward the black race.

To my mind, the current distrust between many, but not all, African and European Americans points to one of the biggest needs in contemporary rhetorical and historical scholarship. The races have difficulty communicating largely because we are collectively ignorant of the cultural assumptions that guide and inform the deliberative practice of the other race. This project represents one small portion of a historical narrative that informs black consciousness. Unfortunately, it has left many areas uncovered. More research needs to be done on the rhetoric and lives of particular participants. Charles Sumner, James Rapier, Robert Elliott, Alexander Stephens, and John Harris all deserve rhetorical investigations of their own. The purpose of such scholarship is not to document oppression or even black success. Instead, this research is necessary so that we can begin to understand those rhetorical perspectives that currently keep us apart. When we understand how these past rhetorical events influence cultural assumptions and our linguistic contexts, we can begin to grapple with the divergent rationalities that hinder open and honest discussion.

Appendix A

The Civil Rights Act of 1875

Whereas, it is essential to just government we recognize the equality of all men before the law, and hold that it is the duty of government in its dealings with the people to mete out equal and exact justice to all, of whatever nativity, race, color, or persuasion, religious or political; and it being the appropriate object of legislation to enact great fundamental principles into law: Therefore,

Sec. 1. *Be it enacted by the Senate and House of Representatives of the United States of America in Congress assembled,* That all persons within the jurisdiction of the United States shall be entitled to the full and equal enjoyment of the accommodations, advantages, facilities, and privileges of inns, public conveyances on land or water, theatres, and other places of public amusement; subject only to the conditions and limitations established by law, and applicable alike to citizens of every race and color, regardless of any previous condition of servitude.

Sec. 2. That any person who shall violate the foregoing section by denying to any citizens, except for reasons by law applicable to citizens of every race and color, and regardless of any previous condition of servitude, the full enjoyment of any of the accommodations, advantages, facilities, or privileges in said section enumerated, or by aiding or inciting such denial, shall for every such offence forfeit and pay the sum of five hundred dollars to the person aggrieved thereby, to be recovered in an action of debt, with full costs; and shall also, for every such offence, be deemed guilty of a misdemeanor, and, upon conviction thereof, shall be fined not less than five hundred nor more than one thousand dollars, or shall be imprisoned not less than thirty days nor more than one year: *Provided,* That all persons may elect to sue for the penalty aforesaid, or to proceed under their rights at common law and by State statues; and having so elected to proceed in the one mode or the other, their right to proceed in the other jurisdiction shall be barred. But this provision shall not apply to criminal proceedings, either under this act or the criminal law of any State: *And provided further,* That a judgment for the penalty in favor of the party aggrieved, or a judgment upon an indictment, shall be a bar to either prosecution respectively.

Sec. 3. That the district and circuit court of the United States shall have, exclusively of the courts of the several States, cognizance of all crimes and offenses against, and violations of, the provisions of this act; and actions for the penalty given by the preceding section may be prosecuted in the territorial, district, or circuit courts of the United States wherever the defendant may be found, without regard to the other party; and the district attorneys, marshals, and deputy marshals of the United States, and commissioners appointed by the circuit and territorial courts of the United States, with powers of arresting and imprisoning or bailing offenders against the laws of the United States, are hereby specially authorized and required to institute proceedings against every person and imprisoned or bailed, as the case may be, for trial before such court of the United States, or territorial court, as by law has cognizance of the offense, except in respect of the right of action accruing to the person aggrieved; and such district attorneys shall cause such proceedings to be prosecuted to their termination as in other cases: *Provided,* That nothing contained in this section shall be construed to deny or defeat any right of civil action accruing to any person, whether by reason of this act or otherwise; and any district attorney who shall willfully fail to institute and prosecute the proceedings herein required, shall, for every such offense, forfeit and pay the sum of five hundred dollars to the person aggrieved thereby, to be recovered by an action of debt, with full costs, and shall, on conviction thereof, be deemed guilty of a misdemeanor, and be fined not less than one thousand nor more than five thousand dollars: *And provided further,* That a judgment for the penalty in favor of the party aggrieved against any such district attorney, or a judgment upon an indictment against any such district attorney, shall be a bar to either prosecution respectively.

Sec. 4. That no citizen possessing all other qualification which are or may be prescribed by law shall be disqualified for service as grand or petit juror in any court of the United States, or of any State, on account of race, color, or previous condition of servitude; and any officer or other person charged with any duty in the selection or summoning of jurors who shall exclude or fail to summon any citizen for the cause aforesaid shall, on conviction thereof, be deemed guilty of a misdemeanor, and be fined not more than five thousand dollars.

Sec. 5. That all cases arising under the provisions of this act in the courts of the United States shall be reviewable by the Supreme Court of the United States, without regard to the sum in controversy, under the same provisions and regulations as are now provided by law for the review of other causes in said court.

Approved, March 1, 1875.

Notes

Preface

1. Eric Foner, *Reconstruction: America's Unfinished Revolution, 1863–1877* (New York: Harper and Row, 1988).
2. William Archibald Dunning, *Reconstruction, Political and Economic, 1865–1877* (New York: Harper and Brothers, 1907); John William Burgess, *The Civil War and the Constitution, 1859–1865* (New York: C. Scribner's Sons, 1901); Claude G. Bowers, *The Tragic Era: The Revolution after Lincoln* (Cambridge, Mass.: Houghton Mifflin, 1929).
3. Eric L. McKitrick, *Andrew Johnson and Reconstruction* (Chicago: University of Chicago Press, 1960); John Hope Franklin, *Reconstruction: After the Civil War,* 2d ed. (Chicago: University of Chicago Press, 1994); LaWanda Cox and John H. Cox, *Politics, Principle, and Prejudice, 1865–1866: The Dilemma of Reconstruction in America* (New York: Free Press, 1963); James M. McPherson, *The Struggle for Equality* (1964; reprint, Princeton: Princeton University Press, 1992); David Herbert Donald, *The Politics of Reconstruction, 1863–1867* (Baton Rouge, La.: Louisiana State University, 1965).
4. August Meier, "Negroes in the First and Second Reconstructions of the South," *Civil War History* 13 (1967): 114–30; Harold M. Hyman, *A More Perfect Union: The Impact of the Civil War and Reconstruction on the Constitution* (New York: Knopf, 1973); Leon F. Litwack, *Been in the Storm So Long: The Aftermath of Slavery* (New York: Random House, 1979); William Gillette, *Retreat from Reconstruction, 1869–1879* (Baton Rouge, La.: Louisiana State University Press, 1979); Michael Les Benedict, *A Compromise of Principle: Congressional Republicans and Reconstruction, 1863–1869* (New York: Norton, 1974); Eric Foner, "Reconstruction Revisited," *Reviews in American History* 10 (1982): 82–100.
5. The terms "politics of equality" and the "rhetoric of place" are critical interpretive labels that identify two discourse formations and patterns of political judgment. Their definition and relevance to the congressional desegregation debate will become clear in the first and ensuing chapters.

6. See Stephen E. Lucas, "The Schism in Rhetorical Scholarship," in *Landmark Essays on American Public Address,* ed. Martin J. Medhurst (Davis, Calif.: Hermagoras Press, 1993), 139.
7. For theoretical discussions about the relationship between rhetorical criticism and history, see the essays in Kathleen J. Turner, ed., *Doing Rhetorical History: Concepts and Cases* (Tuscaloosa: University of Alabama Press, 1998). See, in particular, Turner's introduction, David Zarefsky's "Four Senses of Rhetorical History," and Bruce E. Gronbeck's "The Rhetorics of the Past." See also Robert Hariman, "Relocating the Art of Public Address," in *Rhetoric and Political Culture in Nineteenth-Century America,* ed. Thomas W. Benson (East Lansing: Michigan State University Press, 1997), 222–48; Bruce E. Gronbeck, "Popular Culture, Media, and Political Communication," in *New Directions in Political Communication,* ed. David L. Swanson and Dan Nimmo (Newbury Park, Calif.: Sage Publications, 1990), 195–96. Philosophers and historians are also familiar with the potential impact of rhetoric. See A. Cook, "Reference and Rhetoric in Historiography," in *Criticism, History, and Intertextuality,* ed. Richard Fleming and Michael Payne (Lewisburg, Pa: Bucknell University Press, 1988), 159–82; Hyden V. White, *Metahistory: The Historical Imagination in Nineteenth-Century Europe* (Baltimore: Johns Hopkins University Press, 1973). Those who are familiar with the history of rhetoric will note a "dramatistic" orientation in this study. Although Kenneth Burke's terminology is not evident, the perspective that he advanced is a considerable influence on this project. See Kenneth Burke, s.v. "Dramatism," in *International Encyclopedia of the Social Sciences,* ed. David L. Sills (New York: Macmillan Co. and Free Press, 1968), 7:445–52.
8. See David Theo Goldberg, *Racist Culture: Philosophy and the Politics of Meaning* (Cambridge, Mass.: Blackwell, 1993); Stephen Jay Gould, *The Mismeasure of Man,* rev. and expanded ed. (New York: Norton, 1996); Henry Louis Gates Jr., ed., *"Race," Writing, and Difference* (Chicago: University of Chicago Press, 1986); Kenan Malik, *The Meaning of Race: Race, History and Culture in Western Society* (Washington Square, N.Y.: New York University Press, 1996); and Anthony Appiah and Amy Gutmann, *Color Conscious: The Political Morality of Race* (Princeton: Princeton University Press, 1996).
9. I. F. Haney López, "The Social Construction of Race," *Harvard Civil Rights-Civil Liberties Law Review* 29 (1994): 27. For additional resources in critical race theory see Derrick Bell, "Racial Realism—After We're Gone: Prudent Speculations on America in a Post-racial Epoch," *St.*

Louis University Law Journal 34 (1990) 393–405; Derrick Bell, *Faces at the Bottom of the Well: The Permanence of Racism* (New York: Basic Books, 1992); Kimberlé Williams Crenshaw, "Race, Reform, and Retrenchment: Transformation and Legitimation in Anti-discrimination Law," *Harvard Law Review* 101 (1988): 1331–87; and Richard Delgado, ed., *Critical Race Theory: The Cutting Edge* (Philadelphia: Temple University Press, 1995).

10. For a discussion about the retrenchment of racism and white privilege after civil rights movements, see Philip A. Klinkner and Rogers M. Smith, *The Unsteady March: The Rise and Decline of Racial Equality in America* (Chicago: University of Chicago Press, 1999). For a general discussion about the continued problem of racism, see Christopher H. Foreman Jr., ed, *The African American Predicament* (Washington, D.C.: Brookings Institution Press, 1999); Andrew Hacker, *Two Nations: Black and White, Separate, Hostile, Unequal* (New York: Ballantine Books, 1992); and Derrick A. Bell, *And We Are Not Saved: The Elusive Quest for Racial Justice* (New York: HarperCollins, 1987).
11. David Dante Troutt, "Behind the Court's Civil Rights Ruling," *New York Times*, 29 April 2001, secs. 3, 4.
12. In *Alexander v. Sandoval* the Supreme Court restricted the scope of the Civil Rights Act of 1964, Title VI, to exclude suits based on the effects of discrimination. The court argued that it would only allow arguments based on intentional discrimination. See *Alexander v. Sandoval*, 532 U.S.—, 149 L Ed. 517, 121 Ct.— (2001).
13. Cornel West, *Race Matters* (New York: Vintage Books, 1994), 6.

Chapter 1

1. See "Reviving Race Issues," *Washington Post*, 23 October 1883, 1.
2. See *Civil Rights Cases*, 109 U.S. 3 (1883).
3. "Civil Rights," *Chicago Tribune*, 16 October 1883, 1; "The Civil Rights Decision," *New York Times*, 16 October 1883, 4; "Civil Rights Bill," *New York Times*, 18 October 1883, 4; "Civil Rights," *Atlanta Constitution*, 16 October 1883, 1; "The *Civil Rights Cases*," *New Orleans Times Picayune*, 16 October 1883, *New Orleans Times Picayune*, 1. See also Ali N. Mohamed, "Attitudes of Northern Papers toward the Egalitarian Laws of Reconstruction," *Newspaper Research Journal* 19 (1998): 52–60.
4. Frederick Douglass, "Speech at Lincoln Hall," 22 October 1883, in *Proceedings of the Civil Rights Mass Meeting* (Washington, D. C.: C. P. Farrell, 1883), 4.

5. Frederick Douglass, "Speech at the Thirty-sixth Anniversary of the American Anti-slavery Society," *National Slavery Standard,* 29 May 1869, 1.
6. For a brief account of this incident see "Editorial Notes," *National Standard,* 1 April 1871, 1.
7. For additional details see the letter to the editor, C. W. Denison, "The Outrage on Mr. Frederick Douglass," *National Standard,* 8 April 1871, 6.
8. Douglass, "Speech at Lincoln Hall," in *Proceedings,* 13.
9. John Hope Franklin and Alfred A. Moss Jr., *From Slavery to Freedom: A History of Negro Americans,* 6th ed. (New York: Knopf, 1988), 136–57; Richard Kluger, *Simple Justice: The History of "Brown v. Board of Education" and Black America's Struggle for Equality* (New York: Knopf, 1976), 38; Philip S. Foner, *History of Black Americans* (Westport, Conn.: Greenwood Press, 1975), 1:206–9.
10. Leon F. Litwack, *North of Slavery: The Negro in the Free States, 1790–1860* (Chicago: University of Chicago Press, 1961), 97.
11. John. H. Mooer, "Jim Crow in Georgia," *South Atlantic Quarterly* 66 (1967): 554–65; Gilbert T. Stephenson, *Race Distinctions in American Law* (New York: AMS Press, 1910); Litwack, *North of Slavery,* 66–67.
12. C. Vann Woodward, *The Strange Career of Jim Crow,* 3d rev. ed. (New York: Oxford University Press, 1974), 14.
13. Leonard P. Curry, *The Free Black in Urban America, 1800–1850: The Shadow of the Dream* (Chicago: University of Chicago Press, 1981), 90–91; Foner, *History of Black Americans,* chapters 9 and 10.
14. Woodward, *The Strange Career of Jim Crow,* 17–21; Litwack, *North of Slavery,* chapter 4.
15. Litwack, *North of Slavery;* 71; Roger A. Fischer, "Racial Segregation in Ante Bellum New Orleans," *American Historical Review* 74 (1969): 926–57. Statistics are taken from the United States Census Bureau and are reported in Curry, *The Free Black in Urban America;* see especially appendix A and C. See also Herbert Aptheker, *Anti-racism in U.S. History: The First Two Hundred Years* (Westport, Conn.: Praeger, 1993), 4.
16. See Gary H. Mills, "Miscegenation and the Free Negro in Ante-bellum 'Anglo' Alabama: A Re-examination of Southern Race Relations," *Journal of American History* 67 (1980): 41–60; *Aptheker, Anti-racism in U.S. History.*
17. Frederick Douglass, "American Prejudice and Southern Religion: An Address Delivered in Hingham, Massachusetts," 4 November 1841, in *The Frederick Douglass Papers: Speeches, Debates, and Interviews,* ed. John

W. Blassingame (New Haven, Conn.: Yale University Press, 1979), 1:12. For a description of the speech and comments about his experiences with the Eastern Railroad line, see Gregory P. Lampe, *Frederick Douglass: Freedom's Voice, 1818–1845* (East Lansing, Mich.: Michigan State University Press, 1998), 77–82.

18. For a history of black abolitionism and the efforts of African Americans to abolish slavery *and* secure their civil rights, see C. Peter Ripley, introduction to *The Black Abolitionist Papers* (Chapel Hill, N.C.: University of North Carolina Press, 1991), 3:3–69; Herbert Aptheker, *Abolitionism: A Revolutionary Movement* (Boston: Twayne Publishers, 1989).
19. Charles Lenox Remond, "The Rights of Colored Citizens in Traveling," in *Lift Every Voice: African American Oratory, 1787–1900,* ed. Philip S. Foner and Robert J. Branham (Tuscaloosa, Ala.: University of Alabama Press, 1998), 191.
20. For a history of these campaigns and an analysis of their implications for legal theory, see J. Morgan Kousser, "'The Supremacy of Equal Rights'": The Struggle against Racial Discrimination in Antebellum Massachusetts and the Foundations of the Fourteenth Amendment," *Northwestern University Law Review* 82 (1988): 941–1010.
21. Theodore S. Wright, "Prejudice against the Colored Man," in *Lift Every Voice,* 170.
22. W. E. B. Du Bois, *The Souls of Black Folk* (1903; reprint, New York: Alfred A. Knopf, 1993), 7.
23. For an analysis of Du Bois's theory of racial identity, see Kirt H. Wilson, "Towards a Discursive Theory of Racial Identity: *The Souls of Black Folk* as a Response to Nineteenth-Century Biological Determinism," *Western Journal of Communication* 63 (1999): 193–215.
24. For a concise overview of the Reconstruction era, see Eric Foner and Olivia Mahoney, *America's Reconstruction: People and Politics after the Civil War* (New York: HarperPerennial, 1995); John Hope Franklin, *Reconstruction: After the Civil War,* 2d ed. (Chicago: University of Chicago Press, 1994). For three excellent histories of this period that include both national and regional histories, see Eric Foner, *Reconstruction: America's Unfinished Revolution, 1863–1877* (New York: Harper and Row, 1988); W. E. B. Du Bois, *Black Reconstruction in America, 1860–1880* (1935; reprint, New York: Atheneum, 1992); and Michael Perman, *The Road to Redemption: Southern Politics, 1869–1879* (Chapel Hill, N.C.: University of North Carolina Press, 1984).
25. See Foner, *Reconstruction,* 28, 258; James M. McPherson, *The Struggle for Equality,* (1964; reprint, Princeton: Princeton University Press,

1992); Earl M. Maltz, "Fourteenth Amendment Concepts in the Antebellum Era," *The American Journal of Legal History* 32 (1988): 306–9; Eric Foner, *Free Soil, Free Labor, Free Men: The Ideology of the Republican Party before the Civil War* (New York: Oxford University Press, 1970); and Herman Belz, *Abraham Lincoln, Constitutionalism, and Equal Rights in the Civil War Era* (New York: Fordham University Press, 1998), 184–85.

26. U.S. Constitution, amend. 13
27. Robert J. Kaczorowski, "The Enforcement Provisions of the Civil Rights Act of 1866: A Legislative History in Light of *Runyon v. McCrary*," *Yale Law Journal* 98 (1989): 567–69.
28. W. R. Brock, "The Waning of Radicalism," in *Reconstruction: An Anthology of Revisionist Writings*, ed. Kenneth M. Stampp and Leon F. Litwack (Baton Rouge, La.: Louisiana State University Press, 1969), 497.
29. Du Bois, *Black Reconstruction in America*, 55.
30. See Claude F. Oubre, *Forty Acres and a Mule : The Freedmen's Bureau and Black Land Ownership* (Baton Rouge, La.: Louisiana State University Press, 1978); Jacqueline Jones, *Labor of Love, Labor of Sorrow* (New York: Basic Books, 1985); Dorothy Sterling, *The Trouble They Seen: The Story of Reconstruction in the Words of African Americans* (New York: Da Capo Press, 1994); and Foner, *Reconstruction*, 282–86.
31. Joel Williamson, *The Crucible of Race* (New York: Oxford University Press, 1984), 28–29, quotation from 79–80.
32. South Carolina, *An Act to Establish and Regulate the Domestic Relations of Persons of Color, and to Amend the Law in Relation to Paupers and Vagrancy*, secs. 35, 295 (1865).
33. Mississippi, *An Act to Confer Civil Rights on Freedmen, and for Other Purposes, Laws*, chapter 4: 82–86 (1965); Mississippi, *An Act to Regulate the Relation of Master and Apprentice, as Relates to Freedmen, Free Negroes, and Mulattoes*, chapter 5, 86–90 (1965).
34. Stetson Kennedy, *After Appomattox: How the South Won the War* (Gainseville, Fla.: University Press of Florida, 1995); George C. Rable, *But There Was No Peace: The Role of Violence in the Politics of Reconstruction* (Athens, Ga.: University of Georgia Press, 1984).
35. Foner, *Reconstruction*, 119–23. See also Joel Williamson, *After Slavery: The Negro in South Carolina during Reconstruction, 1861–1877* (1965; reprint, Hanover, N.H.: University Press of New England, 1990), 96–98; Franklin, *Reconstruction after the Civil War*, 51.
36. John C. Lester, D. L. Wilson, and Walter L. Fleming, *Ku Klux Klan: Its Origin, Growth and Disbandment* (New York: Neale Publishing Co.,

1905); William Peirce Randel, *The Ku Klux Klan: A Century of Infamy* (Philadelphia: Chilton Books, 1965).

37. Stampp, *The Era of Reconstruction*, 200, 201.
38. House, *Report of and Testimony Taken by the Joint Select Committee to Inquire into the Condition of Affairs in the Late Insurrectionary States*, 13 vols., 42d Cong., 2d sess., 1871–72. See, for example, stories in the *New National Era* on 12 January 1871, 25 May 1871, 14 March 1872, and 2 January 1873.
39. Thomas Nast, "Slavery Dead?" *Harper's Weekly*, 11, 12 January 1867, 24. See also Thomas Nast, "Slavery Dead?" Library of Congress, Prints and Photographs Division, LC-USZ62–108003.
40. Perman, *Road to Redemption*.
41. Howard N. Rabinowitz, ed., *Southern Black Leaders of the Reconstruction Era* (Urbana, Ill.: University of Illinois Press, 1982); Annjennette Sophie McFarlin, *Black Congressional Reconstruction Orators and Their Orations, 1869–1979* (Metuchen, N.J.: Scarecrow Press, 1976).
42. Douglass, "Speech at Lincoln Hall," in *Proceedings*, 12.

Chapter 2

1. See, for instance, James M. McPherson, "Abolitionists and the Civil Rights Act of 1875," *Journal of American History* 52 (1965): 493–510; and William Gillette, *Retreat from Reconstruction, 1869–1879* (Baton Rouge, La.: Louisiana State University Press, 1979), 190–210.
2. Rabinowitz argues that with the exception of public accommodations, most of the Jim Crow laws that were passed from 1865 to 1890 were championed by white Republicans with the tacit approval of African Americans. Howard N. Rabinowitz, *Race Relations in the Urban South, 1865–1890* (New York: Oxford University Press, 1978); Howard N. Rabinowitz, "More Than the Woodward Thesis: Assessing *The Strange Career of Jim Crow*," *Journal of American History* 75 (1988): 842–56; C. Vann Woodward, *The Strange Career of Jim Crow*, 3d rev. ed. (New York: Oxford University Press, 1974); C. Vann Woodward, "*Strange Career* Critics: Long May They Persevere," *Journal of American History* 75 (1988): 857–68; Joel Williamson, *The Crucible of Race* (New York: Oxford University Press, 1984), 44–50; Gillette, *Retreat from Reconstruction*, 201.
3. Howard N. Rabinowitz, "From Exclusion to Segregation: Southern Race Relations, 1865–1890," *Journal of American History* 63 (1976): 325–50; John William Graves, "Jim Crow in Arkansas: A Reconsider-

ation of Urban Race Relations in the Post-Reconstruction South," *Journal of Southern History* 55 (1989): 421–48.

4. Douglass's paper the *New National Era* ran many articles in favor of the desegregation bill. See, for example, "Civil Rights," *New National Era,* 11 January 1872, 2; "Equal Rights," *New National Era,* 14 March 1872, 1.
5. David Herbert Donald, *The Politics of Reconstruction, 1863–1867* (Baton Rouge, La.: Louisiana State University Press, 1965); David Montgomery, *Beyond Equality: Labor and the Radical Republicans, 1862–1872,* (New York: Alfred A. Knopf, 1967); Michael Les Benedict, *A Compromise of Principle: Congressional Republicans and Reconstruction, 1863–1869* (New York: Norton, 1974).
6. Brief of Charles Sumner, *Roberts v. City of Boston,* 59 Mass. 198 (1849); J. Morgan Kousser, "'The Supremacy of Equal Rights': The Struggle against Racial Discrimination in Antebellum Massachusetts and the Foundations of the Fourteenth Amendment," *Northwestern University Law Review* 82 (1988): 973–80. See Leonard W. Levy and Harlan B. Phillips, "The *Roberts* Case: Source of the 'Separate but Equal' Doctrine," *American Historical Review* 56 (1950): 510–18; and David Herbert Donald, *Charles Sumner and the Coming of the Civil War* (New York: Alfred A. Knopf, 1960), 180–81.
7. *Congressional Globe,* 41st Cong., 2d sess., 1870, 42, pt. 4:3434. For a brief legislative history see Edward D. Smith, "The Unfortunate History of America's First Comprehensive Civil Rights Bill, 1870–1883," *Negro History Bulletin* 47 (1984): 42–44. For an extensive analysis of the bill's legislative history, including votes on amendments, see Michael McConnell, "Originalism and the Desegregation Decisions," *Virginia Law Review* 83 (1995): 947–1140. For general accounts see Alfred H. Kelly, "The Congressional Controversy over School Segregation, 1867–1875," *The American Historical Review* 64 (1959): 537–63; William P. Vaugn, "Separate and Unequal: The Civil Rights Act of 1875 and Defeat of the School Integration Clause," *The Southwestern Social Science Quarterly* 48 (1967): 146–54.
8. Bertram Wyatt-Brown, "The Civil Rights Act of 1875," *Western Political Quarterly* 18 (1965): 766; Ronald B. Jager, "Charles Sumner: the Constitution and the Civil Rights Act of 1875," *New England Quarterly* 42 (September 1969): 362; Eric Foner, *Reconstruction: America's Unfinished Revolution, 1863–1877* (New York: Harper and Row, 1988), 505.
9. *Congressional Globe,* 42d Cong., 1st sess., 1871, 44, pt. 1:21.

10. The amnesty measure would have allowed many former Confederate leaders to regain the political power that they lost under the Fourteenth Amendment.
11. Jager, "Charles Sumner," 362. See also Wyatt-Brown, "The Civil Rights Act," 768; James M. McPherson, "Abolitionists and the Civil Rights Act," 501; Foner, *Reconstruction,* 505.
12. The party and state affiliations of congressional members have been cross-referenced with the *Biographical Directory of the United States Congress, 1774–1989,* bicentennial ed. (Washington, D.C.: U.S. Government Printing Office, 1989).
13. *Congressional Globe,* 42d Cong., 2d sess., 1871, 45, pt. 1:241–42.
14. Foner, *Reconstruction,* 278.
15. The tactic of these Grant Republicans was complicated further by the fact that the amnesty measure required a two-thirds majority for passage. Thus, with Sumner's bill attached, both of these unpopular proposals stood little chance of success. See also Patrick O. Gudridge, "Privileges and Permissions: The Civil Rights Act of 1875," *Law and Philosophy* 8 (1989): 88; McPherson "Abolitionists and the Civil Rights Act," 502.
16. For the first vote on Sumner's provision see *Congressional Globe,* 42d Cong., 2d sess., 1872, 45, pt. 2:919. For the second vote see *Congressional Globe,* 42d Cong., 2d sess., 1872, 45, pt. 4:3268. See also Wyatt-Brown, "The Civil Rights Act," 768; McPherson, "Abolitionists and the Civil Rights Act," 502.
17. According to the *Biographical Directory of the United States Congress,* Carpenter had been a Democrat prior to the Civil War. He remained an opponent of desegregation, even after the Republicans united behind the compromises of 1875. The language of his own measure was sufficiently ambiguous to allow for separate but equal accommodations. *Congressional Globe,* 42d Cong., 2d sess., 1872, 45, pt. 5:3705, 3735.
18. For an account of the endgame, see *Congressional Globe,* 42d Cong., 2d sess., 1872, 45, pt. 5:3729–39. See also Edward Pierce, ed., *Memoir and Letters of Charles Sumner* (Boston: Roberts Brothers, 1893), 4:503; J. David Hoeveler Jr., "Reconstruction and the Federal Courts: The Civil Rights Act of 1875," *Historian* 31 (August 1969): 608; Wyatt-Brown, "The Civil Rights Act," 769; Foner, *Reconstruction,* 505.
19. *Congressional Globe,* 42d Cong., 2d sess., 1872, pt. 1:1116; See also McConnell, "Originalism and the Desegregation Decisions," 1060–63.
20. Sumner, despite his ill health, attended sessions whenever possible. He was now the longest serving member, and *Harper's* called him the

"Father of the Senate." See "The Senate Chamber," *Harper's Weekly* 17, 3 January 1874, 21.

21. See Michael Perman, *The Road to Redemption: Southern Politics, 1869–1879* (Chapel Hill, N.C.: University of North Carolina Press, 1984), 139; David McBride, "Fourteenth Amendment Idealism: The New York State Civil Rights Law, 1873–1918," *New York History* 71 (1990): 207–33.
22. There may have been three distinct reasons for this feeling. The first relates to the continued pressure of certain radicals who believed in the principle of equality. Also, a few Republicans had hoped that the bill might reunite a divided party. Finally, African Americans were increasingly insistent that the Republicans owed them this measure. See Gillette, *Retreat from Reconstruction,* 202–3.
23. Figure 2. "The First Colored Senator and Representatives," Library of Congress, Prints and Photographs Division, LC-USZ62–2814.
24. For a brief biographical summary of these and other black congressmen, see Annjennette Sophie McFarlin, *Black Congressional Reconstruction Orators and Their Orations, 1869–1879,* (Metuchen, N.J.: Scarecrow Press, 1976). Figure A shows three of the men—Rainey, Walls, and Elliot—who were active in the desegregation debate.
25. *Congressional Record,* 43d Cong., 1st sess., 1874, 2, pt. 5:4782.
26. Eric Foner, *Freedom's Lawmakers: A Directory of Black Officeholders during Reconstruction,* rev. ed. (Baton Rouge, La.: Louisiana State University Press, 1996).
27. "The Civil Rights Bill," *New York Times,* 5 February 1875, 1.
28. "Hon. Joseph Rainey," *New National Era,* 14 March 1872, 3.
29. *Congressional Record,* 43d Cong., 1st sess., 1874, 2, pt. 1:318.
30. Ibid., pt. 1:337–39.
31. Ibid., pt. 1:341.
32. Ibid., pt. 1:343.
33. Ibid., pt. 1:344.
34. Ibid., pt. 1:376.
35. Ibid., pt. 1:377.
36. "Civil Rights Debate," *Chicago Times,* 8 January 1874, 3.
37. *Congressional Record,* 43d Cong., 1st sess., 1874, 2, pt. 1:383.
38. Peggy Lamson, *The Glorious Failure: Black Congressman Robert Brown Elliott and the Reconstruction in South Carolina* (New York: W. W. Norton and Co., 1973), 174–75.
39. Foner, *Reconstruction,* 14, 246–47.

40. Alexander Hamilton Stephens, *A Constitutional View of the Late War between the States: Its Causes, Character, Conduct, and Results Presented in a Series of Colloquies at Liberty Hall* (Philadelphia: National Pub. Co., Zeigler McCurdy, 1868); personal inscription to the earl of Rosebery from Alexander H. Stephens, 13 December 1873, Alexander H. Stephens Papers, Library of Congress, Manuscript Division, reel 40, microfilm.
41. Foner, *Reconstruction,* 533.
42. The compromise that gave both Stephens and Elliott an hour indicates that the Stephens-Elliott exchange might have been planned from the debate's beginning. At the very least, the two congressmen were paired against each other before Stephens attacked civil rights.
43. "Stephens on Civil Rights," *Chicago Times,* 6 January 1874, 1; *Chicago Tribune,* 6 January 1874, 1; *New York Times,* 6 January 1874, 1.
44. Mrs. H. Whitsill to Alexander H. Stephens, 12 January 1874, Alexander H. Stephens Papers, Library of Congress, Manuscript Division, reel 40, microfilm.
45. Editorial, *Charleston News and Courier,* 7 January 1874, 2.
46. "Debate on the Civil Rights Bill," *New York Times,* 6 January 1874, 1.
47. "Stephens on Civil Rights," *Chicago Times,* 6 January 1874, 1.
48. For an excellent historical account of Elliott's life and political influence, see Peggy Lamson, *The Glorious Failure: Black Congressman Robert Brown Elliott and the Reconstruction in South Carolina* (New York: W. W. Norton and Co., 1973).
49. *Congressional Record,* 43d Cong., 1st sess., 1874, 2, pt. 1:386.
50. Up until Elliott entered the house, most of the black representatives had been biracial and of lighter skin coloration. See Lamson, *The Glorious Failure,* 119.
51. "Washington," *Chicago Times,* 7 January 1874, 8.
52. *Congressional Record,* 43d Cong., 1st sess., 1874, 2, pt. 1:407.
53. Ibid., pt. 1:407–10
54. Lamson, *The Glorious Failure,* 181.
55. "The Civil Rights Bill," *Chicago Tribune,* 7 January 1874, 1.
56. "Washington," *New York Times,* 7 January 1874, 1.
57. Thomas Nast, "The Shackle Broken by the Genius of Freedom," a lithograph in the Library of Congress, Prints and Photographs Division, Washington, D.C. Reproduction number LC-USZ62–2247. Originally published in Baltimore by E. Sachse and Co., 1874.
58. The *Chicago Times* argued that it had made this statement in general and not toward particular cases. In the editorial, however, the *Times* noted that just because Elliott delivered a good speech did not mean

that he had written the speech or that its arguments were accurate. For example, it mentioned that his comments about black military sacrifice were a gross exaggeration. "It is all a myth about Negro gallantry during the rebellion," it reported. Quoted from "Elliott's Speech," *Chicago Times,* 8 January 1874, 4. See also "Washington," *Chicago Times,* 7 January 1874, 8.

59. *Congressional Record,* 43d Cong., 1st sess., 1874, 2, pt. 1:565–67, 901–3; "Judge Sloanaker on Colored Congressmen," *New Orleans Weekly Louisianian,* 23 May 1874, 1.

60. *Congressional Record,* 43d Cong., 1st sess., 1874, 2, pt. 1:416.; see also McFarlin, *Black Congressional Reconstruction Orators,* 321.

61. The actual debate had ceased by this point. Butler, as I explain in the following pages, had recommitted the bill to the judiciary committee; still, Cain, Ransier, and Rapier offered lengthy speeches in support of civil rights during moments of "general discussion" that usually transpired on Saturdays.

62. See Norman W. Walton, "James T. Rapier: Congressman from Alabama," *Negro History Bulletin* 30 (November 1967): 6–10; Eric Foner, *Freedom's Lawmakers,* 176–77.

63. *Congressional Record,* 43d Cong., 1st sess., 1874, 2, pt. 5:4784.

64. Foner, *Reconstruction,* 458.

65. *Congressional Record,* 43d Cong., 1st sess., 1874, pt. 1:458.

66. See the story and illustrations of Sumner's death and funeral in *Harper's Weekly* 18, 11 April 1874. See also W. E. B. Du Bois, *Black Reconstruction in America, 1860–1880* (1935; reprint, New York: Atheneum, 1992), 594.

67. *Harper's Weekly* 18, 9 May 1874, 391; McConnell, "Originalism and the Desegregation Decisions," 1069.

68. Hoeveler, "Reconstruction and the Federal Courts," 610

69. Wyatt-Brown, "The Civil Rights Act," 769–70; McConnell, "Originalism and the Desegregation Decisions," 1069–78.

70. *Congressional Record,* 43d Cong., 1st sess., 1874, 2, pt. 4:3452.

71. *Congressional Record,* 43d Cong., 1st sess., appendix, 233.

72. See "Order of Business," *Chicago Times,* 9 May 1874, 3.

73. *Congressional Record,* 43d Cong., 1st sess., 1874, appendix, 318–23; *Congressional Record,* 43d Cong., 1st sess., 1874, 2, pt. 5:4154–62.

74. "Washington," *New York Times,* 23 May 1874, 4.

75. *Congressional Record,* 43d Cong., 1st sess. 1874, 2, pt. 5:4162–65; *Congressional Record,* 43d Cong., 1st sess. 1874, appendix, 307–18, 361–70.

76. "The Civil Rights Bill," *New York Tribune,* 23 May 1874, 1. According to the *Tribune* Flanagan had fallen so deeply asleep that his head had flopped backward over his chair and he was in danger of dislocating his spine. See "Washington," *Chicago Tribune,* 23 May 1874, 7; "Washington," *New York Times,* 24 May 1874, 1.
77. *Congressional Record,* 43d Cong., 1st sess., 1874, 2, pt. 5:4167.
78. Ibid., pt. 5:4169, 4171–74; McConnell, "Originalism and the Desegregation Decisions," 1078.
79. In spite of his opposition to school desegregation, Sargent voted with the Republican majority. See Gillette, *Retreat from Reconstruction,* 205–7.
80. "Civil Rights," *New York Daily Tribune,* 9 June 1874, 1.
81. *Congressional Record,* 43d Cong., 1st sess., 1874, appendix, 478.
82. McPherson, "Abolitionists and the Civil Rights Act," 506
83. "The Civil Right Bill," *Harper's Weekly* 18,13 June 1874, 490; "Washington," *Chicago Tribune,* 26 May 1874, 1; The *Courier-Journal* is quoted by Wyatt-Brown, "The Civil Rights Act," 770; "Very Latest," *Atlanta Constitution,* 24 May 1874, 1.
84. Wyatt-Brown, "The Civil Rights Act," 771.
85. Hoeveler, "Reconstruction and the Federal Courts," 613; Foner, *Reconstruction,* 549–53. See also Foner, *Freedom's Lawmakers,* xiii.
86. Foner, *Reconstruction,* 553; Gillette, *Retreat from Reconstruction,* 260.
87. *Congressional Record,* 43d Cong., 2d sess., 1875, 3, pt. 1:116. The text of the entire bill can be found at *Congressional Record,* 43d Cong., 2d sess., 1875, 3, pt. 2:939.
88. Gillette, *Retreat from Reconstruction,* 267. See also Foner, *Reconstruction,* 555; Wyatt-Brown, "The Civil Rights Act," 772.
89. With one day of debate guaranteed and because the change did not apply to pork-barrel projects, the proposal gained the support of moderate Republicans. See Wyatt-Brown, "The Civil Rights Act," 773; Foner, *Reconstruction,* 555.
90. See "Washington," the *Chicago Tribune,* 3 February 1875, 5.
91. The general ill will and acrimony between opponents and proponents might fuel some of the cynicism expressed by historians who discuss this bill. Most certainly, the 1875 debate did not conform to our ideals about deliberative political discussion.
92. "Civil Rights," *The New Orleans Weekly Louisianian,* 13 February 1875, 2. Note that this source was far from objective. The black newspaper's motto was "Republican at all times and under all circumstances."

93. "Exciting Scenes over the Civil Rights Bill," *New York Times,* 4 February 1875, 1.
94. *Congressional Record,* 43d Cong., 2d sess., 1875, 3, pt. 2:940–42.
95. Ibid., 2:944–48.
96. "Washington," *Chicago Tribune,* 4 February 1875, 2.
97. *Congressional Record,* 43d Cong., 2d sess., 1875, 3, pt. 2:955–60.
98. Editorial, *Chicago Tribune,* 5 February 1875, 4; "Exciting Scenes over Civil Rights Bill," *New York Times,* 4 February 1875, 1.
99. *Congressional Record,* 43d Cong., 2d sess., 1875, 3, pt. 2:982–85.
100. Ibid., pt. 2:985.
101. "The Civil Rights Bill," *New York Times,* 5 February 1875, 1.
102. "Dementia," *Chicago Tribune,* 5 February 1875, 5.
103. The House knew that Brown's comments were premeditated because the day before he had begun to create the same analogy but had been cut off before he had completed his statements. Several senators investigated the *Congressional Record* to prove that point.
104. *Congressional Record,* 43d Cong., 2d sess., 1875, 3, pt. 2:985–92.
105. Ibid., pt. 2:990
106. Ibid., pt. 2:978–79, 982; *Congressional Record,* 43d Cong., 2d Session, 1875, appendix, 156–59.
107. *Congressional Record,* 43d Cong., 2d sess., 1875, 3, pt. 2:939.
108. Ibid., pt. 2:998.
109. Richard Cain, ibid., pt. 2:981–82.
110. Ibid., pt. 2:271.
111. Ibid., pt. 3:1866–67.
112. These amendments included a proposal to strike down sections 820 and 821 (1862 provisions which excluded Confederate soldiers from serving as jurors) of the "Revised Statues of the United States" and amendments to limit the penalty for violation to five hundred dollars and to strike out the word "theaters" and insert "churches."
113. *Congressional Record,* 43d Cong., 2d sess., 1875, 3, pt. 3:1869–70.
114. *Civil Rights Act of 1875, U.S. Statutes at Large* 18 (1875): 335–337. For the text of the bill see appendix A on page 201.
115. "Passage of the Civil Rights Bill in the House," *New York Times,* 6 February 1875, 1.
116. McPherson, "Abolitionists and the Civil Rights Act," 509.
117. Valeria W. Weaver, "The Failure of Civil Rights, 1875–1883, and Its Repercussions," *Journal of Negro History* (October 1969): 368–69; John Hope Franklin, "The Enforcement of the Civil Rights Act of 1875," *Prologue* 6 (1974): 225–35; Wyatt-Brown, "The Civil Rights Act," 774.

118. See *Civil Rights Cases,* 109 U.S. 3 (1883).
119. Jager, "Charles Sumner," 371
120. Weaver, "The Failure of Civil Rights," 370.
121. "The Civil Rights Decision," *New York Times,* 16 October 1883, 4.
122. See Chester A. Arthur, "Third Annual Message," 4 December 1883, in *Messages and Papers of the Presidents,* ed. James D. Richardson (1897; reprint, New York: Bureau of National Literature, 1917), 10:4775. See also Stanley P. Hirshson, *Farewell to the Bloody Shirt: Northern Republicans and the Southern Negro, 1877–1893* (Bloomington, Ind.: Indiana University Press, 1962), 104–5.
123. Weaver, "The Failure of Civil Rights," 377; Stephen J. Riegel, "The Persistent Career of Jim Crow: Lower Federal Courts and the 'Separate but Equal' Doctrine, 1865–1896," *The American Journal of Legal History* 28 (1984): 17–40. See also G. T. Stephenson, *Race Distinctions in American Law* (New York: AMS Press, 1910), 120–24.
124. Robert J. Kaczorowski, *The Nationalization of Civil Rights: Constitutional Theory and Practice in a Racist Society, 1866–1883* (New York: Garland, 1987); J. Morgan Kousser, "'The Supremacy of Equal Rights'": The Struggle against Racial Discrimination in Antebellum Massachusetts and the Foundations of the Fourteenth Amendment," *Northwestern University Law Review* 82 (1988): 941–1010; McConnell, "Originalism and the Desegregation Decisions," 947–1140.
125. See Raol Berger, *The Fourteenth Amendment and the Bill of Rights* (Norman, Okla.: University of Oklahoma Press, 1989); Raoul Berger, *Government by Judiciary: The Transformation of the Fourteenth Amendment* (Cambridge: Harvard University Press, 1977); Harold M. Hyman, *A More Perfect Union: The Impact of the Civil War and Reconstruction on the Constitution* (Boston: Houghton Mifflin Co., 1975).
126. Riegel, "The Persistent Career of Jim Crow," 29–37.
127. Ward M. McAfee, "Reconstruction Revisited: The Republican Public Education Crusade of the 1870s," *Civil War History* 42 (1996): 133–53.
128. Stanley J. Folmsbee, "The Origin of the First 'Jim Crow' Law," *Journal of Southern History* (1949): 234–47; John W. Graves, "Jim Crow in Arkansas: A Reconsideration of Urban Race Relations in the Post-Reconstruction South," *Journal of Southern History* 55 (1989): 421–48; J. H. Moore, "Jim Crow in Georgia," *South Atlantic Quarterly* 66 (1967): 554–65; G. Tindall, "Negro Disenfranchisement in South Carolina," *Journal of Southern History* (1949): 212–34; L. Mathews, "Keeping Down Jim Crow: The Railroads and the Separate Coach Bills in South Carolina," *South Atlantic Quarterly* 73 (1973): 117–29.

129. Gillette, *Retreat from Reconstruction,* 218.
130. Wyatt-Brown, "The Civil Rights Act," 774–75.
131. Foner, *Reconstruction,* 556; Rabinowitz, "More Than the Woodward Thesis," 847.

Chapter 3

1. *Congressional Globe,* 42d Cong., 2d sess., 1872, 45, pt. 1:385.
2. Ronald B. Jager, "Charles Sumner: The Constitution and the Civil Rights Act of 1875," *New England Quarterly* 42 (September 1969): 350.
3. See David Herbert Donald, *Charles Sumner and the Coming of the Civil War* (New York: Alfred A. Knopf, 1960), 12–21, chapter 3; Carl Schurz, *Charles Sumner: An Essay by Carl Schurz,* ed. Arthur Reed Hogue (Urbana, Ill.: University of Illinois Press, 1951), 15–23; Anna Laurens Dawes, *Charles Sumner* (New York: Dodd, Mead and Co., 1892), 31; Jager, "Charles Sumner," 355–56.
4. Schurz, *Charles Sumner,* 23.
5. Webster maintained that slavery was a local institution that could exist only when sanctioned by local law. Sumner countered that slavery was not solely a local issue, but that it was a national problem; consequently, he believed that Congress could and should regulate the institution. Although it was unpopular to disagree publicly with Webster, Sumner's courage and forthright position increased his visibility and set the stage for his role as a political maverick.
6. Charles Sumner, "The True Grandeur of Nations," in *The Works of Charles Sumner,* vol. 1 (Boston: Lee and Shepard, 1870); Donald, *Charles Sumner,* 109; Schurz, *Charles Sumner,* 23.
7. Sumner, "The True Grandeur of Nations," in *The Works of Charles Sumner,* 1:7–8.
8. Schurz, *Charles Sumner,* 26.
9. Donald, *Charles Sumner,* 111.
10. "Independence," *Daily Evening Transcript,* 5 July 1845, 2.
11. Schurz, *Charles Sumner,* 28.
12. Sumner, "The True Grandeur of Nations," in *The Works of Charles Sumner,* 1:123.
13. Sumner to Winthrop, 6 July 1845, *The Selected Letters of Charles Sumner,* ed. Beverly Wilson Palmer (Boston: Northeastern University Press, 1990), 1:148
14. Sumner, "The True Grandeur of Nations," in *The Works of Charles Sumner,* 1:17

15. Bill Ledbetter, "Charles Sumner: Political Activist for the New England Transcendentalists," *Historian* 44 (1982): 352.
16. McPherson contends that whether Sumner was a "real" abolitionist is a subject of some question, because he maintained a political philosophy quite distinct from the social agitators. Still, from the discourse of this study, I find it difficult to consider Sumner as anything but an abolitionist. See James M. McPherson, *The Struggle for Equality* (1964; reprint, Princeton: Princeton University Press, 1992), 3.
17. Dawes, *Charles Sumner,* 52.
18. Jager, "Charles Sumner" 352.
19. Moorfield Storey, *Charles Sumner* (Boston: Houghton, Mifflin, and Co., 1900), 86.
20. For a detailed account of the 1854 Kansas-Nebraska bill, see David Zarefsky, *Lincoln Douglas and Slavery: In the Crucible of Public Debate* (Chicago: University of Chicago Press, 1990), 2–7.
21. Storey, *Charles Sumner,* 132–36.
22. *Congressional Globe,* 34th Cong., 1st sess., 1856, appendix, 529–47. See also Charles Sumner, "The Crime against Kansas: The Apologies for the Crime, The True Remedy," in *Charles Sumner: His Complete Works* (1882; reprint, Norwood, Mass.: Lee and Shepard, 1900), 5:125–342; and Michael D. Pierson, "'All Southern Society Is Assailed by the Foulest Charges': Charles Sumner's 'The Crime against Kansas' and the Escalation of Republican Anti-slavery Rhetoric," *New England Quarterly* 68 (1995): 531–57.
23. Storey, *Charles Sumner,* 138.
24. Glen Stocker, "Charles Sumner's Rhetoric of Insult," *Southern Communication Journal* 38 (1973): 223–34; Storey, *Charles Sumner,* 144; Donald, *Charles Sumner,* 285–90.
25. Storey, *Charles Sumner,* 146; Donald, *Charles Sumner,* 293–94. Sumner had called Butler the Don Quixote of slavery, dedicated to that ugly mistress that only he could perceive as beautiful. See Donald, *Charles Sumner,* 290.
26. Donald, *Charles Sumner,* 295.
27. Storey, *Charles Sumner,* 148.
28. Stocker, "Charles Sumner's Rhetoric of Insult," 223–43.
29. Pierson, "'All Southern Society,'" 531–57.
30. Margaret D. Zulick, "The Agon of Jeremiah: On the Dialogic Invention of Prophetic Ethos," *Quarterly Journal of Speech* 78 (1992): 126.
31. James Darsey, "The Legend of Eugene Debs: Prophetic 'Ethos' as Radical Argument," *Quarterly Journal of Speech* 74 (1988): 435–36. See also

James Darsey, *The Prophetic Tradition and Radical Rhetoric in America* (New York: New York University Press, 1997).

32. Donald, *Charles Sumner and the Rights of Man* (New York: Alfred A. Knopf, 1970), 300.
33. Ledbetter, "Charles Sumner: Political Activist," 358.
34. James Jasinski, "The Forms and Limits of Prudence in Henry Clay's (1850) Defense of the Compromise Measures," *Quarterly Journal of Speech* 81 (1995): 454–78.
35. Eric Foner, *Reconstruction: America's Unfinished Revolution, 1863–1877* (New York: Harper and Row, 1988), 239.
36. Sumner, "Equal Rights of All," *Congressional Globe,* 39th Cong., 1st sess., 1866, 36, pt. 1:673.
37. Sumner to Smith, 12 February 1866, *The Selected Letters of Charles Sumner,* 357. It is worth noting that Donald offers a slightly different interpretation of Sumner's opposition, suggesting that he had been attacked by Massachusetts radicals for losing his principles. Supporting the Fourteenth Amendment would have strengthened his opponent, John Andrew, so his speech was a response to these political pressures. See David Herbert Donald, *Charles Sumner and the Rights of Man,* 245–46.
38. Donald, *Charles Sumner and the Rights of Man,* 247.
39. Sumner, "The Equal Rights of All," *Congressional Globe,* 39th Cong., 1st sess., 1866, 36, pt. 1:674
40. Donald, *Charles Sumner and the Rights of Man,* 248.
41. Ibid., , 251.
42. For a theoretical explanation of interpretive prophecy, see Michael Walzer, *Interpretation and Social Criticism* (Cambridge: Harvard University Press, 1987), 75.
43. Walzer, *Interpretation and Social Criticism,* 38–39.
44. Zulick, "The Agon of Jeremiah," 140.
45. Henry Schile, "Charles Sumner," Library of Congress, LC-USZ62–89586
46. *Congressional Globe,* 42d Cong., 2d sess., 1872, 45, pt. 1:381.
47. Thomas Nast, "The Past and Future," 24 January 1863, *Harper's Weekly,* 7, 56–57. Figure 4 displays a second version of this lithograph published in 1965. In the second version Abraham Lincoln features more prominently in a second center panel that appears just below a black domestic scene. Thomas Nast, "EMANCIATPION," a lithograph in the Library of Congress Prints and Photographs Division Washing-

ton, D.C. Reproduction number LC-USZ62–2573. Originally published in Philadelphia by King and Baird, Printers, 1865.

48. John Hope Franklin, *The Emancipation Proclamation* (1963; reprint, Wheeling, Ill: Harlan Davidson, 1995); George M. Frederickson, "A Man but Not a Brother: Abraham Lincoln and Racial Equality," *Journal of Southern History* 41 (1975): 39–58; David Herbert Donald, *Lincoln* (New York: Simon and Schuster, 1995); Don E. Fehrenbacker, "The Anti-Lincoln Tradition," in *Lincoln in Text and Context: Collected Essays* (Stanford, Calif: Stanford University Press, 1987).
49. See Bruce Levine, *Half Slave and Half Free: The Roots of the Civil War* (New York: Noonday Press, 1992), chapter 5; Eric Foner, *Free Soil, Free Labor, Free Men: The Ideology of the Republican Party before the Civil War* (New York: Oxford University Press, 1970).
50. *Congressional Globe,* 42d Cong., 2d sess., 1872, 45, pt. 1:381.
51. Ibid., pt. 1:381, 384
52. Ibid., pt. 1:383.
53. Ibid., pt. 1:381–82; James M. McPherson, "Abolitionists and the Civil Rights Act of 1875," *Journal of American History* 52 (1965): 496.
54. *Congressional Globe,* 42d Cong., 2d sess., 1872, 45, pt. 1:429.
55. For the concept of a condensation symbol see Murray Edelman, *The Symbolic Uses of Politics* (1964; reprint, Urbana, Ill.: University of Illinois Press, 1985); and David S. Kaufer and Kathleen M. Carley, "Condensation Symbols: Their Variety and Rhetorical Function in Political Discourse," *Philosophy and Rhetoric* 26 (1993): 201–26. For an explanation of ideographs, see Michael Calvin McGee, "The 'IdeoGraph': A Link between Rhetoric and Ideology," *Quarterly Journal of Speech* 66 (1980): 1–16.
56. Celeste Michelle Condit and John Louis Lucaites, *Crafting Equality: America's Anglo-African Word* (Chicago: University of Chicago Press, 1993), 34.
57. Sumner to Winthrop, 6 July 1845, *The Selected Letters of Charles Sumner,* 147
58. Frederick Douglass, "What, to the Slave, Is the Fourth of July?" in *Lift Every Voice: African American Oratory, 1787–1900,* ed. Philip S. Foner and Robert J. Branham (Tuscaloosa, Ala.: University of Alabama Press, 1998), 257.
59. Gabor S. Boritt, *Lincoln and the Economics of the American Dream* (Memphis, Tenn.: Memphis State University Press, 1978); David Zarefsky, "Consistency and Change in Lincoln's Rhetoric about Equality," *Rhetoric and Public Affairs* 1 (1998): 21–44.

60. Charles Sumner, "The Civil Rights Bill," *Charles Sumner: His Complete Works,* 19: 232.
61. *Congressional Globe,* 42d Cong., 2d session, 1872, 45, pt. 1:385
62. Brief of Charles Sumner, *Roberts v. City of Boston,* 59 Mass. 198 (1849); J. Morgan Kousser, "'The Supremacy of Equal Rights': The Struggle against Racial Discrimination in Antebellum Massachusetts and the Foundations of the Fourteenth Amendment," *Northwestern University Law Review* 82 (1988): 973–80.
63. *Congressional Globe,* 42d Cong., 2d Session, 1872, 45, pt. 1:382.
64. Ibid., pt. 1:382.
65. Ibid., pt. 1:382; Sumner's comments were in reference to Lincoln's speech at Independence Hall on 22 February 1861. See Abraham Lincoln, "Address in Independence Hall, Philadelphia February 22, 1861," in *Abraham Lincoln: His Speeches and Writing,* ed. Roy P. Basler (1946; reprint, New York: Da Capo Press, 1990), 577–79.
66. *Congressional Globe,* 42d Cong., 2d sess., 1872, 45, pt. 1:382.
67. Ibid., pt. 1:382.
68. Ibid., pt. 1:382.
69. Ibid., pt. 1:385.
70. Charles Sumner, "The Civil Rights Bill," in *Charles Sumner: His Complete Works,* 19:257.
71. Proceedings of the National Negro Convention of 1853, in *A Documentary History of the Negro People in the United States,* ed. Herbert Aptheker (New York: Citadel Book Press, 1951), 1:349.
72. Robert Hariman, "Afterward: Relocating the Art of Public Address," in *Rhetoric and Political Culture in Nineteenth-Century America,* ed. Thomas W. Benson (East Lansing, Mich.: Michigan State University Press, 1997), 177
73. *Congressional Globe,* 42d Cong., 2d sess., 1872, 45, pt. 1:385.
74. This philosophy has been called the "Limited Absolute Equality" position. See Earl M. Maltz, "Fourteenth Amendment Concepts in the Antebellum Era," *The American Journal of Legal History* 32 (1988): 308.
75. Sumner's approach to this issue was not without a significant flaw, however. The black equality that he defined depended on the Fourteenth Amendment. The amendment, of course, was passed by an all-white Congress, and, as a result, his emphasis on citizenship actually deflected an equality stance based upon the positive characteristics of African Americans. As we shall see in chapter 4, the black congressmen of the 1874 and 1875 debates redefined equality so that blacks were responsible for their own equality.

76. *Congressional Globe,* 42d Cong., 2d sess., 1872, 45, pt. 1:386.
77. See Booker T. Washington, "Atlanta Exposition Address," in *Lift Every Voice,* 800–5.
78. McPherson *The Struggle for Equality,* 221–23; Foner *Reconstruction,* 25–26.
79. Benjamin Banneker to Thomas Jefferson, 1872, in *A Documentary History,* 1:24–25; Angela Ray, "'In my own hand writing': Benjamin Banneker Addresses the Slaveholder of Monticello," *Rhetoric and Public Affairs* 1 (1998): 387–405; Condit and Lucaites, *Crafting Equality,* 79–84.
80. Frederick Douglass, 11 May 1869, "Speech at the Thirty-sixth Anniversary of the American Anti-slavery Society," 29 May 1869, *National Slavery Standard,* p. 1
81. See Sumner's exchange with Senator Joshua Hill of Georgia; *Congressional Globe,* 42d Cong., 2d sess., 1871, 45, pt. 1:241–42.
82. *Congressional Globe,* 42d Cong., 2d sess., 1872, 45, pt. 1:383.
83. Ibid., pt. 1:383.
84. Ibid., pt. 1:383.
85. Kousser, 'The Supremacy of Equal Rights," 978–79.
86. *Congressional Globe,* 42d Cong., 2d sess., 1872, 45, pt. 1:383.
87. S. G. F. Spackman, "American Federalism and the Civil Rights Act of 1875," *Journal of American Studies* 10 (1976): 317.
88. Bertram Wyatt-Brown, "The Civil Rights Act of 1875," *Western Political Quarterly* 18 (1965): 765–66.
89. *Congressional Globe,* 42d Cong., 2d sess., 1872, 45, pt. 1:382.
90. Ibid., pt. 1:385.
91. David Zarefsky and Victoria J. Gallagher, "From 'Conflict' to 'Constitutional Question': Transformations in Early American Public Discourse," *Quarterly Journal of Speech* 76 (1990): 247–61.
92. Garry Wills, *Lincoln at Gettysburg: The Words that Remade America* (New York: Simon and Schuster, 1992), 101.
93. Wills, *Lincoln at Gettysburg,* 145.
94. Martha Solomon Watson, "The Dynamics of Intertextuality: Re-reading the Declaration of Independence," in *Rhetoric and Political Culture in Nineteenth-Century America,* 91–111.
95. *Congressional Globe,* 42d Cong., 2d sess., 1872, 45, pt. 1:382.
96. Ibid., pt. 1:384.
97. Ibid., pt. 1:385.
98. Sumner's arguments presented an interesting national history so far as equality is concerned. Recall his reasoning that slavery had been

the country's interpretive principle; he also affirmed that the founding fathers believed as he did. His speech implies, then, that somewhere after the original declarations, America went astray and adopted the inequality error. Notably, he does not state when and where this transgression transpired. Focusing on the Declaration and then on slavery's presence and the Civil War, he does not, within the context of this speech, identify where inequality is introduced, although he is quick to affirm that after inequality became the nation's creed it took the Civil War and Reconstruction to set things right.

99. Sumner, *Charles Sumner: His Complete Works,* 19:233–34.
100. Jager, "Charles Sumner" 367.
101. James Jasinski, "Rearticulating History in Epideictic Discourse: Frederick Douglass's 'The Meaning of the Fourth of July to the Negro,'" in *Rhetoric and Political Culture in Nineteenth-Century America,* 75.
102. Ralph Waldo Emerson, "Prudence," in *The Collected Works of Ralph Waldo Emerson,* vol. 2, *Essays: First Series,* ed. Joseph Slater, Alfred R. Ferguson, and Jean F. Carr (1841; reprint, Cambridge: Harvard University Press, 1979).
103. Emerson, "Prudence," in *The Collected Works,* 2:136

Chapter 4

1. *Congressional Globe,* 42d Cong., 2d sess., 1872, 45, pt. 1:385.
2. *Congressional Globe,* 39th Cong., 1st sess., 1866, pt. 1:474–75.
3. See LaWanda Cox and John H. Cox, eds., *Reconstruction, the Negro, and the New South* (Columbia, S.C.: University of South Carolina Press, 1973), xiv. For some commentary on the relationship between racism and desegregation, see Eric Foner, *Reconstruction: America's Unfinished Revolution, 1863–1877* (New York: Harper and Row, 1988), 40, 368–72.
4. See David G. Bramley and Charles F. Longino Jr., eds., *White Racism and Black Americans* (Cambridge: Schenkman Publishing Co., 1972).
5. Although the various categories of racism—cultural, institutional, and linguistic—provide analytical insight, these terms are contemporary categories that the nineteenth century did not acknowledge. This does not mean that debate participants failed to grasp racism's pervasive qualities; the entire controversy implies that civil rights proponents understood how racial prejudice was evident within the legal system of segregation. Rather, one must keep in mind that the nineteenth century did not categorize racial prejudice into these three

forms. Both sides considered white superiority and black inferiority to be either natural truths or a set of personal beliefs.

6. Pierre Van den Berghe, *Race and Racism* (New York: John Wiley and Sons, 1967).
7. See William J. Wilson, "Class Conflict and Jim Crow Segregation in the Postbellum South," *Pacific Sociological Review* 19 (1976): 431–46.
8. Harold D. Woodman, *New South, New Law: The Legal Foundations of Credit and Labor Relations of the Postbellum Agricultural South* (Baton Rouge, La.: Louisiana State Press, 1995); Harold D. Woodman, "Sequel to Slavery: The New History Views the Postbellum South," *Journal of Southern History* 43 (1997): 523–54; Roger L. Ransom and Richard Sutch, "Debt Peonage in the Cotton South after the Civil War," *Journal of Economic History* 32 (1972): 641–69; Foner, *Reconstruction*, 405–7. See also Bradley G. Bond, *Political Culture in the Nineteenth-Century South: Mississippi, 1830–1900* (Baton Rouge, La.: Louisiana State University Press, 1995).
9. Thomas F. Gossett, *Race: The History of an Idea in America* (Dallas: Southern Methodist University Press, 1968); Oscar Handlin, *Race and Nationality in American Life*, 3d ed. (Boston: Little, Brown and Co., 1957).
10. Samuel Morton, *Crania Americana* (Philadelphia: J. Dobson, 1839); Samuel Morton, *Catalogue of Skulls of Man and the Inferior Animals*, 3d ed. (Philadelphia: Merrihew and Thompson, 1849).
11. "Death of Samuel George Morton, MD," *Charleston Medical Journal and Review* 16 (1851): 597.
12. Louis Agassiz, "The Diversity of Origin of the Human Races," *Christian Examiner* 49 (1850): 110–45; Nathaniel Shaler, "The Negro Problem," *Atlantic Monthly* 54, 1884: 703; Nathaniel Shaler, "Nature and Man in America," *Scribner's Magazine* 8, September 1890; Nathaniel Shaler, "African Element in America," *Arena*, September 1890. See Joel Williamson, *The Crucible of Race* (New York: Oxford University Press, 1984), 119–20.
13. *Congressional Record*, 43d Cong., 1st sess., 1874, appendix, 321.
14. *Congressional Record*, 43d Cong., 2d sess., 1875, 3, pt. 2:983.
15. *Congressional Record*, 43d Cong., 1st sess., 1874, 2, pt. 1:406.
16. *Congressional Record*, 43d Cong., 2d sess., 1875, 3, pt. 2:984.
17. *Congressional Record*, 43d Cong., 1st sess., 1874, 2, pt. 1:898.
18. *Congressional Record*, 43d Cong., 2d sess., 1875, 3, pt. 2:982.
19. Ibid., pt. 2:985.

20. Eric Foner, *Freedom's Lawmakers: A Directory of Black Officeholders during Reconstruction,* rev. ed. (Baton Rouge, La.: Louisiana State University Press, 1996), xi–xiii. See also Foner, *Reconstruction,* 423–24; and George C. Rable, *But There Was No Peace: The Role of Violence in the Politics of Reconstruction* (Athens, Ga.: University of Georgia Press, 1984), 81–100.
21. Thomas Nast, "This is a White Man's Government," *Harper's Weekly,* 12, 5 Sept. 1868, 568. Reproduced from the collection of the Library of Congress, Prints and Photographs Division, LC-USZ62-121735.
22. Waldo W. Braden, "Repining over an Irrevocable Past: The Ceremonial Oratory in a Defeated Society, 1865–1900," in *Oratory in the New South,* ed. Waldo W. Braden (Baton Rouge, La.: Louisiana State University Press, 1979), 26–36.
23. *Congressional Record,* 43d Cong., 1st sess., 1874, 2, pt. 1:429.
24. Ibid., pt. 5:4146.
25. Ibid., pt. 1:898.
26. *Biographical Directory of the United States Congress, 1774–1989,* bicentennial ed. (Washington, D.C.: U.S. Government Printing Office, 1989), 1724.
27. *Congressional Record,* 43d Cong., 1st sess., 1874, 2, pt. 1:953; See Thomas Dixon Jr., *The Leopard's Spots: A Romance of the White Man's Burden, 1865–1900* (New York: Doubleday, Page and Co., 1902).
28. Foner, *Freedom's Lawmakers,* xiii.
29. *Congressional Record,* 43d Cong., 2d sess., 1875, 3, pt. 2:983.
30. *Congressional Record,* 43d Cong., 1st sess., 1874, 2, pt. 5:4083.
31. Lerone Bennett Jr., *Before the Mayflower: A History of Black America,* 6th ed. (New York: Penguin Books, 1993); Benjamin Quarles, *The Negro in the Making of America* (New York: Collier Books, 1964).
32. David W. Blight, *Race and Reunion: The Civil War in American Memory* (Cambridge: Harvard University Press, 2001).
33. For theoretical and critical discussions about public memory, see Stephen H. Browne, "Reading Public Memory in Daniel Webster's *Plymouth Rock Oration,*" *Western Journal of Communication* 57 (1993): 464–77; Barbie Zelizer, "Reading the Past against the Grain: The Shape of Memory Studies," *Critical Studies of Mass Communication* 12 (1995): 214–39; and John Bodnar, *Remaking America: Public Memory, Commemoration, and Patriotism in the Twentieth Century* (Princeton: Princeton University Press, 1992).
34. *Congressional Record,* 43d Cong., 1st sess., 1874, 2, pt. 5:4784.
35. Ibid., pt. 1:565–66.
36. Ibid., pt. 1:410.

37. Ibid., pt. 1:899.
38. Ibid., pt. 1:407.
39. Ibid., pt. 5:4784.
40. Ibid., pt. 1:458.
41. Karlyn Kohrs Campbell, *The Rhetorical Act,* 2d ed. (Belmont, Calif.: Wadsworth Publishing Co., 1996), 9–11.
42. Abraham Lincoln to Governor Michael Hahn, 13 March 1864, in *Abraham Lincoln: His Speeches and Writing,* ed. Roy P. Basler (1946; reprint, New York: Da Capo Press, 1990), 745.
43. Blight, *Race and Reunion: The Civil War in American Memory.*
44. *Congressional Record,* 43d Cong., 1st sess., 1874, 2, pt. 1:899–900.
45. Ibid., pt. 1:426.
46. Celeste Michelle Condit and John Louis Lucaites, *Crafting Equality: America's AngloAfrican Word* (Chicago: Chicago University Press, 1993), 81.
47. *Congressional Record,* 43d Cong., 1st sess., 1874, 2, pt. 5:4083.
48. Ibid., pt. 1:407.
49. Ibid., pt. 1:566. See also *Congressional Record,* 43d Cong., 2d sess., 1875, 3, pt. 2:956–57.
50. See Tamar Lewin, "Calls for Slavery Restitution Getting Louder," *New York Times,* 4 June 2001, sec. a, 1; and Diane Cardwell, "Seeking Out a Just Way to Make Amends for Slavery," *New York Times,* 12 August 2000, sec. b, 7.
51. *Congressional Record,* 43d Cong., 1st sess., 1874, 2, pt 5:4783.
52. Ibid., pt. 5:4783.
53. Ibid., pt. 5:4783.
54. Ibid., pt. 1:406.
55. Patricia J. Williams, *The Alchemy of Race and Rights: Diary of a Law Professor* (Cambridge: Harvard University Press, 1991).
56. *Congressional Record,* 43d Cong., 1st sess., 1874, 2, pt. 5:4151.
57. Benjamin Butler, "Address in an African Church," Richmond, Va., 13 January 1868, Benjamin F. Butler Papers, Library of Congress, Manuscript Division, container 180.
58. *Congressional Record,* 43d Cong., 1st sess., 1874, 2, pt. 1:382.
59. See the authors' discussion of Barbara Jordan and Virginia Woolf, in Karlyn Kohrs Campbell and Kathleen Hall Jamieson, *Form and Genre: Shaping Rhetorical Action* (Falls Church: Speech Communication Association, 1978), 9–11.
60. Karlyn Kohrs Campbell notes as well that "enactment is both proof and a way to present evidence vividly." Thus enactment as a rhetori-

cal strategy involves both the procedural and product dimensions of argument. It is a procedure in the sense that it presents or acts a claim. Enactment is a product in the sense that the person speaking becomes an argument in and of herself. See Campbell, *The Rhetorical Act,* 309–10.

61. Kathleen Campbell, "Enactment as a Rhetorical Strategy in *The Year of Living Dangerously,*" *Central States Speech Journal* 39 (1988): 258–68.
62. Campbell, "Enactment as a Rhetorical Strategy," 260–61.
63. *Congressional Record,* 43d Cong., 1st sess., 1874, 2, pt. 5:4782.
64. It is important to note that Whitehead did offer his own testimony, stating that he had seen black riders in the ladies' car of several trains in his state. See *Congressional Record,* 43d Cong., 2d sess., 1875, 3, pt. 1:955.
65. Ibid., pt. 2:957–58.
66. *Congressional Record,* 43d Cong., 1st sess., 1874, 2, pt. 5:4782.
67. Ibid., pt. 1:410.
68. Ibid., pt. 5:4782.
69. This was a reference to the captivity suffered by Judah after the Babylonian invasion around 586 B.C. Ibid., 5:4784. One might note also that the same reference exists in Frederick Douglass, "What to the Slave Is the Fourth of July," 5 July 1852, in *Three Centuries of American Rhetorical Discourse: An Anthology and Review,* ed. Ronald F. Reid (Prospect Heights, Ill.: Waveland Press, 1988), 372.
70. Kenneth Cmiel, *Democratic Eloquence: The Fight over Popular Speech in Nineteenth-Century America* (New York: William Morrow and Co., 1990), 218.
71. Lamson, *The Glorious Failure,* 124.
72. *Congressional Record,* 43d Cong., 1st sess., 1874, 2, pt. 5:4783.
73. Ibid., pt. 5:4784.
74. Ibid., pt. 1:410.
75. Ibid., pt. 5:4785.
76. Ibid., pt. 5:4783.
77. Ibid., pt. 1:407.
78. Ibid., pt. 1:455.
79. Ibid., pt. 1:409.
80. Ibid., pt. 5:4784.
81. Ibid., pt. 5:4785.
82. Ibid., pt. 5:4784.
83. Ibid., pt. 1:376–77.

84. Cal M. Logue and Thurmon Garner, "Shift in Rhetorical Status of Blacks after Freedom," *Southern Communication Journal* 54 (1988): 1–39.
85. Elliott's letter is recorded in Lamson, *The Glorious Failure,* 132. See also page 284.
86. *Congressional Record,* 43d Cong., 1st sess., 1874, 2, pt. 4:3451, 3452.
87. Ibid., pt. 5:4784.
88. Ibid., pt. 5:4784.
89. Foner, *Reconstruction,* 412.
90. Condit and Lucaites, *Crafting Equality,* 116–17.
91. Cal M. Logue, "The Rhetorical Appeals of Whites to Blacks during Reconstruction," *Communication Monographs* 44 (1977): 241–51.
92. The New South was a particularly powerful myth that became popular toward the end of Reconstruction and into the 1880s and 1890s. See Waldo W. Braden, ed., *Oratory in the New South* (Baton Rouge, La.: Louisiana State University Press, 1979). See also the following speech by Henry Grady—one of the New South's most popular spokesmen. Henry Grady, "The New South," in *American Voices: Significant Speeches in American History, 1640–1945,* ed. James Andrews and David Zarefsky (New York: Longman, 1989), 352–59.
93. As quoted by Wirt Armistead Cate in *Lucius Q. C. Lamar: Secession and Reunion,* (1935; reprint, New York: Russell and Russell, 1969), 183.
94. *Congressional Record,* 43d Cong., 1st sess., 1874, appendix, 316.
95. Ibid., appendix, 316.
96. For work in the field of communication studies that examines these relationships, see Robert L. Scott, "On Viewing Rhetoric as Epistemic," *Central States Speech Journal* 18 (1967): 9–17; Robert L. Scott, "On Viewing Rhetoric as Epistemic: Ten Years Later," *Central States Speech Journal* 27 (1976): 258–66; Sonja K. Foss and Ann Gill, "Michel Foucault's Theory of Rhetoric as Epistemic," *Western Journal of Speech Communication* 51 (1987): 384–401; and Ronald F. Wendt, "Answers to the Gaze: A Genealogical Poaching of Resistances," *Quarterly Journal of Speech* 82 (1996): 251–73.
97. *Congressional Record,* 43d Cong., 1st sess,, 1874, 2, pt. 1:379.
98. Ibid., pt. 1:379.
99. *Congressional Record,* 43d Cong., 1st sess., 1874, appendix, 316.
100. See Phillip C. Wander, "The Savage Child: The Image of the Negro in the Pro-slavery Movement," *Southern Communication Journal* 37 (1972): 335–60.
101. *Congressional Record,* 43d Cong., 1st sess., 1874, appendix, 321.

102. *Congressional Record,* 43d Cong., 1st sess., 1874, 2, pt. 1:421.
103. *Congressional Record,* 43d Cong., 1st sess., 1874, appendix, 3.
104. Martha Hodes, *White Women, Black Men* (New Haven, Conn.: Yale University Press, 1997), 166.
105. *Congressional Record,* 43d Cong., 1st sess., 1874, appendix, 3.
106. Hodes, *White Women, Black Men,* 165.
107. *Congressional Record,* 43d Cong., 1st sess., 1874, 2, pt. 5:4157–58.
108. Ibid., pt. 1:556.
109. Williamson, *Crucible of Race,* 32; Hodes, *White Women, Black Men,* 96–122.
110. *Congressional Record,* 43d Cong., 1st sess., 1874, appendix, 316.
111. Howard N. Rabinowitz, *Race Relations in the Urban South, 1865–1890* (New York: Oxford University Press, 1978), 34, 45.
112. The presence of this argument does not mean that Southern whites began to treat pure African Americans better than those who were biracial. Rather, this argument reveals a shift in their rhetoric, not in their action.
113. *Congressional Record,* 43d Cong., 1st sess., 1874, 2, pt. 5:4169.
114. *Congressional Record,* 43d Cong., 1st sess., 1874, 1, pt. 1:556.
115. *Congressional Record,* 43d Cong., 1st sess., 1874, appendix, 4.
116. Ibid., appendix, 316.
117. Earl M. Maltz, "Fourteenth Amendment Concepts in the Antebellum Era," *American Journal of Legal History* 32 (1988): 307.
118. Abraham Lincoln, "Ottawa: Lincoln's Reply," 21 August 1858, in *The Complete Lincoln-Douglas Debates of 1858,* ed. Paul M. Angle (Chicago: University of Chicago Press, 1991), 117.
119. See G. S. Boritt, *Lincoln and the Economics of the American Dream* (Memphis, Tenn.: Memphis State University Press, 1978). Lincoln's views of black equality evolved from 1858 to the time of his death. See David Zarefsky, "Consistency and Change in Lincoln's Rhetoric about Equality," *Rhetoric and Public Affairs* 1 (1998): 21–44.
120. *Congressional Record,* 43d Cong., 1st sess., 1874, 1, pt. 1:376.
121. Abraham Lincoln, "Speech at Springfield, IL," 26 June 1857, in *Collected Works of Abraham Lincoln,* ed. Roy P. Basler (New Brunswick, N.J.: Rutgers University Press, 1953), 2:405–6.
122. *Congressional Record,* 43d Cong., 1st sess., 1874, appendix, 316.
123. *Congressional Record,* 43d Cong., 1st sess., 1874, 2, pt. 1:379.
124. Ibid., pt. 5:4154.
125. Allen Thurman, ibid., pt. 5:4088; Eli Saulsbury, ibid., pt. 5:4158.
126. Bond, *Political Culture,* 152.

127. *Congressional Record,* 43d Cong., 1st sess., 1874, 2, pt. 1:565–66.
128. Ibid., pt. 1:899.
129. See Augustus Merrimon, *Congressional Record,* 43d Cong., 1st sess., 1874, appendix, 316.

Chapter 5

1. Aristotle *The Rhetoric* 1.3.1358b22–25, trans. W. Rhys Roberts (New York: Random House, 1984). See also Kennedy's comments in footnote 81 of Aristotle's *The Rhetoric,* trans. George A. Kennedy (New York: Oxford University Press, 1991), 49.
2. Perelman and L. Olbrechts-Tyteca, *The New Rhetoric: A Treatise on Argumentation,* trans. John Wilkinson and Purcell Weaver (Notre Dame, Ind.: University of Notre Dame Press, 1969), 266–70. Cited passage on page 267.
3. See especially chapter 3 in Richard Weaver, *The Ethics of Rhetoric* (Davis, Calif.: Hermagoras Press, 1985). See also John R. E. Bliese, "Richard Weaver's Axiology of Argument," *Southern Communication Journal* 44 (1979): 275–88; and John R. E. Bliese, "The Conservative Rhetoric of Richard M. Weaver: Theory and Practice," *Southern Communication Journal* 54 (1989): 403–5.
4. The most prominent and controversial example is their emphasis on the universal audience. See Perelman and Olbrechts-Tyteca, *The New Rhetoric,* 31–35.
5. *Congressional Record,* 43d Cong., 1st sess., 1874, appendix, 3.
6. By textual context I mean an interpreted situation as defined and managed by the arguments of a debate's texts.
7. I described these incidents in chapter 2. See James M. McPherson, "Abolitionists and the Civil Rights Act of 1875," *Journal of American History* 52 (1965): 496.
8. Rainey had served in the South Carolina Senate during the early days of Reconstruction, and he was the first black seated in the House, arriving early to fill a vacancy on 12 December 1870. Known as a strong advocate of desegregation, he once refused to leave a segregated restaurant, causing the management to evict him physically. See Peggy Lamson, *The Glorious Failure: Black Congressman Robert Brown Elliott and the Reconstruction in South Carolina* (New York: W. W. Norton and Co., 1973), 68, 188, 121.
9. *Congressional Record,* 43d Cong., 2d sess., 1875, 3, pt. 2:955–57.
10. Ibid., pt. 2:959.

11. *Congressional Record,* 43d Cong., 1st sess., 1874, 2, pt. 1:341.
12. Historians suggest that Richard "Daddy" Cain was familiar with the South and racial tension. Once a Methodist preacher and the editor of the *South Carolina Leader,* he and his family lived in "constant fear" and had their home guarded by armed men. Cain left the House and South Carolina in 1879 and eventually helped to found Paul Quinn College in Waco, Texas, later becoming its second president. See Lamson, *The Glorious Failure,* 284; and Eric Foner, *Reconstruction: America's Unfinished Revolution, 1863–1877* (New York: Harper and Row, 1988), 426.
13. *Congressional Record,* 43d Cong., 1st sess, 1874, 2, pt. 1:565.
14. Ibid., pt. 1:566.
15. Ibid., pt. 5:4782.
16. Ibid., pt. 1:340.
17. See ibid., pt. 5:4784.
18. Ibid., pt. 1:565.
19. Ibid., pt. 1:566.
20. Ibid., pt. 1:423–24.
21. Ibid., pt. 1:426.
22. *Congressional Record,* 43d Cong., 2d sess., 1875, 3, pt. 3:1869.
23. Ibid., pt. 2: 957.
24. Interestingly, proponents of slavery before the war had argued that if only the abolitionists would stop their agitation, then the tensions between the North and South also would cease.
25. *Congressional Record,* 43d Cong. 1st sess., 1874, appendix, 310.
26. Ibid., appendix, 310.
27. See Waldo W. Braden, "Repining over an Irrevocable Past: The Ceremonial Orator in a Defeated Society, 1865–1900," in *Oratory in the New South,* ed. Waldo W. Braden (Baton Rouge, La.: Louisiana State University Press, 1979).
28. *Congressional Record,* 43d Cong., 1st sess., 1874, 2, pt. 1:381.
29. Ibid., pt. 1:899.
30. Ibid., pt. 1:381.
31. Ibid., pt. 1:375.
32. *Congressional Record,* 43d Cong., 1st sess., 1874, appendix, 3.
33. *Congressional Record,* 43d Cong., 1st sess., 1874, 2, pt. 5:4160.
34. *Congressional Record,* 43d Cong., 1st session, 1874, appendix, 320.
35. Ibid., 3.
36. *Congressional Record,* 43d Cong. 1st sess., 1874, 2, pt. 1:406.
37. Ibid., pt. 5:4088.

38. Ibid., pt. 5:4115.
39. Ibid., pt. 5:4114.
40. Ibid., pt. 5:4089.
41. Ibid., pt. 1:381.
42. *Congressional Record,* 43d Cong., 2d sess., 1875, 3, pt. 2:953.
43. *Congressional Record,* 43d Cong., 1st sess., 1874, 2, pt. 1:425.
44. Ibid., pt. 5:4153.
45. Both Gillette and Wyatt-Brown argue that these congressmen knew the bill would be ineffective. See William Gillette, *Retreat from Reconstruction, 1869–1879* (Baton Rouge, La.: Louisiana State University Press, 1979), 271; and Bertram Wyatt-Brown, "The Civil Rights Act of 1875," *Western Political Quarterly* 18 (1965): 774–75.
46. *Congressional Record,* 43d Cong., 1st sess., 1874, 2, pt. 5:4154.
47. Ibid., pt. 1:414.
48. Ibid., pt. 5:4785–86.
49. Ibid., pt. 1:410.
50. *Congressional Record,* 43d Cong., 2d sess., 1875, 3, pt. 2:981.
51. Ibid., pt. 2:1002.
52. *Congressional Record,* 43d Cong., 1st sess., 1874, 2, pt. 1:416.
53. Eric Foner, *Freedom's Lawmakers: A Directory of Black Officeholders during Reconstruction,* rev. ed. (Baton Rouge, La.: Louisiana State University Press, 1996), 138–39.
54. *Congressional Record,* 43d Cong., 2d sess., 1875, 3, pt. 2:944.
55. See Joseph Rainey, ibid., pt. 2:960; Alonzo Ransier, *Congressional Record,* 43d Cong., 1st sess., 1874, 2, pt. 1:382.
56. *Congressional Record,* 43d Cong., 2d sess., 1875, 3, pt. 2:944.
57. Ibid., pt. 2:957.
58. *Congressional Record,* 43d Cong., 1st sess., 1874, 2, pt. 1:344.
59. Quotation from page 107 of Celeste Michelle Condit and John Louis Lucaites, *Crafting Equality: America's Anglo-African Word* (Chicago: Chicago University Press, 1993); see also pages 107–8.
60. *Congressional Record,* 43d Cong., 2d sess., 1875, 3, pt. 2:957.
61. See Eric Foner, *Freedom's Lawmakers,* 171–72.
62. Pinchback did, however, become the lieutenant governor and then the acting governor of Louisiana. See James Haskins, *Pinckney Benton Stewart Pinchback* (New York: Macmillan, 1973); and James Haskins, *The First Black Governor: Pinckney Benton Stewart Pinchback* (Trenton, N.J.: Africa World Press, 1996).
63. See Pinckney Pinchback, "Speech on Equal Rights," June 1874, in the

P.B.S. Pinchback Papers, Manuscript Division, Moorland-Springarn Research Center, Howard University, box 1, folder 38.

64. Ibid., 7.
65. Ibid., 12.
66. *Congressional Record,* 43d Cong., 1st sess., 1874, 2, pt. 5:4116.
67. Ibid., pt. 5:4169.
68. *Congressional Record,* 43d Cong., 1st session, 1874, appendix, 302–7.
69. *Congressional Record,* 43d Cong., 2d sess., 1875, 3, pt. 2:952.
70. Ibid., pt. 2:984.
71. Ibid.
72. *Congressional Record,* 43d Cong., 1st sess., 1874, 2, pt. 5:4160.
73. *Congressional Record,* 43d Cong., 2d sess., 1875, 3, pt. 2:954.
74. *Congressional Record,* 43d Cong., 1st sess., 1874, 2, pt. 5:4164.
75. See Allen Thurman, ibid., pt. 5:4088.
76. *Congressional Record,* 43d Cong., 2d sess., 1875, appendix, 105.
77. *Congressional Record,* 43d Cong., 2d sess., 1875, 3, pt. 2:982.
78. *Congressional Record,* 43d Cong., 1st sess., 1874, appendix, 3.
79. *Congressional Record,* 43d Cong., 1st sess., 1874, 2, pt. 5:4146.
80. Ibid., pt. 5:4146; ibid., pt. 1:378.
81. Foner, *Reconstruction,* 525–26.
82. See Augustus Merrimon, *Congressional Record,* 43d Cong., 1st sess., 1874, appendix, 317.
83. Gillette, *Retreat from Reconstruction,* 200–1.
84. *Congressional Record,* 43d Cong., 1st sess., 1874, 2, pt. 5:4089.
85. Ibid., pt. 1:421.
86. Ibid., pt. 1:415.
87. Gillette, *Retreat from Reconstruction,* 200.
88. *Congressional Record,* 43d Cong., 2d sess., 1875, 3, pt. 2:944.
89. *Congressional Record,* 43d Cong., 1st sess., 1874, 2, pt. 5:4153.
90. *Congressional Record,* 43d Cong., 1st sess., 1874, appendix, 305.
91. Gillette, *Retreat from Reconstruction,* 204–5. While Gillette has a good point, I believe his eventual conclusion is a bit hasty. He calls this "hedging" a "travesty" against Sumner's principles, but one need not see it as such. Rather, ambiguity such as this is commonplace in political discourse. Even the most principled of congressmen utilize strategic ambiguity to further their cause.
92. *Congressional Record,* 43d Cong., 2d sess., 1875, 3, pt. 2:978.
93. *Congressional Record,* 43d Cong., 1st sess., 1874, appendix, 305.
94. See for instance Eli Saulsbury, *Congressional Record,* 43d Cong., 1st sess., 1874, 2, 5: 4158–59.

95. Ronald Beiner, *Political Judgment* (Chicago: University of Chicago Press, 1983).
96. James Jasinski, "Rhetoric and Judgment in the Constitutional Ratification Debate of 1787–1788: An Exploration of the Relationship between Theory and Critical Practice," *Quarterly Journal of Speech* 78 (1992): 206–14.
97. *Congressional Record,* 43d Cong., 2d sess., 1875, 3, pt. 2:998.
98. Ibid., pt. 5:4172.
99. See Robert Elliott, ibid., pt. 1:408; see Richard Cain, *Congressional Record,* 43d Cong. 2d sess., 1875, 3, pt. 2:957; Frederick T. Frelinghuysen, *Congressional Record,* 43d Cong., 1st sess., 1874, 2, pt. 4:3451.
100. *Congressional Record,* 43d Cong., 2d sess., 1875, 3, pt. 1:1796.
101. By temporal perspective I mean the textual context or the sense of time developed within the text of each side. See Stephen E. Lucas, "The Renaissance of American Public Address: Text and Context in Rhetorical Criticism," in *Landmark Essays on American Public Address,* ed. Martin J. Medhurst (Davis, Calif.: Hermagoras Press, 1993), 191.
102. *Congressional Record,* 43d Cong., 1st sess., 1874, appendix, 3.
103. *Congressional Globe,* 42d Cong., 2d sess., 1872, 45, pt. 1:383.
104. *Congressional Record,* 43d Cong., 1st sess., 1874, 2, pt. 1:425.
105. Ibid., pt. 1:379.
106. See, for instance, Alexander Stephens's emphasis on his own ethical character in ibid., pt. 1: 381.
107. See Richard Cain, *Congressional Record,* 43d Cong., 2d sess., 1875, 3, pt. 2: 981–82

Chapter 6

1. Robert J. Kaczorowski, *The Politics of Judicial Interpretation: The Federal Courts, Department of Justice and Civil Rights, 1866–1876* (New York: Oceana Publications, 1985); Robert J. Kaczorowski, *The Nationalization of Civil Rights: Constitutional Theory and Practice in a Racist Society, 1866–1883* (New York: Garland, 1987); Robert J. Kaczorowski, "The Enforcement Provisions of the Civil Rights Act of 1866: A Legislative History in Light of *Runyon v. McCrary,*" *Yale Law Journal* 98 (1989): 565–95; Howard Jay Graham, *Everyman's Constitution: Historical Essays on the Fourteenth Amendment, The "Conspiracy Theory," and American Constitutionalism* (Madison, Wisc.: State Historical Society of Wisconsin, 1968); Jacobus Ten-Broek, *Equal under Law* (New York: Collier Books, 1965).

2. See Michael W. McConnell, "The Originalist Case for *Brown v. Board of Education*," *Harvard Journal of Law and Public Policy* 19 (1996): 457–64; and Michael W. McConnell, "Originalism and the Desegregation Decisions," *Virginia Law Review* 81 (1995): 947–1140.
3. Earl M. Maltz, *Civil Rights, the Constitution, and Congress, 1863–1869* (Lawrence, Kans.: University Press of Kansas, 1990); Earl M. Maltz, "Reconstruction without Revolution: Republican Civil Rights Theory in the Era of the Fourteenth Amendment," *Houston Law Review* 24 (1987): 221–79; S. G. F. Spackman, "American Federalism and the Civil Rights Act of 1875," *Journal of American Studies* 10 (1976): 313–28.
4. Alexander M. Bickel, "The Original Understanding and the Segregation Decision," *Harvard Law Review* 69 (1955): 1–58; Jonathan Lurie, "The Fourteenth Amendment: Use and Application in Selected State Court Civil Liberties Cases, 1870–1890," *American Journal of Legal History* (1984): 295–313.
5. McConnell, "Originalism and the Desegregation Decisions," 947–1140; Michael J. Klarman, "*Brown,* Originalism, and Constitutional Theory: A Response to Professor McConnell," *Virginia Law Review* 81 (1995): 1881–936; Michael W. McConnell, "The Originalist Justification for *Brown:* A Reply to Professor Klarman," *Virginia Law Review* 83 (1995): 1937–55; Earl M. Maltz, "Originalism and the Desegregation Decisions—A Response to Professor McConnell," *Constitutional Commentary* 13 (1996): 223–31; Michael W. McConnell, "Segregation and the Original Understanding: A Reply to Professor Maltz," *Constitutional Commentary* 13 (1996): 233–41.
6. Paul A. Cimbala, *Under the Guardianship of the Nation: The Freedmen's Bureau and the Reconstruction of Georgia, 1865–1870* (Athens, Ga.: University of Georgia Press, 1997). See also LaWanda Cox, *Freedom, Racism, and Reconstruction: Collected Writings of LaWanda Cox,* ed. Donald G. Nieman (Athens, Ga.: University of Georgia Press, 1997), 41–60; Foner, *Reconstruction: America's Unfinished Revolution, 1863–1877* (New York: Harper and Row, 1988), 68–69.
7. Herman Belz, *Abraham Lincoln, Constitutionalism, and Equal Rights in the Civil War Era* (New York: Fordham University Press, 1998), chapter 6.
8. Foner, *Reconstruction,* 246.
9. Andrew Johnson, "Freedmen's Bureau Veto Message," *The Papers of Andrew Johnson,* ed. Paul H. Bergeron (Knoxville, Tenn.: University of Tennessee Press, 1992), 10:120–27; LaWanda Cox, "Civil Rights: The Issue of Reconstruction," in *Freedom, Racism, and Reconstruction: Col-*

lected Writings of LaWanda Cox, ed. Donald G. Nieman (Athens, Ga.: University of Georgia Press, 1997), 76–93.

10. Andrew Johnson, "Washington's Birthday Address," in *The Papers of Andrew Johnson,* 10:145–57.
11. *Congressional Globe,* 39th Cong., 1st sess., 1866, pt. 1:474–75.
12. Bickel, "The Original Understanding," 19–28; Maltz, *Civil Rights,* 66–67; Foner, *Reconstruction,* 242–51.
13. Cox, "Civil Rights," in *Freedom, Racism, and Reconstruction,* 94–124.
14. Jacob D. Cox to Andrew Johnson, 22 March 1866, in *The Papers of Andrew Johnson,* 10:288.
15. Bickel, "The Original Understanding," 12–13; McConnell, "Originalism and the Desegregation Decision," 958–60.
16. Andrew Johnson, "Veto of the Civil Rights Bill," in *The Papers of Andrew Johnson,* 10:312–20.
17. Brooks D. Simpson, *The Reconstruction Presidents* (Lawrence, Kans.: University Press of Kansas, 1998), 97.
18. Michael Les Benedict, *A Compromise of Principle: Congressional Republicans and Reconstruction, 1863–1869* (New York: Norton, 1974); Kenneth M. Stampp, *The Era of Reconstruction, 1865–1877* (1965; reprint, New York: Vintage Books, 1967), 123–31; Maltz, *Civil Rights,* 71–72.
19. Foner, *Reconstruction,* 252–53; Bickel, "The Original Understanding," 32–40.
20. Maltz, *Civil Rights,* 80.
21. Foner, *Reconstruction,* 238, 254–57; Bickel, "The Original Understanding," 40–56.
22. Foner, *Reconstruction,* 269; John Hope Franklin, *Reconstruction: After the Civil War,* 2d ed. (Chicago: University of Chicago Press, 1994), 65–67.
23. Maltz, *Civil Rights,* 128.
24. Maltz "Reconstruction without Revolution," 253–54.
25. Ibid., 254.
26. Kaczorowski, "The Enforcement Provisions," 567–69.
27. Kaczorowski, *The Politics of Judicial Interpretation,* 3.
28. Klarman, "*Brown,* Originalism, and Constitutional Theory," 1887; Foner also argues that "the Fourteenth Amendment can only be understood within the political and ideological context of 1866." See Foner, *Reconstruction,* 256–57.
29. *Congressional Record,* 43d Cong., 1st sess., 1874, 2, pt. 1:378–82.
30. U.S. Const, Amend XIV, § 1.
31. Ibid., § 5.
32. *Congressional Record,* 43d Cong., 1st sess., 1874, 2, pt. 1:379–80.

33. Kaczorowski, "The Enforcement Provisions," 574.
34. See John C. Calhoun's famous speech, "On the Force Bill: Nationalism and States' Rights, 1833," in *American Voices: Significant Speeches in American History, 1640–1945*, ed. James Andrews and David Zarefsky (New York: Longman, 1989), 139–46.
35. Maltz, "Reconstruction without Revolution," 231–32.
36. *The Slaughter–House Cases*, 16 Wallace 36 (1872).
37. Michael A. Ross, "Justice Miller's Reconstruction: The *Slaughter-House Cases*, Health Codes, and Civil Rights in New Orleans, 1861–1873," *Journal of Southern History* 64 (1998): 649–76. See also Robert C. Palmer, "The Parameters of Constitutional Reconstruction: *Slaughter-House, Cruikshank*, and the Fourteenth Amendment," *University of Illinois Law Review* (1984): 739–70.
38. See *The Slaughter-House Cases*, 16 Wallace 77–78 (1872).
39. The rights of national citizenship included protection of interstate travel, diplomatic protection abroad, use of U.S. waters, and the right to obtain a writ of habeas corpus.
40. Students of history and the law are often quite critical of the *Slaughter-House* decision. See Kaczorowski, *Politics of Judicial Interpretation*, 199–229; Akhil Reed Amar, "The Bill of Rights and the Fourteenth Amendment," *Yale Law Journal* 101 (1992): 1259; Michael McConnell, "The Forgotten Constitutional Moment," *Constitutional Commentary* 11 (1994): 133; Leo Pfeffer, *This Honorable Court: A History of the United States Supreme Court* (Boston: Beacon Press, 1965), 200; Michael Kent Curtis, *No State Shall Abridge: The Fourteenth Amendment and the Bill of Rights* (Durham, N.C.: Duke University Press, 1986); Foner, *Reconstruction*, 529–30.
41. See for instance William Finck, *Congressional Record*, 43d Cong., 2d sess., 1875, 3, pt. 2:948–48; Eli Saulsbury, *Congressional Record*, 43d Cong., 1st sess., 1874, 2, pt. 5:4159; James Beck, *Congressional Record*, 43d Cong., 1st sess., 1874, 2, pt. 1:342.
42. Wallace 77 (1872), quoted in *Congressional Record*, 43d Cong., 1st sess., 1874, 2, pt. 1:380.
43. *Congressional Record*, 43d Cong., 1st sess., 1874, 2, pt. 1:380.
44. Wallace 82 (1872), quoted in ibid., pt. 1:380.
45. *Congressional Record*, 43d Cong., 1st sess., 1874, 2, pt. 1:380.
46. *Congressional Record*, 43d Cong., 1st sess., 1874, appendix, 2.
47. *Congressional Record*, 43d Cong., 1st sess., 1874, 2, pt. 1:380.
48. *Congressional Record*, 43d Cong., 2d sess., 1875, 3, pt. 2:948.
49. *Congressional Record*, 43d Cong., 1st sess., 1874, 2, pt. 1:380.

50. Ibid.
51. Ibid., pt. 5:4146.
52. *Congressional Record,* 43d Cong., 1st sess., 1874, appendix, 241.
53. *Congressional Record,* 43d Cong., 2d sess., 1875, 3, pt. 2:949.
54. *Congressional Record,* 43d Cong., 1st sess., 1874, 2, pt. 5:4086.
55. Ibid., pt. 1:379.
56. *Congressional Record,* 43d Cong., 2d sess., 1875, 3, pt. 3:1862.
57. Foner, *Reconstruction,* 256–57.
58. *Congressional Record,* 43d Cong., 1st sess., 1874, 2, pt. 1:407.
59. Ibid.
60. Ross, "Justice Miller's Reconstruction," 650–53, 670–76.
61. *Congressional Record,* 43d Cong., 1st sess., 1874, 2, pt. 1:408.
62. Ibid.
63. Ibid.
64. Wallace 38 (1872).
65. Wallace 67–70 (1872), quoted in part in *Congressional Record,* 43d Cong., 1st sess., 1874, 2, pt. 1:408.
66. Ibid., pt. 1:408.
67. Ibid., pt. 4:3453.
68. Ibid., pt. 1:412–14.
69. See, for example, Eric Foner, *Reconstruction,* 23.
70. Foner, *Reconstruction,* 231–32. The presence of this distinguishing factor supports Maltz's position that while most Republicans understood that absolute state power was obliterated, they still maintained the fundamental belief in federalism and concurrent authority. See Maltz, *Reconstruction without Revolution,* 232.
71. *Congressional Record,* 43d Cong., 1st sess., 1874, 2, pt. 1:410.
72. *Congressional Record,* 43d Cong., 2d sess., 1875, 3, pt. 2:979.
73. *Congressional Record,* 43d Cong., 1st sess., 1874, 2, pt. 5:4147.
74. *Congressional Record,* 43d Cong., 2d sess., 1875, 3, pt. 3:1866.
75. Ibid., pt. 3:1870.
76. Wallace 95–96 (1872).
77. *Congressional Record,* 43d Cong., 1st sess., 1874, 2, pt. 5:4116.
78. Ibid., pt. 5:4148.
79. Palmer, "The Parameters of Constitutional Reconstruction," 741.
80. See Klarman, "*Brown,* Originalism, and Constitutional Theory," 1881–936; McConnell, "The Originalist Justification for *Brown,*" 1937–55; Maltz, "Originalism and the Desegregation Decisions," 223–31; McConnell, "Segregation and the Original Understanding," 233–41.

81. *Congressional Record,* 43d Cong., 1st sess., 1874, 2, pt. 1:381.
82. Ibid.
83. *Congressional Record,* 43d Cong., 1st sess., 1874, appendix, 481.
84. *Congressional Record,* 43d Cong., 1st sess., 1874, 2, pt. 1:408–9.
85. Ibid., pt. 1:408.
86. Ibid., pt. 1:410.
87. *Congressional Record,* 43d Cong., 2d sess., 1875, 3, pt. 2:960.
88. *Congressional Record,* 43d Cong. 1st sess., 1874, 2, pt. 1:409.
89. *Congressional Record,* 43d Cong., 2d sess., 1875, 3, pt. 2:944.
90. See Susan B. Anthony, "Is It a Crime for a U.S. Citizen to Vote," in *Man Cannot Speak for Her,* comp. Karlyn Kohrs Campbell (New York: Praeger, 1989) 2:279–316.
91. I do not mean to suggest that any period in history sustains only one interpretation of the Constitution; multiple theories of its meaning exist during any period. Rather, the scope of its meaning and the interpretations that dominate political discussion regulate what is possible with respect to congressional action.
92. *Congressional Record,* 43d Cong., 1st sess., 1874, 2, pt. 1:380.
93. Ibid., pt. 1:410.
94. Ibid., pt. 1:407.
95. Thurgood Marshall, "Reflections on the Bicentennial of the United States Constitution," *Harvard Law Review* 101 (1987): 2, 4.
96. The court did uphold the fourth section of provision, arguing that the desegregation of juries was within the authority of the Fourteenth Amendment.
97. *The Civil Rights Cases,* 109 U.S. 11 (1883).
98. McConnell argues that the *Civil Rights Cases* would have been decided differently if the bill had been more carefully worded. McConnell could be right, but his conclusion is speculative. See McConnell, "Originalism and the Desegregation Decisions," 1090–91.

Chapter 7

1. David Brion Davis, "The Emancipation Moment," in *Lincoln, the War President: The Gettysburg Lectures,* ed. Gabor S. Boritt (New York: Oxford University Press, 1992), 63–88.
2. Lucian W. Pye, *Politics, Personality and Nation Building* (New Haven, Conn.: Yale University Press, 1962).
3. See, for example, Arthur Asa Berger, ed., *Political Culture and Public Opinion* (New Brunswick, N.J.: Transaction Publishers, 1989); Dennis

J. Coyle and Richard J. Ellis, eds., *Politics, Policy, and Culture* (Boulder, Colo.: Westview Press, 1994); Terry Nichols Clark and Vincent Hoffmann-Martinot, eds., *The New Political Culture* (Boulder, Colo.: Westview Press, 1998); Aaron Wildavsky, "Choosing Preferences by Constructing Institutions: A Cultural Theory of Preference Formation," *American Political Science Review* 81 (1987): 3–21; and Bradley G. Bond, *Political Culture in the Nineteenth-Century South: Mississippi, 1830–1900* (Baton Rouge, La.: Louisiana State University Press, 1995).

4. Thomas B. Farrell, *Norms of Rhetorical Culture* (New Haven, Conn.: Yale University Press, 1993); Michael Leff, "The Habitation of Rhetoric," in *Argument and Critical Practices*, ed. Joseph W. Wenzel (Annandale, Va.: SCA, 1987), 1–8; Robert Hariman, "Relocating the Art of Public Address," in *Rhetoric and Political Culture in Nineteenth-Century America*, ed. Thomas W. Benson (East Lansing, Mich.: Michigan State University Press, 1997), 222–48.
5. See the introduction by G. Thomas Goodnight, "A Theory of Social Controversy: On Reason, Rhetoric and Communication" (Northwestern University, working paper, 1993). See also G. Thomas Goodnight, "Controversy," in *Argument in Controversy: Proceedings of the Seventh SCA/AFA Conference on Argumentation*, ed. Donn W. Parson (Annandale, Va.: Speech Communication Association, 1991), 3.
6. Goodnight, "Controversy," in *Argument in Controversy*, 6.
7. Quoted in Eric Foner, "Time for a Third Reconstruction," *The Nation*, 1 February 1993, 117.
8. Celeste Michelle Condit and John Louis Lucaites, *Crafting Equality: America's Anglo-African Word* (Chicago: Chicago University Press, 1993), 116–19; Cal M. Logue, "Restoration Strategies in Georgia, 1865–1880," in *Oratory in the New South*, ed. Waldo W. Braden (Baton Rouge, La.: Louisiana State University Press, 1979), 38–73; Waldo W. Braden, "Repining over an Irrevocable Past: The Ceremonial Oratory in a Defeated Society, 1865–1900," in *Oratory in the New South*, 26–36.
9. See Wirt Armistead Cate, *Lucius Q. C. Lamar: Secession and Reunion* (1935; reprint, New York Russell and Russell, 1969); and Henry Grady, "The New South," in *American Voices: Significant Speeches in American History, 1640–1945*, ed. James R. Andrews and David Zarefsky (New York: Longman, 1989), 352–59. For a critical discussion of Grady's rhetorical strategy, see Harold D. Mixon, "Henry Grady as a Persuasive Strategist," in *Oratory in the New South*, 74–116.
10. *Congressional Record*, 43d Cong., 1st sess., 1874, appendix, 316.
11. *Congressional Record*, 43d Cong., 1st sess., 1874, 1, pt. 1:555.

12. Lucius Q. C. Lamar, "Ought the Negro to Be Disfranchised? Ought He to Have Been Enfranchised?" in *Lucius Q. C. Lamar: His Life, Times, and Speeches,* ed. Edward Mayers (Nashville, Tenn.: Publishing House of the Methodist Episcopal Church, 1896), 722.
13. Gunnar Myrdal, *An American Dilemma: The Negro Problem and Modern Democracy* (New York: Harper and Brothers, 1944), 573–86.
14. As quoted in William Gillette, *Retreat from Reconstruction, 1869–1879* (Baton Rouge, La.: Louisiana State University Press, 1979), 218.
15. Although these men gave voice to a rhetoric of principle and equality, the author posits that their "real" feelings denied the equalitarian ideals they espoused. Bertram Wyatt-Brown, "The Civil Rights Act of 1875," *Western Political Quarterly* 18 (1965): 775; Gillette, *Retreat from Reconstruction,* 271.
16. W. R. Brock, "The Waning of Radicalism," in *Reconstruction: An Anthology of Revisionist Writings,* ed. Kenneth M. Stampp and Leon F. Litwack (Baton Rouge, La.: Louisiana State University Press, 1969), 496–515.
17. Gillette, *Retreat from Reconstruction,* 364–66
18. Ali N. Mohamed, "Attitudes of Northern Papers toward the Egalitarian Laws of Reconstruction," *Newspaper Research Journal* 19 (1998): 47–62; Ali N. Mohamed, "Civil Rights in the Nineteenth Century: Frederick Douglass vs. the Pro-Republican Press," *Proteus* 12 (1995): 29–34; David Domke, "Journalists, Framing, and Discourse about Race Relations," *Journalism and Mass Communication Monographs* 164 (1997); David Domke, "The Press and 'Delusive Theories of Equality and Fraternity' in the Age of Emancipation," *Critical Studies in Mass Communication* 13 (1996): 228–50.
19. Eric Foner, *Reconstruction: America's Unfinished Revolution, 1863–1877* (New York: Harper and Row, 1988), 524–29.
20. Frederick Douglass, "Speech at Lincoln Hall," 22 October 1883, in *Proceedings of the Civil Rights Mass Meeting* (Washington, D.C.: C. P. Farrell, 1883).
21. John Hope Franklin, "The Enforcement of the Civil Rights Act of 1875," *Prologue* 6 (1974): 225–35; Michael McConnell, "Originalism and the Desegregation Decisions," *Virginia Law Review* 83 (1995): 1087; Gillette, *Retreat from Reconstruction,* 276.
22. Rutherford B. Hayes, "Atlanta Speech," September 1877, in *The Life of Rutherford Birchard Hayes,* ed. Charles R. Williams (Boston: Houghton Mifflin, 1914), 2:252.
23. Brooks D. Simpson, *The Reconstruction Presidents* (Lawrence, Kans.: University Press of Kansas, 1998), chapter 7.

24. Rutherford B. Hayes, "Speeches," 20 May 1880, *R.B. Hayes Papers*, Library of the Rutherford B. Hayes Presidential Center (microfilm edition, roll 293, frame 413).
25. Booker T. Washington, "Atlanta Exposition Address," in *Lift Every Voice: African American Oratory, 1787–1900*, ed. Philip S. Foner and Robert J. Branham (Tuscaloosa, Ala.: University of Alabama Press, 1998), 800–5.
26. William McKinley, "Speech at Tuskegee Normal and Industrial Institute," 16 December 1898, in *Speeches and Addresses of William McKinley* (New York: Doubleday and McClure Co., 1900), 168.
27. John Hope, "We Are Struggling for Equality," in *Lift Every Voice*, 833.
28. For speeches that express incipient visions of black nationalism, see Martin Delany, "The Moral and Social Aspect of Africa," in *Lift Every Voice*, 389–91; Martin Delany, "Advice to Ex-slaves," in *Lift Every Voice*, 445–51; and Henry McNeal Turner, "Justice or Emigration Should Be Our Watchword," in *Lift Every Voice*, 775–89.
29. Howard N. Rabinowitz, "From Exclusion to Segregation: Southern Race Relations, 1865–1890," *Journal of American History* 63 (1976): 325–50; Joel Williamson, *The Crucible of Race* (New York: Oxford University Press, 1984), 44–61.
30. *Congressional Record*, 43d Cong., 2d sess., 1875, 3, pt. 2:945.
31. C. Vann Woodward, *The Strange Career of Jim Crow*, 3d rev. ed. (New York: Oxford University Press, 1974), 62.
32. Williamson, *Crucible of Race*, 69–72, 111–19.
33. Ward M. McAfee, "Reconstruction Revisited: The Republican Public Education Crusade of the 1870s," *Civil War History* 42 (1996): 133–53; David A. Gerber, "Education, Expediency, and Ideology: Race and Politics in the Desegregation of Ohio Public Schools in the Late Nineteenth Century," *Journal of Ethnic Studies* 1 (1973): 1–31. Ronald E. Butchart offers a rather negative evaluation of Northern and Southern public school reform for African Americans in *Northern Schools, Southern Blacks, and Reconstruction: Freedmen's Education, 1862–1875* (Westport, Conn: Greenwood Press, 1980). See also Gilbert T. Stephenson, *Race Distinctions in American Law* (New York: AMS Press, 1910), 120–24.
34. Eric Anderson, "James O'Hara of North Carolina: Black Leadership and Local Government," in *Southern Black Leaders of the Reconstruction Era*, ed. Howard N. Rabinowitz (Urbana, Ill.: University of Illinois Press, 1982), 101–25. See also George W. Reid, "Four in Black: North

Carolina's Black Congressmen, 1874–1901," *Journal of Negro History* 64 (1979): 229–43. Williamson; *Crucible of Race,* 112–13.

35. Hayes, "Atlanta Speech," in *The Life of Rutherford Birchard Hayes,* 252.
36. Benjamin Harrison, "First Annual Message," 3 December 1889, in *Messages and Papers of the Presidents,* ed. James D. Richardson (1897; reprint, New York: Bureau of National Literature, 1920), 11:5491.
37. Williamson, *Crucible of Race,* 116–17; Myrdal, *An American Dilemma,* 560–64; Jane Dailey, "Deference and Violence in the Postbellum Urban South: Manners and Massacres in Danville, Virginia," *Journal of Southern History* 63 (1997): 553–90; Philip A. Klinkner and Rogers M. Smith, *The Unsteady March: The Rise and Decline of Racial Equality in America* (Chicago: University of Chicago Press, 1999), 90–93. For a discussion about the post-Reconstruction presidents' views on race and civil rights, see George Sinkler, *Racial Attitudes;* and Kenneth O'Reilly, *Nixon's Piano* (New York: Free Press, 1995).
38. See Klinkner and Smith, *The Unsteady March,* 92–94; Stanley P. Hirshson, *Farewell to the Bloody Shirt: Northern Republicans and the Southern Negro, 1877–1893* (Bloomington, Ind.: Indiana University Press, 1962), 200–35; Sinkler, *Racial Attitudes of American Presidents,* 260–63; Homer E. Socolofsky and Allan B. Spetter, *The Presidency of Benjamin Harrison,* American Presidency Series (Lawrence, Kans.: University Press of Kansas, 1987), 62–66; and Vincent P. De Santis, "The Republican Party and the Southern Negro, 1877–1897," *Journal of Negro History* 45 (1960): 71–87. See also C. Vann Woodward, *Origins of the New South, 1877–1913* (Baton Rouge, La.: Louisiana State University Press, 1971).
39. "Civil v. Social Rights," *Chicago Tribune,* 9 November 1883, 4.

Epilogue

1. Foner, "Time for a Third Reconstruction," *The Nation,* 1 February 1993, 118.
2. *New York Times,* 10 October 1995, p. A10, col. 1.
3. Frederick Douglass, "Speech at Lincoln Hall," 22 October 1883, in *Proceedings of the Civil Rights Mass Meeting* (Washington, D.C.: C. P. Farrell, 1883), 13.
4. Andrew Hacker, *Two Nations: Black and White, Separate, Hostile, Unequal* (New York: Ballantine Books, 1992), 14.
5. Many contemporary black intellectuals have explored both the reality and the perception of racism among African Americans. See Cornel West, *Race Matters* (New York: Vintage Books, 1994); Cornel West and

Kelvin Shawn Sealey, *Restoring Hope: Conversations on the Future of Black America* (Boston: Beacon Press, 1997); bell hooks, *Black Looks: Race and Representation* (Boston: South End Press, 1992); bell hooks, "Representing Whiteness in the Black Imagination," in *Cultural Studies,* ed. Lawrence Grossberg, C. Nelson and P. Treichler (New York: Routledge, 1992); Derrick Bell, *And We Are Not Saved: The Elusive Quest for Racial Justice* (New York: HarperCollins, 1987); Derrick Bell, *Faces at the Bottom of the Well: The Permanence of Racism* (New York: Basic Books, 1992); Manning Marable, *The Crisis of Color and Democracy* (Monroe, Maine: Common Courage Press, 1992); and Manning Marable, *Beyond Black and White: Transforming African-American Politics* (New York: Verso, 1995).

Selected Bibliography

Agassiz, Louis. "The Diversity of the Human Races." *Christian Examiner* 49 1950: 110–145.

Alexander Stephens Papers, Library of Congress, Manuscript Division.

Amar, Akhil Reed. "The Bill of Rights and the Fourteenth Amendment." *Yale Law Journal* 101 (1992): 1193–284.

Anderson, Eric. "James O'Hara of North Carolina: Black Leadership and Local Government." In *Southern Black Leaders of the Reconstruction Era*, edited by Howard N. Rabinowitz, 101–25. Urbana: University of Illinois Press, 1982.

Anderson, Eric, and Alfred A. Moss Jr., eds. *The Facts of Reconstruction: Essays in Honor of John Hope Franklin.* Baton Rouge: Louisiana State University Press, 1991.

Andrews, James R. "An Historical Perspective on the Study of Social Movements." *Central States Speech Journal* 34 (1983): 67–69.

———. "History and Theory in the Study of the Rhetoric of Social Movements." *Central States Speech Journal* 31 (1980): 274–81.

Andrews, James R., and David Zarefsky, eds. *American Voices: Significant Speeches in American History, 1640–1945.* New York: Longman, 1989.

———. *Contemporary American Voices: Significant Speeches in American History, 1945–Present.* New York: Longman, 1992.

Angle, Paul M., ed. *The Complete Lincoln-Douglas Debates of 1858.* 1958. Reprint, Chicago: University of Chicago Press, 1991.

Appiah, Anthony, and Amy Gutmann. *Color Conscious: The Political Morality of Race* Princeton: Princeton University Press, 1996.

Aptheker, Herbert. *Abolitionism: A Revolutionary Movement.* Boston: Twayne Publishers, 1989.

———. *Anti-racism in U.S. History: The First Two Hundred Years.* Westport, Conn.: Praeger, 1993.

———, ed. *A Documentary History of the Negro People in the United States.* Vol. 1. New York: Citadel Book Press, 1951.

Aritstotle. *The Rhetoric.* Translated by George A. Kennedy. New York: Oxford University Press, 1991.

———. *The Rhetoric.* Translated by W. Rhys Roberts. New York: Random House, 1984.

Ashworth, John. *Agrarians and Aristocrats: Party Political Ideology in the United States, 1837–1846.* Atlantic Highlands, N.J.: Humanities Press, 1983.

Basler, Roy P., ed. *Abraham Lincoln: His Speeches and Writing.* 1946. Reprint, New York: Da Capo Press, 1990.

______. *Collected Works of Abraham Lincoln.* Vol. 2. New Brunswick, N.J.: Rutgers University Press, 1953.

Beiner, Ronald. *Political Judgment.* Chicago: University of Chicago Press, 1983.

Bell, Derrick. *And We Are Not Saved: The Elusive Quest for Racial Justice.* New York: HarperCollins, 1987.

______. *Faces at the Bottom of the Well: The Permanence of Racism.* New York: Basic Books, 1992.

Belz, Herman. *Abraham Lincoln, Constitutionalism, and Equal Rights in the Civil War Era.* New York: Fordham University Press, 1998.

Benedict, Michael Les. *A Compromise of Principle: Congressional Republicans and Reconstruction, 1863–1869.* New York: Norton, 1974.

Benjamin F. Butler Papers, Library of Congress, Manuscript Division.

Bennett, Lerone, Jr. *Before the Mayflower: A History of Black America.* 6th ed. New York: Penguin Books, 1993.

Berger, Arthur Asa, ed. *Political Culture and Public Opinion.* New Brunswick, N.J.: Transaction Publishers, 1989.

Berger, Raoul. *The Fourteenth Amendment and the Bill of Rights.* Norman: University of Oklahoma Press, 1989.

______. *Government by Judiciary: The Transformation of the Fourteenth Amendment.* Cambridge: Harvard University Press, 1977.

Bickel, Alexander M. "The Original Understanding and the Segregation Decision." *Harvard Law Review* 69 (1955): 1–58.

Blassingame, John W., ed. *The Frederick Douglass Papers: Speeches, Debates, and Interviews.* Vol. 1. (New Haven, Conn.: Yale University Press, 1979).

Bliese, John R. E. "The Conservative Rhetoric of Richard Weaver: Theory and Practice." *Southern Communication Journal* 54 (1989): 401–21.

______. "Richard Weaver's Axiology of Argument." *Southern Communication Journal* 44 (1979): 275–88.

Blight, David W. *Race and Reunion: The Civil War in American History.* Cambridge: Harvard University Press, 2001.

Bodnar, John. *Remaking America: Public Memory, Commemoration, and Patriotism in the Twentieth Century.* Princeton: Princeton University Press, 1992.

Bond, Bradley G. *Political Culture in the Nineteenth-Century South: Mississippi, 1830–1900.* Baton Rouge: Louisiana State University Press, 1995.

Boritt, Gabor S. *Lincoln and the Economics of the American Dream.* Memphis: Memphis State University Press, 1978.

Bowers, Claude G. *The Tragic Era: The Revolution after Lincoln.* Cambridge, Mass.: Houghton Mifflin and Co., 1929.

Braden, Waldo J., ed. *Oratory in the New South.* Baton Rouge: Louisiana State University Press, 1979.

———. "Repining over an Irrevocable Past: The Ceremonial Orator in a Defeated Society, 1865–1900." In *Oratory in the New South,* edited by Waldo W. Braden. Baton Rouge: Louisiana State University Press, 1979.

Braden, Waldo W., and Harold Mixon. "Epideictic Speaking in the Post–Civil War South and the Southern Experience." *Southern Communication Journal* 45 (1988): 40–57.

Bramley, David G., and Charles F. Longino Jr., eds. *White Racism and Black Americans.* Cambridge, Mass.: Schenkman Publishing Co., 1972.

Brock, W. R. "The Waning of Radicalism." In *Reconstruction: An Anthology of Revisionist Writings,* edited by Kenneth M. Stampp and Leon F. Litwack. Baton Rouge: Louisiana State University Press, 1969.

Browne, Stephen H. "Reading Public Memory in Daniel Webster's *Plymouth Rock Oration." Western Journal of Communication* 57 (1993): 464–77.

Burgess, John William. *The Civil War and the Constitution, 1859–1865.* New York: C. Scribner's Sons, 1901.

Burke, Kenneth. "Dramatism" In *International Encyclopedia of the Social Sciences,* edited by David L. Sills. Vol. 7. New York: Macmillan Co. and Free Press, 1968.

Butchart, Ronald E. *Northern Schools, Southern Blacks, and Reconstruction: Freedmen's Education, 1862–1875.* Westport, Conn.: Greenwood Press, 1980.

Campbell, Karlyn Kohrs. *The Rhetorical Act.* 2d ed. Belmont, Ca.: Wadsworth Publishing Co., 1996.

———, comp. *Man Cannot Speak for Her.* Vol. 2. New York: Praeger, 1989.

Campbell, Karlyn Kohrs, and Kathleen Hall Jamieson. *Form and Genre: Shaping Rhetorical Action.* Falls Church, Va.: Speech Communication Association, 1978.

Campbell, Kathleen. "Enactment as a Rhetorical Strategy in *The Year of Living Dangerously." Central States Speech Journal* 39 (1988): 258–68

Cate, Wirt Armistead. *Lucius Q. C. Lamar: Secession and Reunion.* 1935. Reprint, New York: Russell and Russell, 1969.

Cimbala, Paul A. *Under the Guardianship of the Nation: The Freedmen's Bureau and the Reconstruction of Georgia, 1865–1870.* Athens: University of Georgia Press, 1997.

Cmiel, Kenneth. *Democratic Eloquence: The Fight over Popular Speech in Nineteenth-Century America.* New York: William Morrow and Co., 1990.

Condit, Celeste Michelle. "Democracy and Civil Rights: The Universalizing Influence of Public Argumentation." *Communication Monographs* 54 (1987): 1–18.

Condit, Celeste Michelle, and John Louis Lucaites, *Crafting Equality: America's Anglo-African Word.* Chicago: Chicago University Press, 1993.

Congress, U.S. *Biographical Directory of the United States Congress, 1774–1989.* Bicentennial ed. Washington, D.C.: U.S. Government Printing Office, 1989.

Congressional Globe, 42d Cong., 2d session, 1872, Vol. 45, pt. 1.

Congressional Record, 43d Cong., 1873–75. Washington, D.C.

Cook, A. "Reference and Rhetoric in Historiography." In *Criticism, History, and Intertextuality,* edited by Richard Fleming and Michael Payne, 159–82. Lewisburg, Pa.: Bucknell University Press, 1988.

Cox, LaWanda. "Civil Rights: The Issue of Reconstruction." In *Freedom, Racism, and Reconstruction: Collected Writings of LaWanda Cox,* edited by Donald G. Nieman. Athens: University of Georgia Press, 1997.

———. *Freedom, Racism, and Reconstruction: Collected Writings of LaWanda Cox.* Edited by Donald G. Nieman. Athens: University of Georgia Press, 1997.

Cox, LaWanda, and John H. Cox. *Politics, Principle, and Prejudice, 1865–1866: The Dilemma of Reconstruction in America.* New York: Free Press, 1963.

———, eds. *Reconstruction, The Negro, and the New South.* Columbia: University of South Carolina Press, 1973.

Coyle, Dennis J., and Richard J. Ellis, eds. *Politics, Policy, and Culture.* Boulder, Colo.: Westview Press, 1998.

Crenshaw, Kimberlé Williams. "Race, Reform, and Retrenchment: Transformation and Legitimation in Anti-discrimination Law." *Harvard Law Review* 101 (1988): 1331–87.

Curry, Leonard P. *The Free Black in Urban America, 1800–1850: The Shadow of the Dream.* Chicago: University of Chicago Press, 1981.

Curtis, Michael Kent. *No State Shall Abridge: The Fourteenth Amendment and the Bill of Rights.* Durham, N.C.: Duke University Press, 1986.

Dailey, Jane. "Deference and Violence in the Postbellum Urban South: Manners and Massacres in Danville, Virginia." *Journal of Southern History* 63 (1997): 553–90.

Darsey, James. "The Legend of Eugene Debs: Prophetic 'Ethos' as Radical Argument." *Quarterly Journal of Speech* 74 (1988): 435–36.

———. *The Prophetic Tradition and Radical Rhetoric in America.* New York: New York University Press, 1997.

Davis, David Brion. "The Emancipation Moment." In *Lincoln, the War President: The Gettysburg Lectures,* edited by Gabor S. Boritt. New York: Oxford University Press, 1992.

Dawes, Anna Laurens. *Charles Sumner.* New York: Dodd, Mead and Co., 1892.

"Death of Samuel George Morton, MD." *Charleston Medical Journal and Review* 16 (1851):597.

Delgado, Richard, ed. *Critical Race Theory: The Cutting Edge.* Philadelphia: Temple University Press, 1995.

De Santis, Vincent P. "The Republican Party and the Southern Negro, 1877–1897." *Journal of Negro History* 45 (1960): 71–87.

Dixon, Thomas, Jr. *The Leopard's Spots: A Romance of the White Man's Burden, 1865–1900.* New York: Doubleday, Page and Co., 1902.

Domke, David. "Journalists, Framing, and Discourse about Race Relations." *Journalism and Mass Communication Monographs* 164 (1997).

———. "The Press and 'Delusive Theories of Equality and Fraternity' in the Age of Emancipation." *Critical Studies in Mass Communication* 13 (1996): 228–50.

Donald, David Herbert. *Charles Sumner and the Coming of the Civil War.* New York: Alfred A. Knopf, 1960.

———. *Charles Sumner and the Rights of Man.* New York: Alfred A. Knopf, 1970.

———. *Lincoln.* New York: Simon and Schuster, 1995.

———. *The Politics of Reconstruction, 1863–1867.* Baton Rouge: Louisiana State University Press, 1965.

Douglass, Frederick. "Speech at Lincoln Hall," 22 October 1883. In *Proceedings of the Civil Rights Mass Meeting.* Washington, D.C.: C. P. Farrell, 1883.

———. "Speech at the Thirty-sixth Anniversary of the American Antislavery Society," 29 May 1869, *National Slavery Standard,* p. 1.

Du Bois, W. E. B. *Black Reconstruction in America, 1860–1880.* 1935. Reprint, New York: Atheneum, 1992.

———. *The Souls of Black Folk.* 1903. Reprint, New York: Alfred A. Knopf, 1993.

Dunning, William Archibald. *Reconstruction: Political and Economic, 1865–1877.* New York: Harper and Brothers, 1907.

Edelman, Murray. *The Symbolic Uses of Politics.* 1964. Reprint, Urbana: University of Illinois Press, 1985.

Emerson, Ralph Waldo. "Prudence." In *The Collected Works of Ralph Waldo Emerson,* edited by Joseph Slater, Alfred R. Ferguson, and Jean F. Carr. Vol. 2. Cambridge: Harvard University Press, 1979.

Farrell, Thomas B. *Norms of Rhetorical Culture.* New Haven, Conn.: Yale University Press, 1993.

Fehrenbacker, Don E. "The Anti-Lincoln Tradition." In *Lincoln in Text and Context: Collected Essays.* Stanford, Calif.: Stanford University Press, 1987.

Fischer, Roger A. "Racial Segregation in Ante Bellum New Orleans." *American Historical Review* 74 (1969): 926–57.

Folmsbee, Stanley J. "The Origin of the First 'Jim Crow' Law." *Journal of Southern History* (1940): 234–47.

Foner, Eric. *Free Soil, Free Labor, Free Men: The Ideology of the Republican Party before the Civil War.* New York: Oxford University Press, 1970.

———. *Freedom's Lawmakers: A Directory of Black Officeholders during Reconstruction.* Rev. ed. Baton Rouge: Louisiana State University Press, 1996.

———. *Reconstruction: America's Unfinished Revolution, 1863–1877.* New York: Harper and Row, 1988.

———. "Reconstruction Revisited." *Reviews in American History* 10 (1982): 82–100.

———. "Time for a Third Reconstruction." *The Nation,* 1 February 1993, 117–18.

Foner, Eric, and Olivia Mahoney. *America's Reconstruction: People and Politics after the Civil War.* New York: HarperPerennial, 1995.

Foner, Philip S. *History of Black Americans.* Vol. 1. Westport, Conn.: Greenwood Press, 1975.

Foner, Philip S., and Robert J. Branham, eds. *Lift Every Voice: African American Oratory, 1787–1900.* Tuscaloosa: University of Alabama Press, 1998.

Foreman, Christopher H., Jr., ed. *The African American Predicament.* Washington, D.C.: Brookings Institution Press, 1999.

Foss, Sonja K., and Ann Gill. "Michel Foucault's Theory of Rhetoric as Epistemic." *Western Journal of Speech Communication* 51 (1987): 384–401.

Foucault, Michel. *The Archaeology of Knowledge.* Translated by A. M. Sheridan Smith. New York: Pantheon, 1972.

Franklin, John Hope. *The Emancipation Proclamation.* Wheeling, Ill.: Harlan Davidson, 1995.

———. "The Enforcement of the Civil Rights Act of 1875." *Prologue* 6 (1974): 225–35.

———. *Reconstruction: After the Civil War.* 2d ed. Chicago: University of Chicago Press, 1994.

Franklin, John Hope, and Alfred A. Moss Jr. *From Slavery to Freedom: A History of Negro Americans.* 6th ed. New York: Knopf, 1988.

Frederickson, George M. "A Man but Not a Brother: Abraham Lincoln and Racial Equality." *Journal of Southern History* 41 (1975): 39–58.

Gates, Henry Louis, Jr., ed. *"Race," Writing, and Difference.* Chicago: University of Chicago Press, 1986.

Gerber, David A. "Education, Expediency, and Ideology: Race and Politics in the Desegregation of Ohio Public Schools in the Late Nineteenth Century." *Journal of Ethnic Studies* 1 (1973): 1–31.

Gillette, William. *Retreat from Reconstruction, 1869–1879.* Baton Rouge: Louisiana State University Press, 1979.

Goldberg, David Theo. *Racist Culture: Philosophy and the Politics of Meaning.* Cambridge, Mass.: Blackwell, 1993.

Goodnight, G. Thomas, "Controversy." In *Argument in Controversy: Proceedings of the Seventh SCA/AFA Conference on Argumentation,* edited by Donn W. Parson. Annandale, Va.: Speech Communication Association, 1991.

———. "The Nuclear Age as an Argument Formation." Working paper presented at the Conference on Methodologies of Survival, Dubrovnik, Croatia, 18–20 June 1987.

———. "A Theory of Social Controversy: On Reason, Rhetoric and Communication." Northwestern University, working paper, 1993.

Gossett, Thomas F. *Race: The History of an Idea in America.* Dallas: Southern Methodist University Press, 1968.

Gould, Stephen Jay. *The Mismeasure of Man.* Rev. and expanded ed. New York: Norton, 1996.

Graham, Howard Jay. *Everyman's Constitution: Historical Essays on the Fourteenth Amendment, the "Conspiracy Theory," and American Constitutionalism.* Madison: State Historical Society of Wisconsin, 1968.

Graves, John William. "Jim Crow in Arkansas: A Reconsideration of Urban Race Relations in the Post-Reconstruction South." *Journal of Southern History* 55 (1989): 421–48.

Gronbeck, Bruce E. "Popular Culture, Media, and Political Communication." In *New Directions in Political Communication,* edited by. David L. Swanson and Dan Nimmo. Newbury Park, Calif.: Sage Publications, 1990.

Gudridge, Patrick O. "Privileges and Permissions: The Civil Rights Act of 1875." *Law and Philosophy* 83 (1989): 83–130.

Hacker, Andrew. *Two Nations: Black and White, Separate, Hostile, Unequal.* New York: Ballantine Books, 1992.

Handlin, Oscar. *Race and Nationality in American Life.* 3d ed. Boston: Little, Brown and Co., 1957.

Haney López, I. F. "The Social Construction of Race." *Harvard Civil Rights-Civil Liberties Law Review* 29(1994): 1–62.

Hariman, Robert. "Relocating the Art of Public Address." In *Rhetoric and Political Culture in Nineteenth-Century America*, edited by Thomas W. Benson, 222–48. East Lansing: Michigan State University Press, 1997.

Haskins, James. *The First Black Governor: Pinckney Benton Stewart Pinchback*. Trenton, N.J.: Africa World Press, 1996.

———. *Pinckney Benton Stewart Pinchback*. New York: Macmillan, 1973.

Hirshson, Stanley P. *Farwell to the Bloody Shirt: Northern Republicans and the Southern Negro, 1877–1893*. Bloomington: Indiana University Press, 1962.

Hodes, Martha. *White Women, Black Men*. New Haven, Conn.: Yale University Press, 1997.

Hoeveler, J. David, Jr. "Reconstruction and the Federal Courts: The Civil Rights Act of 1875." *Historian* 31 (1969): 604–17.

Holt, Thomas. *Black over White: Negro Political Leadership in South Carolina during Reconstruction*. Urbana: University of Illinois Press, 1977

hooks, bell. *Black Looks: Race and Representations*. Boston: South End Press, 1992.

———. "Representing Whiteness in the Black Imagination." In *Cultural Studies*, edited by Lawrence Grossberg, C. Nelson, and P. Treichler. New York: Routledge, 1992.

Hyman, Harold M. *A More Perfect Union: The Impact of the Civil War and Reconstruction on the Constitution*. New York: Knopf, 1973.

Jager, Ronald B. "Charles Sumner: The Constitution and the Civil Rights Act of 1875." *New England Quarterly* 42 (1969): 350–72.

James Rapier Family Papers, Manuscript Division, Moorland-Spingarn Research Center, Howard University.

Jasinski, James. "The Forms and Limits of Prudence in Henry Clay's (1850) Defense of the Compromise Measures." *Quarterly Journal of Speech* 81 (1995): 454–78.

———. "Rearticulating History in Epideictic Discourse: Frederick Douglass's 'The Meaning of the Fourth of July to the Negro.'" In *Rhetoric and Political Culture in Nineteenth-Century America*, edited by Thomas W. Benson. East Lansing: Michigan State University Press, 1997.

———. "Rhetoric and Judgment in the Constitutional Ratification Debate of 1787–1788: An Exploration of the Relationship between Theory and Critical Practice." *Quarterly Journal of Speech* 78 (1992): 206–14.

Johnson, Andrew. *The Papers of Andrew Johnson*. Edited by Paul H. Bergeron. Vol. 10. Knoxville: University of Tennessee Press, 1992.

Jones, Jacqueline. *Labor of Love, Labor of Sorrow*. New York: Basic Books, 1985.

Kaczorowski, Robert J. "The Enforcement Provisions of the Civil Rights Act of 1866: A Legislative History in Light of *Runyon v. McCrary.*" *Yale Law Journal* 98 (1989): 565–95.

———. *The Nationalization of Civil Rights: Constitutional Theory and Practice in a Racist Society, 1866–1883.* New York: Garland, 1987.

———. *The Politics of Judicial Interpretation: The Federal Courts, Department of Justice and Civil Rights, 1866–1876.* New York: Oceana Publications, 1985.

Kaufer, David S., and Kathleen M. Carley. "Condensation Symbols: Their Variety and Rhetorical Function in Political Discourse." *Philosophy and Rhetoric* 26 (1993): 201–26.

Kelly, Alfred H. "The Congressional Controversy over School Segregation, 1867–1875." *The American Historical Review* 64 (1959): 537–63.

Kennedy, Stetson. *After Appomattox: How the South Won the War.* Gainesville: University Press of Florida, 1995.

Klarman, Michael J. "*Brown,* Originalism, and Constitutional Theory: A Response to Professor McConnell." *Virginia Law Review* 81 (1995): 1881–936.

Klinkner, Philip A., and Rogers M. Smith. *The Unsteady March: The Rise and Decline of Racial Equality in America.* Chicago: University of Chicago Press, 1999.

Kluger, Richard. *Simple Justice: The History of "Brown v. Board of Education" and Black America's Struggle for Equality.* New York: Knopf, 1976.

Kousser, J. Morgan. "'The Supremacy of Equal Rights': The Struggle against Racial Discrimination in Antebellum Massachusetts and the Foundations of the Fourteenth Amendment." *Northwestern University Law Review* 82 (1988): 941–1010.

Kousser, J. Morgan, and James M. McPherson, eds. *Region, Race, and Reconstruction: Essays in Honor of C. Vann Woodward.* New York: Oxford University Press, 1982.

Lampe, Gregory P. *Frederick Douglass: Freedom's Voice, 1818–1845.* East Lansing: Michigan State University Press, 1998.

Lamson, Peggy. *The Glorious Failure: Black Congressman Robert Brown Elliott and the Reconstruction in South Carolina.* New York: W. W. Norton and Co., 1973.

Ledbetter, Bill. "Charles Sumner: Political Activist for the New England Transcendentalists." *Historian* 44 (1982): 347–63.

Leff, Michael. "The Habitation of Rhetoric." In *Argument and Critical Practices,* edited by Joseph W. Wenzel. Annandale, Va.: SCA, 1987.

———. "Textual Criticism: The Legacy of G. P. Mohrmann." In *Landmark Essays on American Public Address,* edited by Martin J. Medhurst. Davis:

Hermagoras Press, 1993. First published in *Quarterly Journal of Speech* 72 (1986): 377–89.

———. "Things Made by Words: Reflections on Textual Criticism." *Quarterly Journal of Speech* 78 (1992): 223–31.

Lester, John C., D. L. Wilson, and Walter L. Fleming. *Ku Klux Klan : Its Origin, Growth and Disbandment.* New York: Neale Publishing Co., 1905.

Levine, Bruce. *Half Slave and Half Free: The Roots of the Civil War.* New York: Noonday Press, 1992.

Levy, Leonard W., and Harlan B. Phillips. "The *Roberts* Case: Source of the 'Separate but Equal' Doctrine." *American Historical Review* 56 (1950): 510–18.

Lincoln, Abraham. *Abraham Lincoln: His Speeches and Writing.* Edited by Roy P. Basler. 1946. Reprint, New York: Da Capo Press, 1990.

Litwack, Leon F. *Been in the Storm So Long: The Aftermath of Slavery.* New York: Random House, 1979.

———. *North of Slavery: The Negro in the Free States, 1790–1860.* Chicago: University of Chicago Press, 1961.

Logue, Cal M. "Restoration Strategies in Georgia, 1865–1880." In *Oratory in the New South,* edited by Waldo W. Braden. Baton Rouge: Louisiana State University Press, 1979.

———. "The Rhetorical Appeals of Whites to Blacks during Reconstruction." *Communication Monographs* 44 (1977): 241–51.

Logue, Cal M., and Thurmon Garner. "Shift in Rhetorical Status of Blacks after Freedom." *Southern Communication Journal* 54 (1988): 1–39.

Lucas, Stephen E. "The Renaissance of American Public Address: Text and Context in Rhetorical Criticism." In *Landmark Essays on American Public Address,* edited by Martin J. Medhurst. Davis, Calif.: Hermagoras Press, 1993. First published in *Quarterly Journal of Speech* 74 (1988): 241–60.

———. "The Schism in Rhetorical Scholarship." In *Landmark Essays on American Public Address,* edited by Martin J. Medhurst. Davis, Calif.: Hermagoras Press, 1993. First published in *Quarterly Journal of Speech* 67 (1981): 1–20.

Lurie, Jonathan. "The Fourteenth Amendment: Use and Application in Selected State Court Civil Liberties Cases, 1870–1890." *American Journal of Legal History* (1984): 295–313.

Malik, Kenan. *The Meaning of Race: Race, History and Culture in Western Society.* Washington Square: New York University Press, 1996.

Maltz, Earl M. *Civil Rights, the Constitution, and Congress, 1863–1869.* Lawrence: University Press of Kansas, 1990.

———. "Fourteenth Amendment Concepts in the Antebellum Era." *American Journal of Legal History* 32 (1988): 305–46.

———. "Originalism and the Desegregation Decisions—A Response to Professor McConnell." *Constitutional Commentary* 13 (1996): 223–31.

———. "Reconstruction without Revolution: Republican Civil Rights Theory in the Era of the Fourteenth Amendment." *Houston Law Review* 24 (1987): 221–79.

Marable, Manning. *Beyond Black and White: Transforming African-American Politics.* New York: Verso, 1995.

———. *The Crisis of Color and Democracy.* Monroe, Maine: Common Courage Press, 1992.

Marshall, Thurgood. "Reflections on the Bicentennial of the United States Constitution." *Harvard Law Review* 101 (1987): 1–6.

Mathews, L. "Keeping Down Jim Crow: The Railroads and the Separate Coach Bills in South Carolina." *South Atlantic Quarterly* 73 (1973): 117–29.

Mayers, Edward, ed. *Lucius Q. C. Lamar: His Life, Times, and Speeches.* Nashville, Tenn.: Publishing House of the Methodist Episcopal Church, 1896.

McAfee, Ward M. "Reconstruction Revisited: The Republican Public Education Crusade of the 1870s." *Civil War History* 42 (1996): 133–53.

McBride, David. "Fourteenth Amendment Idealism: The New York State Civil Rights Law, 1873–1918." *New York History* 71 (1990): 207–33.

McConnell, Michael W. "The Forgotten Constitutional Moment." *Constitutional Commentary* 11 (1994): 115–44.

———. "Originalism and the Desegregation Decisions." *Virginia Law Review* 83 (1995): 947–1140.

———. "The Originalist Case for *Brown v. Board of Education.*" *Harvard Journal of Law and Public Policy* 19 (1996): 457–64.

———. "The Originalist Justification for *Brown:* A Reply to Professor Klarman." *Virginia Law Review* 83 (1995): 1937–55.

———. "Segregation and the Original Understanding: A Reply to Professor Maltz." *Constitutional Commentary* 13 (1996): 233–41.

McFarlin, Annjennette Sophie. *Black Congressional Reconstruction Orators and Their Orations, 1869–1879.* Metuchen, N.J.: Scarecrow Press, 1976.

McGee, Michael Calvin. "The 'IdeoGraph': A Link between Rhetoric and Ideology." *Quarterly Journal of Speech* 66 (1980): 1–16.

McKinley, William. *Speeches and Addresses of William McKinley.* New York: Doubleday and McClure Co., 1900.

McKitrick, Eric L. *Andrew Johnson and Reconstruction.* Chicago: University of Chicago Press, 1960.

McPhail, Mark Lawrence. "The Politics of Complicity: Second Thoughts about the Social Construction of Racial Equality." *Quarterly Journal of Speech* 80 (1994): 343–57.

———. *The Rhetoric of Racism.* Lanham, Md.: University Press of America, 1994.

McPherson, James M. "Abolitionists and the Civil Rights Act of 1875." *Journal of American History* 52 (1965): 493–510.

———. *The Struggle for Equality.* 1964. Reprint, Princeton: Princeton University Press, 1992.

Meier, August. "Negroes in the First and Second Reconstructions of the South." *Civil War History* 13 (1967): 114–30.

Mills, Gary H. "Miscegenation and the Free Negro in Ante-bellum 'Anglo' Alabama: A Re-examination of Southern Race Relations." *Journal of American History* 67 (1980): 41–60.

Mixon, Harold D. "Henry Grady as a Persuasive Strategist." In *Oratory in the New South,* edited by Waldo J. Braden. Baton Rouge: Louisiana State University Press, 1979.

Mohamed, Ali N. "Attitudes of Northern Papers toward the Egalitarian Laws of Reconstruction." *Newspaper Research Journal* 19 (1998): 47–62.

———. "Civil Rights in the Nineteenth Century: Frederick Douglass vs. the Pro-Republican Press." *Proteus* 12 (1995): 29–34.

Montgomery, David. *Beyond Equality: Labor and the Radical Republicans, 1862–1972.* New York: Alfred A. Knopf, 1967.

Mooer, John H. "Jim Crow in Georgia." *South Atlantic Quarterly* 66 (1967): 554–65.

Morton, Samuel. *Catalogue of Skulls of Man and the Inferior Animals.* 3d ed. Philadelphia: Merrihew and Thompson, 1849.

———. *Crania Americana.* Philadelphia: J. Dobson, 1839.

Myrdal, Gunnar. *An American Dilemma: The Negro Problem and Modern Democracy.* New York: Harper and Brothers, 1944.

Nast, Thomas. "Emancipation." Library of Congress, LC-USZ62–2573.

———. "Slavery Dead?" Library of Congress, LC-USZ62–108003.

———. "The Past and Future." *Harper's Weekly* 7, 24 January 1863: 56–57.

———. "The Shackle Broken by the Genius of Freedom." Library of Congress, LC-USZ62–2247.

———. "This is a White Man's Government." Library of Congress, LC-USZ62–121735.

O'Reilly, Kenneth. *Nixon's Piano.* New York: Free Press, 1995.

Oubre, Claude F. *Forty Acres and a Mule: The Freedmen's Bureau and Black Land Ownership.* Baton Rouge: Louisiana State University Press, 1978.

Palmer, Robert C. "The Parameters of Constitutional Reconstruction: *Slaughter-House, Cruikshank,* and the Fourteenth Amendment." *University of Illinois Law Review* (1984): 739–70.

P. B. S. Pinchback Papers, Manuscript Division, Moorland-Spingarn Research Center, Howard University.

Perelman, C. and L. Olbrechts-Tyteca. *The New Rhetoric: A Treatise on Argumentation.* Translated by John Wilkinson and Purcell Weaver. Notre Dame, Ind.: University of Notre Dame Press, 1969.

Perman, Michael. *The Road to Redemption: Southern Politics, 1869–1879.* Chapel Hill: University of North Carolina Press, 1984.

Pfeffer, Leo. *This Honorable Court: A History of the United States Supreme Court.* Boston: Beacon Press, 1965.

Pierson, Michael D. "'All Southern Society Is Assailed by the Foulest Charges': Charles Sumner's 'The Crime against Kansas' and the Escalation of Republican Anti-slavery Rhetoric." *New England Quarterly* 68 (1995): 531–57.

Pye, Lucian W. *Politics, Personality and Nation Building.* New Haven, Conn.: Yale University Press, 1962.

Quarles, Benjamin. *The Negro in the Making of America.* New York: Collier Books, 1964.

Rabinowitz, Howard N. "From Exclusion to Segregation: Southern Race Relations, 1865–1890." *Journal of American History* 63 (1976): 325–50.

———. "More Than the Woodward Thesis: Assessing *The Strange Career of Jim Crow.*" *Journal of American History* 75 (1988): 842–56.

———. *Race Relations in the Urban South, 1865–1890.* New York: Oxford University Press, 1978.

———, ed. *Southern Black Leaders of the Reconstruction Era.* Urbana: University of Illinois Press, 1982.

Rable, George C. *But There Was No Peace: The Role of Violence in the Politics of Reconstruction.* Athens: University of Georgia Press, 1984.

Randel, William Peirce. *The Ku Klux Klan: A Century of Infamy.* Philadelphia: Chilton Books, 1965.

Ransom, Roger L., and Richard Sutch. "Debt Peonage in the Cotton South after the Civil War." *Journal of Economic History* 32 (1972): 641–99.

Ray, Angela. "'In My Own Hand Writing': Benjamin Banneker Addresses the Slaveholder of Monticello." *Rhetoric and Public Affairs* 1 (1998): 387–405.

Reid, George W. "Four in Black: North Carolina's Black Congressmen, 1874–1901." *Journal of Negro History* 64 (1979): 229–43.

Reid, Ronald F., ed. *Three Centuries of American Rhetorical Discourse: An Anthology and Review.* Prospect Heights, Ill.: Waveland Press, 1988.

Richardson, James D., ed. *Messages and Papers of the Presidents.* Vols. 10–11. 1897. Reprint, New York: Bureau of National Literature, 1920.

Riegel, Stephen J. "The Persistent Career of Jim Crow: Lower Federal Courts and the 'Separate but Equal' Doctrine, 1865–1896." *American Journal of Legal History* 28 (1984): 17–40.

Ripley, C. Peter. Introduction to *The Black Abolitionist Papers.* Vol. 3. Chapel Hill: University of North Carolina Press, 1998.

Rosenbaum, Walter A. *Political Culture.* New York: Praeger Publishers, 1975.

Ross, Michael A. "Justice Miller's Reconstruction: The *Slaughter-House Cases,* Health Codes, and Civil Rights in New Orleans, 1861–1873." *Journal of Southern History* 64 (1998): 649–76.

Schile, Henry. "Charles Sumner." Library of Congress, LC-USZ62–89586.

Schurz, Carl. *Charles Sumner: An Essay by Carl Schurz.* Edited by Arthur Reed Hogue. Urbana: University of Illinois Press, 1951.

Scott, Robert L. "On Viewing Rhetoric as Epistemic." *Central States Speech Journal* 18 (1967): 9–17.

———. "On Viewing Rhetoric as Epistemic: Ten Years Later." *Central States Speech Journal* 27 (1976): 258–66.

Shaler, Nathaniel. "African Element in America." *The Arena* 12 November 1890: 660–673.

———. "Nature and Man in America: Part I." *Scribner's Magazine* 8 September 1890, 360–376.

———. "The Negro Problem." *Atlantic Monthly* 54 (1884): 696–709.

Simpson, Brooks D. *The Reconstruction Presidents.* Lawrence: University Press of Kansas, 1998.

Sinkler, George. *The Racial Attitudes of American Presidents.* Garden City, N.Y.: Doubleday and Co., 1971.

Smith, Edward D. "The Unfortunate History of America's First Comprehensive Civil Rights Bill, 1870–1883." *Negro History Bulletin* 47 (1984): 42–44.

Socolofsky, Homer E., and Allan B. Spetter. *The Presidency of Benjamin Harrison.* Lawrence: University Press of Kansas, 1987.

Spackman, S. G. F. "American Federalism and the Civil Rights Act of 1875." *Journal of American Studies* 10 (1976): 313–28.

Stampp, Kenneth M. *The Era of Reconstruction, 1865–1877.* New York: Vintage Books, 1967.

———. *The Peculiar Institution: Slavery in the Ante-bellum South.* New York: Alfred A. Knopf, 1961.

Stephens, Alexander Hamilton. *A Constitutional View of the Late War between the States: Its Causes. Character, Conduct, and Results.* Presented in a Series of Colloquies at Liberty Hall. Philadelphia: National Pub. Col., Zeigler McCurdy, 1868.

Stephenson, Gilbert T. *Race Distinctions in American Law.* New York: AMS Press, 1910.

Sterling, Dorothy. *The Trouble They Seen: The Story of Reconstruction in the Words of African Americans.* New York: Da Capo Press, 1994.

Stocker, Glen. "Charles Sumner's Rhetoric of Insult." *Southern Communication Journal* 38 (1973): 223–34.

Storey, Moorfield. *Charles Sumner.* Boston: Houghton, Mifflin, and Co., 1900.

Sumner, Charles. *Charles Sumner: His Complete Works.* Vols. 5, 13, and 19. 1882. Reprint, Norwood, Mass.: Lee and Shepard, 1900.

———. *Memoir and Letters of Charles Sumner.* Edited by Edward L. Pierce. Vol. 4. Boston: Roberts Brothers, 1893.

———. *The Selected Letters of Charles Sumner.* Edited by Beverly Wilson Palmer. Boston: Northeastern University Press, 1990.

———. *The Works of Charles Sumner.* Vol. 1. Boston: Lee and Shepard, 1870.

Ten-Broek, Jacobus. *Equal under Law.* New York: Collier Books, 1965.

"The First Colored Senator and Representatives," Library of Congress, LC-USZ62–2814.

Tindall, G. "Negro Disenfranchisement in South Carolina." *Journal of Southern History* (1949): 212–34.

Turner, Kathleen J., ed. *Doing Rhetorical History: Concepts and Cases.* Tuscaloosa: University of Alabama Press, 1998.

Van den Berghe, Pierre. *Race and Racism.* New York: John Wiley and Sons, 1967.

Vaugn, William P. "Separate and Unequal: The Civil Rights Act of 1875 and Defeat of the School Integration Clause." *The Southwestern Social Science Quarterly* 48 (1967): 146–54.

Walton, Norman W. "James T. Rapier: Congressman from Alabama." *Negro History Bulletin* 30 (1967): 6–10.

Walzer, Michael. *Interpretation and Social Criticism.* Cambridge: Harvard University Press, 1987.

Wander, Phillip C. "The Savage Child: The Image of the Negro in the Proslavery Movement." *Southern Communication Journal* 37 (1972): 335–60.

Watson, Martha Solomon. "The Dynamics of Intertextuality: Re-reading the Declaration of Independence." In *Rhetoric and Political Culture in Nineteenth-Century America,* edited by Thomas W. Benson. East Lansing: Michigan State University Press, 1997.

Weaver, Richard. *The Ethics of Rhetoric.* Davis, Calif.: Hermagoras Press, 1985.

Weaver, Valeria W. "The Failure of Civil Rights, 1875–1883, and Its Repercussions." *Journal of Negro History* 54 (1969): 368–82.

Wendt, Ronald F. "Answers to the Gaze: A Genealogical Poaching of Resistances." *Quarterly Journal of Speech* 82 (1996): 251–73.

West, Cornel. *Race Matters.* New York: Vintage Books, 1994.

West, Cornel, and Kelvin Shawn Sealey. *Restoring Hope: Conversations on the Future of Black America.* Boston: Beacon Press, 1997.

White, Hyden V. *Metahistory: The Historical Imagination in Nineteenth-Century Europe.* Baltimore, Md.: Johns Hopkins University Press, 1973.

Wildavsky, Aaron. "Choosing Preferences by Constructing Institutions: A Cultural Theory of Preference Formation." *American Political Science Review* 81 (1987): 3–21.

Williams, Charles R., ed. *The Life of Rutherford Birchard Hayes.* Vol. 2. Boston: Houghton Mifflin, 1914.

Williams, Patricia J. *The Alchemy of Race and Rights: Diary of a Law Professor.* Cambridge: Harvard University Press, 1991.

Williamson, Joel. *After Slavery: The Negro in South Carolina during Reconstruction, 1861–1877.* 1965. Reprint, Hanover, N.H.: University Press of New England, 1990.

———. *The Crucible of Race.* New York: Oxford University Press, 1984.

Wills, Garry. *Lincoln at Gettysburg: The Words That Remade America.* New York: Simon and Schuster, 1992.

Wilson, Kirt H. "Towards a Discursive Theory of Racial Identity: *The Souls of Black Folk* as a Response to Nineteenth-Century Biological Determinism." *Western Journal of Communication* 63 (1999): 193–215.

Wilson, William J. "Class Conflict and Jim Crow Segregation in the Postbellum South." *Pacific Sociological Review* 19 (1976): 431–46.

Woodman, Harold D. *New South, New Law: The Legal Foundations of Credit and Labor Relations of the Postbellum Agricultural South.* Baton Rouge: Louisiana State Press, 1995.

———. "Sequel to Slavery: The New History Views the Postbellum South." *Journal of Southern History* 43 (1997): 523–54.

Woodward, C. Vann. *Origins of the New South, 1877–1913.* Baton Rouge: Louisiana State University Press, 1971.

———. "*Strange Career* Critics: Long May They Persevere." *Journal of American History* 75 (1988): 857–68.

———. *The Strange Career of Jim Crow.* 3d ed. New York: Oxford University Press, 1974.

Wyatt-Brown, Bertram. "The Civil Rights Act of 1875." *Western Political Quarterly* 18 (1965): 763–75.

Zarefsky, David. "Consistency and Change in Lincoln's Rhetoric about Equality." *Rhetoric and Public Affairs* 1 (1998): 21–44.

———. *Lincoln Douglas and Slavery: In the Crucible of Public Debate.* Chicago: University of Chicago Press, 1990.

Zarefsky, David, and Victoria J. Gallagher. "From 'Conflict' to 'Constitutional Question': Transformations in Early American Public Discourse." *Quarterly Journal of Speech* 76 (1990): 247–61.

Zelizer, Barbie. "Reading the Past against the Grain: The Shape of Memory Studies." *Critical Studies of Mass Communication* 12 (1995): 214–39.

Zinn, Howard. *A People's History of the United States, 1492–Present.* New York: HarperPerennial, 1995.

Zulick, Margaret D. "The Agon of Jeremiah: On the Dialogic Invention of Prophetic Ethos." *Quarterly Journal of Speech* 78 (1992): 125–48.

Index